HOW TO SUCCEED IN THE MUSIC BUSINESS

By Allan Dann & John Underwood
(Revisions by Alex Batterbee)

D0273702

Exclusive Distributors
Music Sales Limited,
14/15 Berners Street,
London, W1T 3LJ.

Music Sales Corporation,
257 Park Avenue South,
New York, NY 10010, USA.

Macmillan Distribution Services,
56 Parkwest Drive
Derrimut, Vic 3030,
Australia.

Every effort has been made to trace the copyright holders of the photographs in this book but one or
two were unreachable. We would be grateful if the photographers concerned would contact us.

Typeset by Phoenix Photosetting, Chatham, Kent
Printed by Gutenberg Press Ltd, Malta

A catalogue record for this book is available from the British Library.

Visit Omnibus Press on the web at www.omnibuspress.com

CONTENTS

INTRODUCTION

There are many big names in the music world who, despite all their apparent success, have come out of it with very little to show in the way of financial reward. The man in the street would firmly believe that they 'must have made a fortune', yet hasty signing of unfavourable contracts has been the downfall of many stars.

Sometimes their problems have become public knowledge, as when contractual wrangles get as far as the courts, but many more have simply not succeeded when they could have done, or have 'succeeded' but just not made the money they should have made.

The temptation is obvious, when you first enter the business, to sign the first piece of paper thrust in front of you, just so that you can wave it about and say, 'I've been signed up, I've got a recording/publishing contract!' This is especially so when often the record company or publisher appears to be doing you a huge favour by 'giving you a chance'. The days have virtually gone when professional songwriters would sell hit songs outright for a few pounds, or important artists would make hit records for just the fee paid at the session, but it still can and does happen. The music stars who have succeeded in becoming famous AND rich, are the ones who had their heads screwed on.

This book is based on the personal experience of two professionals who between them have had more years in the music business than they care to say. It is not intended to be a definitive work on the subject (such a book would be many times this size and very difficult to read). Because of this we should stress from the outset that this book should not be solely relied upon in place of professional legal advice, for which there really is absolutely no substitute in each individual case. This book will, however, help you to find your way around the business and to know what questions to ask, and how to avoid many of the most obvious mistakes that are still, amazingly, common. It will help you to 'have your head screwed on' in the music business.

This book doesn't presume to teach you how to write a hit song or to sing or to play your instrument (you probably don't need any guidance on this – you probably already know what you can and cannot do, musically) although there are sections giving a general guide as to how you can best sell your songs to music publishers and yourself to record companies, pointing out some of the pitfalls.

You may not need to read the book cover to cover, but we strongly urge you to read thoroughly whichever of the following sections is relevant for you. These days very few writers are not also producers and very few singers are not also writers etc. so at the very least we'd suggest that you skim through the headings in the other sections to see what might be relevant.

For quick reference a rough guide to royalty rates and terms offered by publishers, record companies, managers, agents etc. is included towards the back of this book.

RECORDING

GETTING A RECORD CONTRACT

Perhaps more than anything else for a singer or musician hoping to be a star, getting a recording contract is their greatest ambition. In the eyes of friends and relatives, once offered a contract they will already have 'made it'. Unfortunately this may be a very long way from the truth, especially if the contract is a bad one.

Do I need a record company?

It might seem to you that as the Internet comes into its own and physical products like CDs become less and less important that you don't need a record company to produce those CDs, package them and get them into shops. And you may be right. Certainly there are many websites and online music download retailers who would have you believe that this is the case. In reality, though, if you are to have any commercial success (ie. make money from your music) you will need something like a record company to do all the other things that have always been a big part of the record company's job. These things include PR, marketing, protecting your rights from 'pirates' and people who try to use your music for free and, most importantly, collecting the money from consumers and businesses who want to listen to or use your music. If you don't have a 'record company' to do these things for you then you'll either have no time to make music or else you'll need to pay for a whole team of people, equipment and a place for them all to work (ie. form your own record company). Finally, and perhaps most convincingly, the old-fashioned physical products side of the music business might be in decline from a massive high point, but there are still hundreds of millions of records being sold worldwide every year and the traditional record company has the infrastructure to get a part of that vast market for you.

Which record company is right for me?

The reason behind most people's choice of record company is that 'they know someone who knows someone...'. In a business where a lot of the time it's not what you know but who you know this has some merit, but if the company is unsuitable then it's really a waste of time. Even the major companies have different labels, sometimes separately run and specialising in different types of material. Most of the independent labels ('indies') are to some extent specialised, so aim first for one that is successful with your type of music. If, for instance, you are a dance artist, take a look at the dance records that you or your friends may already have and look to approach these companies first. The only time when this might not be advisable is if you model yourself on one particular distinctive artist. A company is less likely to be interested in signing you up if it already has an artist just like you but who is already successful; then again for the exact same reason you might be just the thing their competitors are looking for.

How can I get their attention?

Unless you are very lucky then the chances are, no matter how talented you are, you will face a good deal of rejection before you get anything like a sniff of interest from a record company. If the first few don't show interest, remember you've lost nothing, and don't despair. Many famous artists, including The Beatles, were turned down by very knowledgeable and successful people in the music business before finally being signed up.

By far the best way to be 'discovered' in this day and age is to build your following, and the buzz around your music, to the point that a record company thinks it will be able to build on that base and take you to the next level. That means getting as much exposure for your music as possible.

So if your music is the sort best heard live, then get yourself as many gigs as you can and get names and email addresses from the people who come and are interested to hear more. Then follow up and make sure those people know about future gigs.

Get yourself a website and keep it up to date with news of gigs, a blog, samples of your music, photos etc... Set yourself up on Internet social networking sites such as MySpace (which offers great music-related tools). If you can, put clips from videos of your performances on YouTube or the like. The possibilities offered by the Internet are almost limitless and it can be quite daunting at first, but it can also be a very productive way to get the public and record companies to hear your music. Just remember not to spread yourself too thinly, for example by joining dozens of sites and then not having time to service them with new information. Pay attention to the feedback that you get about your sites and your music; this doesn't mean you have to follow all the advice you're given, but at least you will begin to know your audience. Also, if you put up a cover version of someone else's song, make sure that the website has the appropriate licences from the PRS (Performing Rights Society); if you plan to make money from your music, it makes sense to respect copyright laws.

At the same time of course, you'll want to get your music heard by the record companies you have targeted. Ideally they'll be in touch with you because of all the buzz you've created but, if not, you shouldn't hesitate to get in touch with them. The A&R (Artists & Repertoire) team are the people at the record company you need to contact, and you'll be able to get names and contact details from the company's website (we've

included a short list in the next chapter to get you started, but you can find others that you need with the aid of your favourite search engine).

The best thing you can do when approaching A&R is to get a professional-looking and attractive package together, including your demos, pictures, a short bio, any reviews you have and details of upcoming gigs. Whether you send it physically or by email is a decision you should try to make knowing what the A&R team prefer but, if you can't find that out, there's little harm in doing both. Any demo tracks you include should of course be recorded to the highest possible standard; it's not that a good A&R person can't hear through a bad demo but they listen to a lot of music and chances are that if your demo makes a bad first impression then they won't get past that to hear the good beneath. What's more a good recording shows you have confidence in your music which is half the battle.

If your first demo is rejected by all of the major companies and those you have targeted, then you will most likely face an uphill struggle with a second demo, and it will take something pretty dynamic to get over this prejudice.

You could take the drastic step to change your name, but the price you pay for this is that you will sacrifice at least some of the following you have already built up. Alternatively, you could leave it for, say, a year before you try a second time, and you may well find that the actual people listening to your demo are entirely different from those who heard it before. Faces change quickly in the music business and you'll again have the advantage of being an unknown quantity. Keep an eye on the websites for new contact names.

Where can I get help in getting a record deal?

Rather than go it alone, you would be well advised, with this crucial step in your career, to get help, and there are five main sources: publishers, lawyers, managers, producers and mutual friends.

Most acts these days write their own material, and most, though not all, artists in the charts are there because they wrote, or had access to, good songs. Noel Gallagher of Oasis said that it was more important to be a good songwriter than a great musician, and he was absolutely right.

So if you have good material and you can impress a publisher first, then he may well be able to use his contacts to try to get you a record deal. He may even fund or co-fund the creation of masters or high quality demos to license or promote your music to a record company.

The downside of course is that had you come to the publisher with a record

deal in hand you'd have got a better publishing deal, but it is a chicken and egg situation and this may be a small price to pay for a good record deal.

Should I consider entering a reality TV competition like The 'X Factor'?

Lately this sort of television programme has become big business, both in terms of ratings and record sales. Not only that, it has brought about a revival in the market for non-musician and non-songwriter artists, which harks back to the 'doo-wop' groups of the late Fifties and 'Motown'-style acts in the Sixties. The first point to remember is that it doesn't hurt to be a member of a 'put-together group' as winners of a talent show. Stars, whether they wrote, or co-wrote, their own hits, have always tended to come out of successful bands. In fact, this goes right back to people like Frank Sinatra, who started off by singing with dance bands. It really didn't harm Robbie Williams' career that he was once in Take That, and Geri Halliwell and Melanie C. etc. were successful with their solo albums despite (or perhaps because of) the fact that they were members of the all-conquering Spice Girls. So don't worry if it's a 'band' talent show or 'put-together' act or a solo one – if you're really good and/or really good looking and/or good at marketing yourself, then it's quite possible that you'll be successful. In the end these shows provide just one more way for an artist to get attention; once the initial excitement has died down, though, it's up to you to build on that success with your talent and that's what will decide if you can build on that success like Leona Lewis, Will Young or Girls Aloud have.

It doesn't matter which show, if you think you're good at that sort of thing then apply. They can only say no, in which case you just try for the next one!

What do I have to sign to be in a show or put-together act like that?

There's obviously always someone behind these shows and put-together acts, and you could reasonably expect them to want to manage you, and for their production company to record you and, if by any chance you are offered the chance to co-write any of your songs, to publish you, normally for a period of three years or so. This would be a prerequisite of your entering the competition and provided that you know that the company and/or the competition is run by a reputable television production company and tied to a reputable record company, then you'll appreciate that they won't want to be seen to be ripping you off and you'll get a reasonable deal – maybe not the best but you can live with that.

Obviously, the artist's share of income in any of these sorts of deals is going to be less than it would be if you got the deal directly based on your building your own following and largely using your own material. But many artists have shown that this can all come later in their careers, and the 'big break' is worth the price.

What not to do is to enter a 'talent competition' run by some local organisation without very seriously checking that they're not going to tie you to some very dodgy or simply amateur and inexperienced management/recording/publishing organisation in a long-term deal with onerous conditions. Check the small print, and if you don't understand it, get someone you trust who does to check it, before even thinking about signing.

Whatever you do don't pay someone a fee to enter a contest or an audition; it smacks of shady practice and is more than likely a money-making scheme that will get you nowhere except out of pocket.

Suppose someone offers to put one of my tracks on a 'promo' CD or website?

There are companies that produce CDs of unsigned artists and send them around the business and put them on the Internet in the hope that someone will hear something they like and sign it. These companies make their money either by charging the artists to be on the CD or by asking for a royalty on the artist's first album etc. This can be a perfectly legitimate way to get noticed but, as with the *X Factor*-style talent shows, it's very important to check what you're signing and check out the reputation of the company you're signing with. If they're charging you, it's unlikely that the company has much motivation to exercise any quality control (the more tracks they send out, the more fees they make), so the less likely it is that the record companies take any notice. If they're not charging you, then be sure that anything you sign doesn't have the potential to deprive you of any long-term rights, or rights (eg. to the best track you've written/recorded so far) that you might need to give or license to the company you eventually sign to.

Can I expect a lawyer actually to go out and get me a record deal?

In short, sometimes yes. These days a music business lawyer will often act almost like a manager and use his contacts to get you a deal. You will need a lawyer anyway at some point, so it can be a great advantage.

The downside is that their close contacts may be more limited than those of a publisher or manager. In addition, lawyers can be expensive and they'll charge you by the hour (it can easily cost upwards of £1,000 to negotiate a record deal for you). Finally, the limited range of close contacts may give rise to anxieties about conflicts of interest or may mean they don't shop around for the best deal for you.

That said, your lawyer might do the work on a contingency basis if they think they can get you a deal (so instead of a fee, they'll take a percentage of your earnings); though this will probably be much more expensive if you're successful, it may be a price worth paying to get that first deal. It is also possible that, as with publishers, your lawyer can persuade the record label to pay some or all of your legal costs anyway.

Wouldn't I be better off with a manager?

A really good manager will have contacts galore and would be the best person of all to get you a deal. He can also advise best on the presentation of you and your songs, organising showcases etc. The downside is that you're more likely to attract a good manager once you've already got some record company interest (chicken and egg again). Most managers will take commission on all your income from the music business, but if you did already have the record deal all wrapped up, your manager might well be prepared to reduce his commission from record income. Dance acts may well only have one hit single (plus lots of uses of their track on compilation albums) and then disappear, maybe to reappear under a different guise a year or so later. However, rock acts, who will need more investment to make them successful, tend to sign record (and publishing) deals for longer and it's much harder to convince record companies and publishers to invest in them – hence a persuasive manager is more helpful.

Getting a good manager (and you'll hear about good and bad ones by word of mouth) can be as hard as getting a record deal, but while one doesn't necessarily lead to the other, it certainly helps a great deal. So for all the effort you put in to promoting your music to A&R teams, you should consider putting the same into getting a good manager.

Won't a record producer only get involved once I'm signed to a label?

Not necessarily. Although this is the usual way round, it is possible that you could interest a producer who you feel understands your music and who you can work with. These days, more and more acts, especially dance acts, more-or-less produce themselves, usually with the help of remixers once a track is due to be released (see 'How could I get to be a producer?' in 'General Q & A'). But there are plenty of professional producers of all types who may be prepared to make a recording of you to take to a record company, especially if they own or have a deal with a particular studio. Many belong to an organisation called MPG (contact details in our 'Useful Addresses' list), which could advise on which producers might be prepared to listen to you, especially if they happen to be local.

With a 'name' producer singing your praises you're much more likely to get record company interest. In return, the producer will expect to be able to go on and produce at least your first album. He may even want to sign you himself and license your first recordings to the record company (see 'lease-tape deals' in 'Recording Q & A') although this is less likely.

Suppose I know someone (anyone) in the music business?

Finally, personal contacts can be extremely valuable. The cost may be no more than a round of drinks, but remember that the contacts your friend has may be with an unsuitable record company, and you increase the risk that if your contact at the company leaves, his successor may well hate your music (always an occupational hazard). Nonetheless, it's worth asking around in local record shops, musical equipment shops and certainly in the local studio where you make your demos, whether anyone has any contacts in the business. Do remember that you still have to impress all the above people so much that they'll risk their credibility with their valuable contacts on your behalf, no matter how low a royalty or advance you're prepared to accept!

How can I organise a showcase?

For a band, a showcase can open doors. With luck a manager or publisher will organise and pay for one for you. If you can get to play at a suitable venue in your nearest city (even if you have to pay to play there), it's worth inviting as many suitable record company, publishing and music press people as possible. Nothing works better for getting them excited about you than to have those people standing in the midst of a crowd going mad for your music.

Don't rush into it. You may only get one really big bite of the cherry. Try to get some local press and possibly local airplay of your demos beforehand, build up that mailing list and your online following and time it to follow other gigs so you can fine-tune your repertoire and build up a fan base. You must be convinced about your material and your performance and that you're guaranteed a hardcore of adoring fans. Again, don't underestimate the importance of your material. Record companies are ideally looking for a minimum of three or four potential hit singles per album. Even a rock band will be expected to have some hits. If you don't honestly think you're halfway there, then work on the songs first; don't refuse help if necessary from friends or acquaintances, especially ones in the business.

Choose your venue wisely and remember that at any given time some clubs are much more credible than others. The fact that your band is playing at some sites is almost a disincentive for someone to sign you.

Many industry bodies (see the list in our 'Useful Addresses' list) have initia-

tives providing showcases for unsigned bands. Check their websites regularly for new opportunities, but even more than your own showcase these can be a one-shot deal for you, so make sure you're ready before accepting an invitation to play.

Similarly, several radio stations, national and local, offer opportunities for bands and individuals to play short live sets; if you get one of these chances and it goes well, make sure to get a high quality copy of the show to add to your package.

How can I make a really good demo?

Studios are not all the exclusive property of record companies. Most of them are independent, and smaller ones can be hired privately for as little as £100 a day (plus cost of tape, equipment hire and incidental expenses). A competent band should be able to put down three songs in a day. If you can do it during an ordinary working day (so the engineer at the studio doesn't have to be paid overtime etc.), the total cost could be as low as £250 for 16 or 24-track demos, so long as you don't have to go for too many retakes.

The better (and generally the more expensive) the studio, the better your demos will probably be, though there's no point in wasting very expensive studio time on fairly basic demos, especially if you could have made them yourself in a home studio. Getting a good mix is as important as getting a good recording, so don't underestimate the time it could take to mix down the tracks once you've recorded them.

The above is all very fine for groups. A solo singer could hire or cajole a pianist or guitarist to accompany them if they don't feel confident enough of their own playing, but the hiring of professional musicians is expensive and may not be worthwhile at this stage if costs are to be kept low.

Dance acts almost by definition start out with their own home recording equipment sufficient to lay down the basic tracks. A day's studio time should be quite enough to mix down the tracks and add vocals if you know the studio's capability and have planned in advance.

There are now so many studios around the country (not just in London) that a list would be enormous. Check the Internet or the phone book for local ones. Obviously, some outside London are large residential studios for recording your second album when the first has gone multi-platinum, but any studio will quote their rates to you on request. If you have queries, you would be well advised to seek the help of an organisation called APRS (contact details in the 'Useful Addresses' list below). It has its own list of member recording studios and will be able to advise you.

There is also the option of home recording, but even with the increased level of technology available today, it's worth considering the cost of this equipment, the complexity of using it properly and your level of skill as a recording engineer (as opposed to your talent as an artist). So unless you're absolutely confident of your skills, the professional studio may well be the quickest and cheapest route to a professional-sounding demo.

A LIST OF UK RECORD COMPANIES

One of the most important factors in selling your services to a record company is, of course, to know who and where the record companies are. For this reason we have included here a list of addresses of UK & Irish record companies. Don't think that just because a company is not on this list it's automatically not worth signing with. This list is by no means comprehensive; small to medium-sized independents are springing up all the time, and just as frequently some go out of business or are swallowed up by larger companies.

For other names, websites and addresses you can also refer to current telephone directories, industry association websites (see the Useful Addresses section below) and the latest trade publications, such as Music Week. The Music Week Directory is an annual directory widely used within the industry; an up-to-date version is always available on Music Week's subscription website (see the Useful Addresses section below).

In any case, if by this time you have already enlisted the support of a lawyer and an accountant, both of these will know about the latest comings and goings, and who is worth talking to and who isn't likely to be interested.

Not all the companies on this list, or in any other publication, are crying out for new acts all the time. Some specialise in licensing recordings from other companies or in American or Continental-European acts. Or they may have more than they can cope with at a certain time, or you may not really be what they're looking for, even if they admit that you're good. So if they don't want to sign you, there may be a perfectly good reason unrelated to your music.

Many big artists and producers now have their own labels, which are actually a subsidiary of one of the majors. Some will try to sign new acts, others just exist to issue records by one established act. This list includes most of those that are properly in the business of releasing records (and have had their share of hits) and for the most part have been around for a while. If there's a name you were expecting to see that's missing from the list, this may be because it's part of, or run by, another company – check the websites listed below to see lists of labels run by the larger companies.

Ace Records
42–50 Steele Road
London NW10 7AS
www.acerecords.co.uk (020 8453 1311)

Amazon Records
PO Box 5109
Hove
E Sussex BN52 9EA
www.amazonrecords.co.uk
(01273 726 414)

Beggars Banquet Records
17–19 Alma Road
London SW18 1AA
www.beggars.com (020 8870 9912)

Blacklist Entertainment
Fulham Palace, Bishop's Avenue
London SW6 6EA
www.blacklistent.com (020 7751 0175)

Champion Records
181 High St.
Harlesden
London NW10 4TE
www.championrecords.co.uk
(020 8961 5202)

Cherry Red Records
3a Long Island House
Warple Way
London W3 0RG
www.cherryred.co.uk (020 8740 4110)

Cleveland City
52a Clifton Street
Chapel Ash
Wolverhampton WV3 0QT
www.clevelandcity.co.uk
(01902 838 500)

Cooking Vinyl
10 Allied Way,
London W3 0RQ
www.cookingvinyl.com (020 8600 9200)

Curb Records
45 Great Guildford St.
London SE1 0ES
www.curb.com (020 7401 8877)

DB Records
PO Box 19318
Bath BA1 6ZS
www.dbrecords.co.uk (01225 782 322)

The Decca Music Group
347–353 Chiswick High Road
London W4 4HS
www.deccaclassics.com (020 8747 8787)

Deltasonic Records
102 Rose Lane
Mossley Hill
Liverpool L18 8AG
www.deltasonic.com (0151 724 4760)

Demon Music Group
33 Foley St
London W1W 7TL
www.demonmusicgroup.co.uk
(020 7612 3300)

Distinctive Records
35 Drury Lane
Covent Garden
London WC2B 5RH
www.distinctiverecords.com
(020 7689 0079)

Eagle Rock Entertainment
Eagle House, 22 Armoury Way
London SW18 1EZ
www.eagle-rock.com (020 8870 5670)

EMI Records Group
43 Brook Green
London W6 7EF
www.emimusic.co.uk (020 7605 5000)

EMI Music Ireland
1 Aliesbury Road
Dublin 4
Eire
www.emimusic.co.uk (+353 1 203 9900)

Fellside Recordings
PO Box 40
Workington
Cumbria CA14 3GJ
www.fellside.com (01900 61556)

First Night Records
3 Warren Mews
London W1T 6AN
www.first-night-records.com
(020 7383 7767)

4AD
17–19 Alma Road
London SW18 1AA
www.4ad.com (020 8870 9724)

Genetic Records
A303.5 Tower Bridge Business Complex
100 Clements Road
London SE16 4DG
www.geneticrecords.co.uk
(020 7394 3399)

Glasgow Records
Lovat House
Gavell Rd
Glasgow G65 9BS
www.glasgowrecords.com
(01236 826555)

Grönland Records
9–10 Domingo Street
London EC1Y 0TA
www.gronland.co.uk (020 7553 9166)

Gut Records
Bryon House
112a Shirland Road
London W9 2EQ
www.gutrecords.com (020 7266 0777)

Hyperion Records
PO. Box 25
London SE9 1AX
www.hyperion-records.co.uk
(020 8318 1234)

Incentive Music
Reverb House
Bennett Street
London W4 2AH
www.incentivemusic.com
(020 8994 8918)

Independiente
The Drill Hall
3 Heathfield Terrace
London W4 4JE
www.independiente.com
(020 8747 8111)

Inferno Records
32–36 Telford Way
London W3 7AX
www.infernorecords.co.uk
(020 8742 9300)

Kennington Recordings
44 Norwood Park Road
London SE27 9UA
www.kenningtonrecordings.com
(020 8670 4082)

Lakota Records
43 Donnybrook Manor
Donnybrook
Dublin 4
Eire
www.lakotarecords.com
(+353 1 283 9071)

Lavolta Records
Unit F2, Shepherds Building
Rockley Road
London W14 0DA
www.lavoltarecords.com
(020 7371 1311)

Lismor Recordings
PO Box 7264
Glasgow G46 6YE
www.allcelticmusic.com (0141 637 6010)

Ministry of Sound
103 Gaunt St.
London SE1 6DP
www.ministryofsound.com
(0870 0600 010)

Mute Records
from website:
43 Brook Green
London W6 7EF
www.mute.com (020 8964 2001)

Nude Records
120–124 Curtain Road
London EC2A 3SQ
www.nuderecords.com
(020 7426 5151/3)

One Little Indian Records
34 Trinity Crescent
London SW17 7AE
www.indian.co.uk (020 8772 7600)

Park Records
PO Box 651
Oxford OX2 9RB
www.parkrecords.com (01865 241 717)

President Records
Units 6 & 7
11 Wyfold Road
London SW6 6SE
www.president-records.co.uk
(020 7385 7700)

Revolver Music Ltd
152 Goldthorn Hill
Penn
Wolverhampton
W Midlands WV2 3JA
revolverrecords.com (01902 345 345)

Rollercoaster Records
Rock House
London Road
St. Mary's
Chalford
Gloucs. GL6 8PU
www.rollercoasterrecords.com
(0845 456 9759)

Rough Trade Records
66 Golborne Road
London W10 5PS
www.roughtraderecords.com
(020 8960 9888)

Rykodisc
329 Latimer Road
London W10 6RA
www.rykodisc.com (020 8960 3311)

Skint Records
PO Box 174
Brighton
E.Sussex BN1 4BA
www.skint.net (01273 738 527)

Snapper Music
1 Star Street
London W2 1QD
www.snappermusic.com (020 7563 5500)

Sony BMG Music Entertainment
Bedford House
69–79 Fulham High Street
London SW6 3JW
www.sonybmg.com (020 7384 7500)

Sony BMG Music Entertainment Ireland
Embassy House
Ballsbridge
Dublin 4
Eire
(+353 1 647 3430)

Splash Records
29 Manor House
250 Marylebone Road
London NW1 5NP
www.the-demon.com (020 7723 7177)

3 Beat Music
5 Slater Street
Liverpool L1 4BW
www.threebeatrecords.co.uk
(0151 709 3355)

Universal Music
364–366 Kensington High Street
London W14 8NS
www.umusic.com (020 7471 5000)

Universal Music Ireland
9 Whitefriars, Aungier Street
Dublin 2
Eire
www.universalmusic.com
(+353 1 402 2600)

VP Records UK Ltd
Unit 12B, Shaftsbury Centre
85 Barlby Road
London W10 6BN
www.vprecords.com
(020 8962 2760)

Warner Music (UK)
The Warner Building
28a Kensington Church Street
London W8 4EP
www.warnermusic.com
(020 7368 2500)

Warner Music (Ireland)
2nd Floor, Skylab
2 Exchange Street Upper
Dublin 8
Eire
www.warnermusic.com
(+353 1 881 4500)

XL Recordings
1 Codrington Mews
London W11 2EH
www.xlrecordings.com (020 8870 7511)

ZTT Records Ltd
The Blue Building
8–10 Basing Street
London W11 1ET
www.ztt.com (020 7229 1229)

ZYX Records UK
Unit 11, Cambridge Court
210 Shepherd's Bush Road
London W6 7NL
www.zyxmusic.co.uk
(020 7371 6969)

RECORD COMPANIES

In these days of digital home recording, cheaply pressed CDs and digital distribution on the Internet, it is easier than ever to call yourself a record company and 'issue' records to the public. In the last few years a great many new record companies have mushroomed in the world's major music centres, some offering new and experimental financial models for relations between 'record company' and artist. Some of these are owned by managers, producers, publishers or artists themselves, partly hoping to become independent of the remaining so-called 'majors', who have for decades dominated the market in most countries, and partly to cash in on the very large profits that can be made by issuing successful records. Often these start-ups fail to appreciate the very heavy costs involved in recording, pressing, distribution (even without a physical product to manufacture, there are costs such as hardware, network bandwidth and software licensing to be met) and, often most expensive of all, advertising and PR, without which no one will know your recordings are out there to be bought.

What sort of advance will they give me?

It's almost impossible to say. It depends entirely on how 'hot' they think you are and on how much they like the songs that would go on your first album. It also depends (crucially) on whether they're giving you a sum of money as an advance (to live on) or whether the recording budget for your first album has to come out of that. You shouldn't expect a guarantee of millions for your first album – if you can get £100–200,000 that wouldn't be too bad, though you might be offered a lot more. Always remember, however, that if your recording costs form part of your upfront advance or are added to your 'unrecouped balance', the cash you have in hand may (unless the album is immediately wildly successful) be the last you'll see for quite a while. It may not seem very rock 'n' roll to watch your budget, especially with a big number in the bank, but recording and promotion costs (sometimes also added to those unrecouped balances) can mount up notoriously quickly. So you can end up spending that advance very quickly or having to wait quite a time before your royalties exceed your unrecouped balance, and so having to eke out the money you have to live on. Then again, if you are renegotiating with a success under your belt then the sky can be the limit. EMI reportedly re-signed Robbie Williams in 2002 for a staggering £80 million, working on the assumption (projected on the sales of his previous albums) that he would sell at least 18 million copies worldwide of new albums covered by the new deal.

Lastly, it's worth making sure that an advance is termed non-returnable (this is usual practice, but better safe than sorry), so if you fail to recoup you won't be under an obligation to pay it back with no clear means of doing so. (See also 'Who pays the recording costs?')

Will they always want to give me an exclusive contract?

Publishers won't always be looking to sign you to an exclusive long-term contract, but with recording this is almost always the case. A record company will not normally chance making and releasing one record to 'see what happens' without having options to keep you for a longer term if you turn out to be a sensation. (Equally these days, the bigger labels especially will want the option to drop you as quickly as possible if you have little success first time out.) All this is understandable as issuing recordings can be expensive. A quite straightforward first single can easily cost from £10,000 to produce plus the cost of manufacture and marketing, even without the cost of a promo video for which you can often put an extra nought on the end of that figure. So you will be offered a contract, generally for one or two years, under the terms of which the company should be required to record a minimum number of tracks per contract year in exchange for your exclusive services.

What recording or release commitment will they give me?

With dance or dance-orientated chart acts, it is more likely you will be offered a so-called 'singles deal'. The first single may be one you, your publisher, manager, producer or accountant has brought to them. Although they'll usually want options for albums if you're successful, they'll only commit to releasing one, or possibly two singles.

A rock or indie act (guitar-based bands and the like) is more likely to be offered an album deal or nothing. As it costs more to release an album, the record company will want to be that much more certain of your potential (and thus it's more likely that they'll reject you). If they do take you on and start spending money, however, they're unlikely not to make and release a whole album. Remember, a three-album deal doesn't necessarily mean that the company is guaranteeing to make and release three albums – it just gives them the option to do so on terms already agreed.

Under an album deal, the company will commit to making recordings (or giving you a budget to organise the recording yourself) of enough tracks for a 12–14-track album, plus a couple of 'bonus' tracks and maybe two or three 'spares' if they think you haven't enough potential hits, or if you've had a great idea just before delivery of the album to the company.

What options will they expect?

The company is likely to want one album per year or every 18 months for up to seven years plus maybe one or two 'overcall' albums (extra live or 'greatest hits' albums to fulfil demand from the public). Most companies will renegotiate terms with an artist who has had success with their first album to give the artist a higher royalty rate, bigger advances or a less tight delivery schedule, in return for delivery of extra albums over a longer period. Such escalations may be minutely specified in your original deal if they think you have long-term potential but, generally, tying yourself down at that early stage when you have less power should be avoided. Remember, touring and other commitments will soon eat into your time, and neither you nor the company wants to release a 'throwaway' album. For this reason, as with publishing deals, each 'year' will if necessary extend till a few months after the album for that year has been released (even if for some reason it's taken up to about three years since the 'year' began for the album to be released).

Surprisingly, a pop act may be 'dropped' in spite of having had a couple of sizeable hits, as each company has only so much money to go round and may have a better prospect lined up (they think). One hit, however, and of course other doors open. The press want to know about you and you can put a nought on the end of the amount you're getting per gig almost overnight. How much of that you will see is another matter (see 'Artist Management' section).

One provision that is well worth considering asking for in a recording contract is that the contract terminates after, say, one 'year', unless a recording produced during that year featuring you has been included in the Top 30 or 50 of a recognised UK (or overseas) album chart. If your record has made the charts then most likely both you and the company will wish to renew the contract for further periods; if it hasn't made the charts then you are simply free to go elsewhere at the end of that first 'year'.

Suppose my record is not released, or only in certain countries?

If the record company really hates the album it has paid for and doesn't release it by a given date, then your negotiated contract should specify that it forfeits any options, and ideally you should be able to buy back the masters. Methods of calculating the price vary and will probably include more than just recording costs.

If a major company's UK people loves your album but, for example, its Italian people don't, some companies will allow you to shop the rights to other Italian companies as long as royalties flow through your UK record company. This is not likely with new artists and could be embarrassing for the Italian branch if it turned it down and it became huge in Italy on another label. This lack of overseas commitment was one of George Michael's arguments in his much-publicised battle with Sony Records in the mid-Nineties.

What royalties will I get under a recording contract?

With a smaller company you may be on a form of 'profit sharing' (50/50 after all costs have been recovered, maybe 60/40 or 70/30 in your favour, especially if you made the initial recording or paid for part of it). Otherwise the amount will be shown as a percentage, which used to be based on the retail price but is now almost always based on the price to dealers. The dealer price is about 2/3rds of retail, so 16% of PDP (published price to dealers) is about the same as 11% of retail (less VAT of course, and a host of other reductions and deductions that make it very hard to work out what you can really expect to receive). It's nice to

know what you'll get in pounds and pence per single or album but never have the royalty expressed in pounds and pence as you'll sooner or later be left behind by inflation. Remember, these royalties are payable for the whole life of copyright in the record (currently 50 years from date of first release) and a lot of 50-year-old records are still selling consistently.

A new artist may start with a royalty of around 16–18% of PDP, depending on the buzz surrounding you and the negotiating skill of your manager or lawyer, but this will only be for full-price albums in the UK. This would equate, on a full-price album with a PDP (before VAT) of about £8, to £1.25–£1.30p. (Some companies' PDP for a full-price album may be up to £1 more, in which case you'll need to add slightly more than 10% to these figures, but if your royalty is based on the 'actual realised price' that the record company gets from record stores, chains etc., then it will probably be less.) Remember, this is split between all of you if you're a band, so it pays to be a three- or four-piece and pay session fees to the horn players and backing vocalists! All other releases will be at a reduced rate, even singles usually. Other than in the case of dance music, most singles are regarded as a necessary loss-leader purely to gain airplay and promote sales of the album they're from. Although they *can* make big money, they're not expected to.

The downward pressure on prices for physical product and online, both from retailers and consumers, probably means that these figures will represent a high water mark for some time to come. That said, it's the fervent hope of the music industry that online will pick up sufficiently in units sold to make up for this reduced unit price.

Note that if you have a hit at the end of the contract with a record you made at the beginning, you'll invariably be paid at the rate that applied when the recording was made. The rates for foreign sales can be lower. They may be expressed as the same rate but based on the price at which your UK company is paid, which might include more deductions (Eire should count as UK by the way). Foreign rates may be around 75% of whatever the UK company receives from its overseas affiliates or licensees (without saying how much that's likely to be).

Will I be paid for every record sold?

You may only be paid on 90% of actual sales, occasionally less. This is to cover returns, breakages and faulty records etc. Suppose you know that your record has sold 100,000 copies or units (incidentally, beware of sales figures shown in the press, as publicity people tend to exaggerate and a high chart entry could be down to hyping). Further suppose your royalty works out at £1.25p per record, but don't expect to get £125,000. Why? Firstly, the 100,000 gross sales becomes 90,000 (or less) net. Then there will be 'container charges' on all forms of actual disc or tape (even still sometimes on Internet downloads where there is no container at all but there are licence fees to pay, for example for DRM) of up to say 20% for a CD in a Perspex 'jewel case'. Now we're down to 72,000 from 90,000. Then there will be no payment on albums distributed for promotional purposes (even though many of these may ultimately be sold somewhere down the line) so now we're down to say 70,000 units. (i.e. your royalty is now down to around £90,000).

All of this is for full-price albums. For almost any other kind of release, your royalty will usually be reduced to the following:
50%–75% of your royalty for CD singles (maybe up to a certain limit);
up to 50% for Internet (much less common in recent years);
50% for double albums, soundtrack albums and compilation albums (pro-rated across the tracks on a compilation album, on which your track can be one of as many as 40);

50% for 'budget' albums;
50% for TV-advertised albums;
50% for sales through mail order and record clubs;
50% for sales to libraries, charities, government organisations and the like.

These may be shown as a percentage of your full-price album rate, or the agreement may specify that, for example, singles are at 12% PDP etc.

Then you may get nothing at all for records deleted, records sold as scrap, promotional records solely promoting your records, coloured vinyl and other unconventional releases. Remember, this could include records given away or sold cheaply to chain stores to encourage sales. As a writer you get paid on most of them, but as an artist you won't.

As budget albums are cheaper and therefore the normal royalty would in any case be low, this may seem a bit tough, but it's normal. Additionally, budget frequently means anything up to 75% of the price of normal chart albums – try to get the definition of budget in your agreement down to half or two-thirds of full price if possible, and try to get the company to pay you as high a royalty as possible on albums they sell cheaply to chain stores to try to increase your overall sales. They may give your records away free, in which case you'll get nothing, but you should at least know what they're doing. Also, if there's a limit to the number of TV-advertised albums at half royalty before you get the full royalty, this will usually be for each separate release, not all your singles or albums added together, and will be for sales in each country of each release, not all countries added together. It should also apply only to accounting periods during and just after the advertising campaign. These reductions are fairly usual, especially for a new artist, but are not set in stone. For a dance act with a successful single, see the quick reference section.

In 2002, BMG Records (now Sony BMG), one of the major record labels, declared it would offer a much simpler formula across the board (Universal Records did the same, notably with regard to internet usages), which is something for which the MMF had been campaigning for years (basically making it much simpler to work out what the artist is owed). Under the sort of agreement BMG was referring to, there would be no packaging deductions, no '75% of statutory rate controlled composition clauses' in the USA, less delays before you are paid, shorter deals, far fewer deductions for budget records, TV-advertised records etc., and even a set amount of recording costs per album that are not recoupable from your royalties. Don't automatically expect this 'alternative' from your record company, but it's worth asking about it, or something like it.

Needless to say the record companies are not giving something for nothing – they will expect the basic royalty rate to be lower and will regard the above as giving them the right to own your recordings for longer without the possibility of a legal challenge to their rights (something the managers' and artists' organisations have always resisted, if ultimately the cost of the recordings comes out of the artists' royalties). Also, it reduces the record companies' administration costs – remember, they have to pay to employ people to work out exactly how much *not* to pay you under the old-style complicated deals!

Who pays the recording costs?

This is the biggest deduction of all. Except in the new-style deals mentioned above, generally you do (or rather the record company pays them, and of course takes all the risks in doing so, but will recover them all from your royalties if and when they start to be generated). If a record label pays you £200,000 as an advance/recording budget for a first album, using our calculations you'd have to sell well over that number of albums before you're in credit. If you as a band managed to make the album for £150,000 and use the rest to live on, you can see

that between you it probably won't keep you going for more than a year at the outside. Incidentally, the advance may well be split 50% on signing and the rest on delivery and/or on the date of release of the album.

However, almost anything else the record company paid out, specifically on your behalf, whether it be photo sessions, showcases, TV and radio advertising, independent promoters, even tour support to promote the album and the cost of company staff accompanying you, will all be added to the costs it recovers before paying you (subject to precise negotiations). Do try to avoid missing engagements, sessions etc., as all the costs will be deducted from your royalties. Being a so-called 'bad boy or girl of rock' may attract publicity but can be very expensive, even without the traditional wanton acts of destruction like smashing guitars on stage or riding a Harley Davidson round your hotel room. If you're going to end up losing a fortune, don't let it be through simply not getting out of bed early enough in the morning.

Who pays for promo videos?

Again, the record company pays, and this time it should generally only deduct half the cost from your record royalties (hooray!). The other half will, however,

17

be deducted from any income (and this may be considerable) from retail sales and other uses of the video. Again, the record company will continue to own it. Clearly, if you can get away with an 'artistic' live video for your first single on an independent label at £10,000 or so and don't need too many takes, you'll be making money sooner than if you spend the £100,000 or so that established artists can easily spend, especially if they insist on using a well-known video or film producer or an unnecessarily exotic location. If each of three videos for three singles from your album costs £100,000, then at 50% recoupable from general royalties that's another £150,000 before you see a penny (i.e. around another 200,000 copies that your album will have to sell).

If you want to make your own promo video as part of your 'sales pitch' to a record company, it's often possible to find an art college or film student prepared to help you make a good basic video for a fraction of the proper commercial cost. If it turns out really well then the record company might want to use it, and you'll have saved several thousand pounds and launched another career into the bargain.

So do I end up owning the recordings?

Ah, that's the catch. Under a renegotiation you might be able to come to some arrangement on this where you lease the masters back to the company at some time in the future, for example. Otherwise, the record company continues to own them, even though in practice you've paid for them if they're successful. They will own the actual physical multi-track master tape, or data, used in making the masters, and also the separate right to remix, release and exploit these, but the owner of the actual recording doesn't automatically own the right to exploit it unless it's covered in his agreement. If you, or your manager, can do a deal where the recordings are just licensed (rather than assigned) to the record company for, say, 10–20 years,

then if the record company is in 'material' (i.e. serious) breach of its obligations to you and doesn't put this right during the 'cure' period, then you could actually get your rights back and start exploiting them yourself. Record companies are gradually relenting on this point, but they remain highly resistant.

Some artists, most recently Simply Red, once established and free of their existing contracts but unable to get back the rights to their original masters, have taken the huge step of embarking on a wholesale re-recording of their back catalogue, so that they have masters that they own themselves. Truth is, though, that it's notoriously hard to reproduce a performance exactly in every nuance, and the record-buying public and advertisers alike have a strong preference for original recordings.

Who pays the producer or remixer's royalty?

Again, the record company normally makes the agreement with the producer and any remixers and pays the costs, advances and royalties, but they'd expect to deduct that from your royalties. If the royalty is 16% and the producer wants 4% for UK, 2% or 3% overseas, then your royalty goes down accordingly. If a remixer wants another 1%, again it comes out of your share unless the producer allowed it to be deducted from his, which is possible. Producers will probably want a fee, too, which may or may not be an advance against their royalty, and be payable part upfront and part on completing the recordings. This is partly because the record company will have the option to reject some of the tracks and replace them with the same or different tracks by another producer. In some cases, remixers may take a flat fee and no royalty, but all of this goes down as part of recording costs, and normally comes out of your royalty as an artist. Even if you owned the original recording and licensed it to the record company, it would insist on owning any remixes that it saw fit to make and pay for itself (and that's assuming the remixers themselves, if they were big names, didn't want to retain an interest in their mix).

Who chooses the producer and can I cut him out and produce myself?

Depending on the deal, and your experience, either you will ask to use a particular producer, generally one you're already in contact with, or the label will recommend someone. Sometimes the label will only sign you if you agree to a particular producer. They'll probably have a list of producers who have worked for them before and who they can trust to do the job well and within budget. If so, he should hopefully be someone you rate highly already, and you should ask the label what his royalty will be – see the last question. He should be interested enough to want to hear you play the tracks live and discuss them with you before going into the studio.

If you know what sounds it's possible to get out of the average collection of outboard equipment in a studio, and have a good rapport with the studio's resident sound engineer, then you could produce yourself. The engineer will know how to get the sounds you want as long as you know what sounds you actually do want. However, it's not to be recommended. Even major artists who could produce themselves and have done so, still like to use a producer, partly because it's easy to become self-indulgent or unnecessarily perfectionist, and it helps to have an expert's outside opinion.

What if I can't help missing a session etc.?

The record company should always give 'reasonable prior notice' of any sessions etc. they want you to attend. They'll usually be as helpful as possible in finding a date and time that is convenient to you although the contract will state that pro-

vided they give you reasonable notice, you must be there.

Some contracts state that if you fail to turn up for no good reason, then you have to pay, or have deducted from your royalties, the entire cost of the session booked, including cancellation fees to the studio, backing musicians, orchestras etc. If you have a perfectly good excuse for your absence then this could be grossly unfair on you. If, on the other hand, you continually fail to appear at sessions that you have previously agreed were perfectly convenient for you, then of course you are being grossly unfair to the record company. It will probably lose patience and drop you, unless you are a megastar, in which case it may excuse you on the grounds of 'artistic temperament', but the costs will still come out of your royalties!

When will I be paid?

Royalties should be paid at least twice yearly, both you and your manager (as specified in your contract) should receive a statement at your last known address and, if monies are at last due (all advances and costs having been recouped), the company should have up-to-date bank details so it can make electronic payments. Even years later, it's important to make sure that every record company that should be paying you royalties has your up-to-date contact and bank details. If you haven't taken reasonable measures to keep in touch they have no legal obligation to pay you more than six years in back royalties. The contract may say that they'll pay you 'as soon as possible' after June 30 and December 31, which really is too vague. Try to make sure that it says 'within X days after...' (60 is perfectly normal, although it may sound a long time). Make sure that the record company will continue to pay you on records made by you that are sold by the label or its licensees after the contract has finished. Generally, they should be payable for the whole of the remaining period in which the recording remains copyright. You'd think this would be obvious, but at least one international record company has issued contracts in the past stating that the royalties cease at the end of the contract, even though it can go on selling the artist's records! Some companies will pay quarterly, or make 'payments on account' on March 31 and September 30. It's as much down to their administration as to your bargaining power.

Can they stop paying my artist royalties for any reason?

Another major company's contract allowed it to withhold your royalties if you lost your voice or talent, or if you die before the contract has finished. As these reasons are beyond your control this is totally unfair to you (or your next of kin), as is the withholding of royalties if you are unable, through no fault of yours, to turn up for sessions as we mentioned earlier (it's possible to insure against such things – see 'General Q & A'). If the company is hit with a lawsuit by, for example, another company claiming to control your recording services exclusively, then it would have the right to suspend payment, though it should only do so once a writ has been issued, and payments should resume, including royalties accrued, with interest, once the case has been tried or settled in the company's favour (if that is the outcome). In any event, it should continue to send you statements telling you what you've earned.

What happens about websites, photographs and publicity?

Under the contract, you give the company the right to use your name, biography, photographs etc. for publicity purposes, often the right to set up a website in your name (or that of the band) and even control of your online fan club. These should be scrutinised and approved by you or your manager. The company may well expect to own the photos etc. that it has arranged for you, or expect you to supply it with photos, which it can use however it likes, free of payment to you. Try to limit the use to album inserts, posters, press advertisements etc. (i.e. only things directly connected with their advertising and sale of recordings of you). The record company will also want to produce electronic press kits (something on DVD to give to the press to promote you, which will include your songs, or extracts from them, together with interviews etc.), and there's no reason not to allow them to do this – at the start, publicity is all-important.

Can I stop my tracks appearing on a compilation album?

Generally, the record company has the right to license your recordings to any compilation company or to include them in their own compilations, whether this means a high-price package of 20 hits currently in the charts, or a very low-priced collection of 100 old reggae hits from the Seventies, New Romantic hits from the Eighties or whatever. If you get to the stage of renegotiating a better deal, you could ask for approval (not to be unreasonably withheld or delayed) before your tracks are used on any compilation.

What are compilation album sales worth?

Albums of chart hits may sell two or three times as well as your current hit single itself! So the royalties can be quite substantial. If your track is dance or mainstream pop, it could wind up on 10 or more UK compilations and 30 or 40 worldwide, all while the single is still in the charts. If you're with a smaller company they're less likely to worry which other companies they license their tracks to, so you'll probably end up on more compilations than if you were with a 'major'. Your royalty will probably be lower on compilations by other companies than compilations by your own, but, cumulatively, this can be a huge source of income. All this additional income can help to recover the recording and other costs that will be deducted before you get paid, and can make a big difference.

That said, the actual royalty from each sale of a compilation album for your one track will be relatively lower than those on your own album or even a single, because there are more tracks across which the royalty is pro-rated and only one of the tracks is yours. So, say you get 16% PDP for your album of 10 tracks, for one track on a 40 track *Now* compilation album, you would get 16% PDP divided by 40, which is 0.4% PDP, on top of which your actual entitlement may be further reduced (see above) because the release is a compilation album.

So it follows that just one track of yours on one very cheap, budget compilation, even if it sells several hundred thousand copies, will probably only bring in a few hundred pounds in royalties for you as the artist, just as it would for you as the songwriter.

What happens if I am part of a duo or band?

Try to establish whether the company is really interested in the group, or just one member. If that's you, then you will have to do some heart-searching and decide whether you really want to succeed without your friends.

The company will probably want each of you to sign identical contracts individ-ually, then there will be one 'collateral' agreement that deals with advances etc. You will end up sharing the total royalty equally. The individual contract may well say that the artist royalty is, in effect, '16%' or suchlike, but it will then go on to say that the royalty is reduced pro rata with other artists performing on the recording who are entitled to receive royalties. The 'other artists' of course will be the rest of the group, who each have identical agreements. Although this wording will also cover the record company if it wants you to record with another of its contract artists, it definitely shouldn't mean that your royalties are reduced pro rata with any session musicians playing on your records.

What happens if the band splits up?

If you leave the band before it has any success, then a record company will probably not be interested in you and will not take up the option on your contract. But you'll still be under contract to them till that time. If you went off and joined a group under contract to some other company during that time, then the first record company may well feel it is entitled to participate in the revenues from that band's recordings and may take legal action against you and/or the new company to enforce those rights; at the very least there will have to be a negotiation between all parties. So if you leave a band, it's best to make sure that everyone who has a hand in your career knows of your intentions and that you are absolutely clear of one company before recording for another. It's worth asking for something in writing confirming this.

If the company wants to keep you on as a solo artist, or do so while keeping the band going with you as a member, then your contract should make it clear that you won't just get your pro-rata share of the advances and royalties as you would with the band but rather that you get the full artists share on your solo albums. If the band splits completely, remember that unless you're very successful there's every chance you'll all be dropped. There are only so many acts any company can cope with on its roster at any one time.

If someone else joins your band, he'll be expected to sign the same agreements as the existing members. If he's already signed to another label and your company has to negotiate with his to get him free, it's likely you'll all end up having the legal costs deducted from your royalties, plus any percentage of future earnings that the new company has to pay to his old label (for further information on band names, see the next section).

Is it right that some bands don't play on their own records?

It used to be very common. Standards of musicianship are improving and technology makes it easier to 'drop in' and re-record over any mistakes, but it can still happen. Acts making their own albums and 'delivering' them as finished products to the label also means this happens less these days. But studio time is expensive and a band member who's perfectly OK live might have a 'block' in the studio. If by any chance this does happen to you, don't worry about your royalties – you will get your share of whatever is due under the contract regardless, though the cost of the session musicians will be deducted from your royalties.

Will I have any say in album designs or notes?

You won't have the final say, but the label should take your views into consideration. You shouldn't end up like Spinal Tap, being shown their 'none more black' album cover as a *fait accompli*, but remember that the design is a major selling factor and the record company will perhaps rightly see this as their area of expertise. It's the kind of point that can be changed in your favour on renegotiation, but remember you wind up paying

out of your royalties for any re-designs or complex packaging, and if you're too self-indulgent, then your sales and your royalties might suffer. If you can commission the artwork yourself (art colleges being the place to look first) then, provided the record company is happy with it, there'll be less cost to deduct from your royalties and you should be able to retain the ownership of it and use it yourself for merchandising – logos on sweatshirts, posters etc. (Just make sure you've paid for it and you own it outright or have a suitable royalty agreed, otherwise your art college friend could hold you to ransom in the future over the use of it.)

The record company would expect to spend £1,000+ on the artwork (recoupable from your royalties) for your album, and they would definitely own it if they commissioned it or produced it in-house, so it's worth trying to come up with something yourself.

Should songwriting and merchandising be mentioned in the contract?

There should be no mention in the contract of your songwriting services, unless you are consciously entering into something like the new '360' deals, and if they are and you are happy with that, you should ensure that the terms are at least equal to those you would get from a separate publishing company. Even today, some companies try to pick up publishing rights in the record contract as though it were quite normal, and on what could most politely be described as old-fashioned terms (or less politely as outrageous). In fact, it's not at all normal to have your publishing and recording rights with the same company, and if you were already signed to a publisher under an exclusive deal and you then signed a record contract with this in it, you'd end up in the middle of a legal wrangle!

If your songs are to be published by your record label's publishing company, it should be under a totally separate agreement with that company, not least because the rights involved are radically different and the term, retention period, rights, prior approvals, rates and types of income will all be very different.

Some record companies' contracts also allow them to market goods such as T-shirts with your name, image or logo, but you should try to limit the label to audio products and music videos only (see 'What should I know about merchandising?' in the next section), as the label will probably pay you a fraction of what your manager could get for you, and a significant source of income for you will be tied up in the offset against your recording costs etc.

> To you – a quid... seein' as it's yours anyway!

Who decides which songs I should record and which get released?

The record company will have the final decision, but it's only really 'put together' acts who are more or less told what to record. Country acts frequently record other people's songs, but these days they're usually new songs chosen by the artist or producer. Newly signed acts will be expected as a matter of course to write or at least co-write almost all their own material, even, to be honest, if writing isn't their strong point.

The producer may bring in some songs from contacts he has with writers or publishers, or he might be a writer himself. With dance acts or 'put together' bands this is that much more likely. Don't dismiss ideas for outside songs if the label or the producer suggests them, but equally if you really don't like them, do say so.

If they want you to re-record a track you did a few years back for a previous label, check to make sure your agreement with that label doesn't prevent you from doing so. About three to five years from the date your last deal ended would be the normal length of time that has to elapse before you can re-record a track. Much more than that would probably be a restraint of your trade and the company couldn't stop you, but the copyright people at your new company will usually be prepared to check old agreements if necessary to ensure you're OK to do it.

The record company will also have the final say as to which tracks go on the album and which are released as singles, but again they should consult you.

How do the records get promoted?

Record labels have promotion budgets for all their releases. Majors have internal promo departments but still sometimes also employ outside independent promoters. These usually ask a set fee per week per record, plus big bonuses if the records reach a certain chart position. Even if your label won't commit to spend a certain amount, try to ask for your records to be A-list priorities or that the label will use its 'best endeavours' to promote them.

You or your manager or publisher can employ promoters separately, though try to ensure that they work with the label; you don't want them to imply that the label's people can't or won't do the job properly. Independent promoters are not cheap. Good ones can even expect to get a royalty of, say, 1% of PDP on sales of the record they are promoting, but they are well worth the money because media exposure is all-important. One hit can change your life and they know that.

Is there any alternative to the normal recording agreement?

It's possible these days to try to negotiate an agreement under which you and the record company jointly own your masters. One major act from the Nineties not so long ago re-signed to a major label with a deal under which the artist would bear a substantial part of the huge marketing budget for their new album, in return for a huge (over 300%) increase in their potential earnings (percentage-wise) from the label for the new album. This was on the basis that it would be exploited in all media to the maximum reasonable extent and that the artist would get the rights back sooner rather than later, and certainly that the label wouldn't acquire the rights, as normal, for life of copyright, subject to possible reversions for inactivity.

You should certainly get back your own master recordings, though not necessarily the multi-tracks, to enable you to remix them within a few years if you are renegotiating or you have any kind of a track record at all. This may even be possible for 'manufactured' bands or for pop/dance records, on the basis that the record company takes a share (say 50%) in a jointly owned company with you, and that company then also negotiates the publishing of your songs, manufacture and distribution of merchandise/streaming of live concerts etc. The idea would be that the record company would pay you an advance (though not a fortune) but would then help to negotiate these other deals and would share in them (i.e. recoup their advance to you from their share of income from them), and thus be prepared to sign you to an album deal when they otherwise might not have bothered. This and other new models for contracts are out there to be had, but they may not be available from the record company you want to be with or from the one offering you a deal. It's up to you and your advisors to strike a deal that suits you best both in terms of the method and proportion of income you get paid and the services (such as selling records) that the record company offers.

How would I get out of a recording contract?

Ultimately, of course, a record company can't physically force you to go into a studio and record. If you've hardly earned anything from your records, and don't expect to, then you may not be bothered with any threat to withhold your royalties. Then again, this is bound to become known around the industry and may hamper your chances of getting a new deal in the future, and even if you get a new deal, chances are your old record company will end up participating in your income.

So the best way out of a recording contract, as with a publishing contract, is by mutual agreement, although you should expect to be asked to pay back any advance payment that the record company has given you and that they haven't yet recovered from your royalties. Of course, there are occasionally instances where the record company itself is happy for the deal to end, to save having to pay you further huge advances that it promised you but now can't be sure of getting back. Thus Mariah Carey was famously paid a reported $28million as part of an agreement whereby her recording contract with EMI was terminated early (only to record a highly successful album for her next label, which EMI got no part of).

If you're at all unsure, consult with your lawyer, especially before putting anything in writing when trying to get out of an agreement or before entering into another agreement elsewhere, even if it's only a brief phone call. He'll always try to estimate what his charge is likely to be if he has to get involved, although he won't of course be able to tell you very precisely until he knows exactly how you stand. If you are wanted by another record company, they may put their business affairs people onto the case for you. In your particular circumstances there may be some other way of getting free from your contract, but record companies have very good lawyers and even the most powerful artist can end up having to settle for less than an outright win. If you need proof, you need only look at George Michael's epic court battle with Sony and Prince's more surreal contests with Warners.

Have the record company exercised their options on time?

They may not have taken up one of their options to extend the contract. This may mean waiting till a certain date and hoping that the letter of extension doesn't arrive. If it doesn't, then write to them straight away, telling them politely that you note that they haven't taken up their option to renew and, in view of this, you intend to place your services elsewhere. Do remember, though, that if you carry on recording for them for some time after the renewal date, even though the contract was not properly renewed, your position may be less strong, as you may be taken to have accepted the extension of contract at the very least for those recordings you have already made.

It's possible that the company will still have a chance to take up the option, if it maintains that the prior period (contract year) hasn't yet come to an end, or if you were required to tell them that the option is due to give them a chance to exercise it. Also, they may have sent notice to your old address because you failed to tell them you'd moved, although normally they'd also have to have sent a courtesy copy of this sort of correspondence to your lawyer, so he'd be aware of it.

Ultimately, it's very important that you keep copies of all correspondence and fully understand the sequence of events that has to happen either for the option to be exercised, the option to be passed up on or the option to expire.

Have the record company failed to account to you properly?

If they have, and they fail to repair the error within a certain time period, you may (depending on your negotiated contract) have the right to terminate the deal; you may even have a right to get out without repayment of advances or to 'get your masters back'. Most modern contracts are very explicit as to what constitutes a 'material breach' and the remedies that you have; they also usually offer a 'cure' period (often 30 days) from you giving notice for the record company to fix the breach before you can ask for your remedies.

A record company may have repeatedly failed to send royalty statements to you at the times set out in the contract (usually twice a year). Then again, if the contract says that they are not obliged to send a statement when there is little or no money due to you, then this is probably the reason if you have had no statements for a while. Otherwise the statements should have arrived even if no money was due. Similarly, if they have failed to actually pay you when you believe that your advance is recouped or have added costs to your unrecouped balance that are not justified by the contract, cleared licences that your contract gives you prior approval of, or done anything that seriously contradicts the terms of your contract, you may have a remedy. Finally, it may be that you have a right to audit their books at your own expense, and if your accountant discovers that their accounting is out by more than a certain percentage, you will almost certainly be entitled to that money, plus interest, and possibly gain the right to terminate the deal.

Have the record company failed to record or release what they promised?

It may be that the record company has failed to record or release the agreed number of tracks with you during the current term of the agreement to enable them to renew. (Obviously, you will have to wait until the end of the current term before you can say this for certain and, perversely, that may be some time if the current period is itself dependant on you making recordings.) Even if they're only committed to record the tracks, not release them, if they didn't release them within a certain period after 'delivery' or 'completion', this could be a restraint of your trade. If, of course, you just haven't met your delivery dates because you never got round to doing final mixes, or some such reason, then you can't blame them for not releasing on time. Make sure you know what's expected of you.

Will I be completely tied to the company?

Your services will be exclusive to the record company, so make sure you ask them first if you want to do even one session for another company (they'll often go along with this provided they get a royalty and credit on the record). If a record company wishes to sign you up, but you're playing regularly on sessions elsewhere, you may be able to get them to sign you exclusively under your own name, but leave you free to work elsewhere unnamed or under pseudonyms (there's no limit to the number of these you can have as an artist).

They'll require you not to re-record for another company any song that you recorded for them for a number of years after the contract has finished, as we mentioned in the last section. Incidentally, until recently, record companies in the US were trying to regard their artists, in legal terms, as people who just hap-

pened to be employed by them (under 'contracts for hire') to come in and make records as employees. Happily, this came to court in 2002 and the artists won.

Should I sign with an independent record production company?

Independent producers are very often management/publishing concerns or established record producers who are sometimes prepared to invest in the making of masters speculatively rather than 'to order' from record labels, especially if they have studio facilities on tap. Unlike most of the record companies, good independent producers are not restricted to London or other major music centres. It's possible you could be recording a demo in a local studio and find that they are so knocked out that they're prepared to give free studio time if they can have the recording to sell to a label.

They will most likely lease the records to the label in return for a royalty of well over 20% of PDP (a lot more than you could expect to get as an artist) out of which they should pay you roughly what you'd have got if you'd signed directly to a label. This could be, say, 17% of PDP or 66.66% of what they get (more in the case of production companies that are part of management companies trying to do an all-in deal with you – see Management section). Or it could be that they will do a deal with the record company to make the first singles and album and then you'll sign directly to the label for any future options. If so, this will be covered in the inducement letter.

They will want to sign you up for a number of years just as a record company would, because the record company they lease your records to will expect options on further singles or albums. There is no reason at all for you not to sign with an independent producer, but you should know or find out exactly what his track record is and discuss closely what he intends to try to do for you. Try to make especially sure that your agreement with an independent producer gives you some protection in case nothing happens at all.

If you are signing exclusively to an independent producer, rather than just making a single or two to 'see what happens', then he should guarantee to record a certain number of tracks just as a label would. What he can't of course do is guarantee that they will be released. And herein lies a problem. The most straightforward royalty split will be a straight division between you of all royalties he gets in, less the recording and any other direct costs that are agreed. However, until he's found an interested label and done the deal, neither of you knows what the overall royalty to be split will be, or how many options over how many years the label will want, or if they're prepared to sign you through another party. It's another chicken and egg situation. A label may be interested in you but may insist that you sign with them direct rather than through the independent producer. In that case, he may be prepared to let you go, provided that the label pays him a separate royalty (an 'override'). If the independent producer is prepared not to sign a contract with you until he knows all this, then fine, but that's not very likely, otherwise he's in no position to guarantee your services to a label (or to guarantee he won't be cut out of the deal).

If I'm signed to an independent producer, will I have to sign an 'inducement letter'?

The record company itself will probably ask you to sign a small agreement, called an inducement letter, directly between you and them. Under this, if you and your independent production company split, or he goes out of business before the end of his deal with the record company, then you have to record directly for the record company for the duration of that deal. If the inducement letter states that you will, at that point, sign the record company's standard artist agreement or a similar phrase then ask to see it, as it may contain certain clauses whereby you end up with less than the royalty the independent producer was paying you! If that turns out to be the case, you should make clear that you need at least the terms you are already on. As ever, read and try to understand everything you are asked to sign, don't be afraid to ask questions and/or get advice from your lawyer.

Should I let them record me before I've signed anything?

It does happen, more often than you'd think, that a company will pay to record and release records prior to getting the artist or producer to sign an agreement. This certainly avoids having to pay an advance before release, and you may not be able to dispute their ownership of the recordings later if you co-operate now on an *ad hoc* basis.

However, this could ultimately be to your advantage. If the first release is successful then they'll want another and will have to offer you more by way of advances, royalties, promotion etc. than you'd have asked for, or you'd have got, before you'd had that first hit. If they don't offer it, some other company will, and your current label will have trouble stopping you leaving, even though they may try to make it awkward. Some companies offer 'development' money or studio time to record you prior to taking the plunge and signing you. This is quite deliberate and you could walk away from it, but they hope that it'll buy them some time to assess your potential while making you feel beholden to them. If you do leave, they may be prepared to sell you the recordings, but they'll have no right to release them without your permission, and you could go off and re-record the same songs elsewhere immediately if you wished.

GENERAL QUESTIONS & ANSWERS ON RECORDING

Could I just sell downloads of my music online?

Despite falling physical sales the world over, it's still a valid exercise to make and sell CDs as they still represent the vast majority of recorded music sales. This is not to say online is not worthwhile, just that you shouldn't entirely discount physical product (see the next question). There are websites (including iTunes) that allow unsigned artists to upload their music and make it available for sale, and you can even set this up directly from your own website or with a link to such a service. Remember, though, that if you sign a deal with a record company, they will want you to take your own service down and remove the tracks from other online sites, so try not to sign or commit to anything long term with these services.

Could I make and sell my own records?

You may be thinking of starting your own label (physical, online or both), whether because no one else will release your records, because you want to keep ownership of your own masters, or because you think it would work out best financially. If so, then think about your act's personnel, your material, the quality of your recordings, the size of your following and your general image first. If you're still convinced you're right and they're all wrong, then start looking for finance to go it alone. Even though it's cheaper to sell online (and even to manufacture your own CDs) than ever before, to operate at any size big enough to make real money will require some capital. In recent years many independent producers, including

many outside London, have taken to pressing their own records in small quantities and getting someone else to distribute them. Some of these small labels have become very successful, usually with a specific type of music, up to the point where they've been bought out by one of the majors. Some are actually owned and run by a band or artist themselves, who have had some money behind them but were unable or unwilling to get a deal with an established record company. These are not to be confused with 'labels', which some record companies give to their established stars who think they've discovered someone else amazing (this really does happen eg. Diana Ross 'discovering' The Jackson 5, Madonna signing Alanis Morissette to her own label etc.). At the other end of the scale from this is a one-off album or single recorded and pressed by a semi-professional act to sell at gigs or for charity (see next but one question).

As we said in the Songwriting section, it is possible, especially with dance or mainstream pop, to make a credible recording on home studio equipment. More and more people own digital all-in-one studios or have computers with software such as Cuebase or Protools, together with CD burners, and they really only need studios for mixing down and adding the outboard effects they can't afford to buy.

It's then perfectly easy to take your finished master recording to a pressing plant and have CDs produced from it. For dance/pop recordings on vinyl, before you can ask for vinyl to be pressed, you need a 'stamper' from which the pressings can be made (these are made from lacquered discs, which have to be 'cut' from the master recording). At this stage, certain frequencies can predominate and make a big difference to the sound of the finished discs, so you should supervise the cutting rather than leave it to others.

The minimum sensible quantity you can expect to have pressed up is normally 500 (plus or minus around 10%, as they can't always stop the machine exactly at the required figure), although it's a lot cheaper per pressing to have 1,000 and so on. The pressing plant can advise on printing of labels and sleeves/cases if necessary, and on the likely cost. Around 1,000 CDs of a 40-minute album should still cost £1 each or less, and 1,000 12″ vinyl singles would be about 40p each, though with mastering, labels, sleeves and artwork/reproduction costs for labels etc., you'd be looking at about £1,500–2,000 in total. You obviously wouldn't have any artist royalties to pay on sales if you're the artist but, if your songs are handled by a publisher (or you've covered works by another writer), then the MCPS will have to collect mechanical royalties (or in certain circumstances their commission) on pressings, even though the bulk of the royalties would eventually find their way back to you. MCPS liaises with the pressing plants, so they'll know which songs you've recorded, and if you call them they'll help you with the straightforward paperwork. Incidentally, beware of giving away free gifts ('widgets') with copies of your record if you're hoping that it will make the charts, as there are rules about this and, from time to time, records are disqualified for having an unfair advantage over their competitors through some add-on or giveaway.

How can I get my records distributed?

If you're selling them at gigs or distributing white-label 12″ singles to DJs and specialist record shops yourself, then fine. But, assuming you've managed to get some airplay, even just locally, it's no use the public going to record shops to buy it if the dealers have never heard of it

and don't know where to order it. At this stage you really need professional distribution.

The distribution companies used to be owned and run by the major record companies, but they have since sold them off, no doubt looking to the future of digital downloads. However, most music is still sold in the old way and the distribution companies are still there. They will charge around 25–30% of PDP to distribute for you, and they will want you to agree to distribute all your follow-up recordings through them for a given period (if you sign to a major record label in the meantime, this will probably override that provision, but check!). This is especially true if you were so 'hot' that the distributor gave you an advance on the strength of it, which is possible. They may require you to supply 'dealer mailings' to be sent to all the dealers in Britain or they may include you on theirs. Some will be more amenable to one-off or small numbers of releases than others. The one thing you should ensure is that you remain throughout the actual owner of the recording.

If you want to stand a chance of making the charts you'll have to register your 'label' with the chart compilers (the current compilers' name and address will be listed in the trade magazine *Music Week*). Incidentally, you should check any P&D deal you have to release your records to see whether they intend to charge you (or offset against the amounts they owe you) for publicity or advertising that they organise.

Is it any different with charity records?

If an established artist wishes to appear on a 'Live Aid' type record or video, his or her record company will usually have no problem. If you want to release your own charity record you'll need to go through the process of recording, manufacture and distribution mentioned in the last two questions. If you can persuade any of the people involved to do it for nothing, or at least for no profit or at a discount, so much the better. Just because your cause is very deserving, however, doesn't guarantee that they'll say yes (not least because they get similar requests every day and can only afford to say yes to so many, and the request might involve many others down the line, who are less able to afford it, working for nothing), any more than that the local radio station will play the record. As we've said, the publishers who own the songs can't waive their right to let MCPS collect the royalties on their behalf, but they might well be prepared to pay their share (and the writers' shares if they're agreeable to it) straight to your charity, once they've received the royalties from MCPS.

Who owns the copyright in my recordings?

In principle you own your recordings, but you assign all rights to your record company when you sign to them (though you might be able to negotiate to get those rights back after a period of years). Just as there is a copyright in a song as soon as it exists in 'tangible form' (i.e. a recording or manuscript), there is also copyright in the recordings themselves, even though they may of course contain someone else's copyright, namely the song. Copyright in the recording in most countries now lasts 50 years from the end of the year when it was first made available to the public (in other words first released). In the US the situation is more complex but in essence is about 95 years, which is the revised length of time that has been suggested in Europe too. If a track is remixed and re-released years later, then the copyright in that mix in theory starts from the first release of the mix. Even a cleaned-up, remastered version of the original recording may have 50 years from the date of the first release of that version too.

There is also copyright in television programmes, films etc., which in turn will usually contain both copyrighted recordings and also copyrighted songs. All this makes clearance of rights by audio-visual producers and multi-media companies so complex that they frequently resort to commissioning their own music to ensure they're not exceeding the bounds of the licence they've been given for an already existing recording or song. This makes everything from feature films to video games a potential source of new commissions for music writers and producers.

A record company will put a (P) or P in a circle plus the year of first release of the recording on each of their records, together with the company that first produced or now owns the master recording. Right from the start the copyright in the recording effectively belongs to the label and not to you, unless you made it at your own expense and only leased it to the label. Otherwise they will own the right to reproduce that recording, the phonographic performance right in it (the right to broadcast or perform it in public), the rental right and all other so-called 'neighbouring rights' that exist in recordings, although you as an artist or producer now have legal rights to a share of the income from these too.

Is anything payable when a record is broadcast?

Yes. As well as the PRS collecting from broadcasters for use of the songs, sums are also collected by an organisation called PPL (Phonographic Performance Ltd.). This is then paid equally to the record company, provided it's a member, and the artist separately. Many artists collect their shares through an organisation called PAMRA to which PPL pays their money and there is another organisation called AURA, which was set up by the Music Managers' Forum to do the same thing. Since the time that this right was granted directly to artists by law, it has taken years for PPL to work out precisely who played on which records. All the musicians and singers in theory should be credited and receive a share whenever the record is broadcast, even if it turns out to be a very small amount. That said, the total to be divided up amounts to several million pounds a year, so don't think this isn't worth bothering about.

Your record company can tell you what you need to do, or you can contact PAMRA or AURA or PPL directly (addresses in our 'useful address' list). If your record is getting airplay, then you should be assured of these fees provided the organisations know who and where you are. If you're a 'featured' artist (i.e. either your name or the name of a group of which you are a regular member appears on the record label), then you'll get more than if you were just a session musician. There's also an organisation called VPL (Video Performance Ltd.), which performs the same function when music videos are broadcast. PPL have introduced a database called CatCo that enables its members (3,000 or thereabouts) to register their catalogues of recordings directly online to PPL and in theory most recordings should be there, together with vital information regarding the artists, helping to streamline the payment of PPL royalties (check out the website listed in 'useful addresses').

If I'm offered either a royalty or session fee, which should I take?

If you are not signed exclusively to one record company, but you are a musician playing on sessions for various companies or a diva singing 'guest' vocals on records for various producers, there may be occasions when you will be offered either a session fee or a royalty on a particular recording. Generally, if you are a 'featured' artist (i.e. your name will appear on the record label) you should choose the royalty just in case the record becomes a hit. There have been a number of occasions over the years where the featured artist on a big hit only received a session fee, and their stories have

reached the press. Obviously, if you really need the ready money and you don't think the record stands an earthly chance of selling, or if you really don't trust the company to account royalties to you properly, you'll have to decide the case on its merits.

Is it a good idea to give my writing and recording services to the same company?

Not necessarily. There is always the risk of a conflict of interest, and you should certainly try to avoid cross-collateralisation of your publishing and recording royalties (unless you really feel the deal for other reasons is the right one for you). That said, the majors run their publishing arms as entirely separate operations and shouldn't try to cross-collateralise your royalties from recording and publishing. Then again, some artists/writers feel, perhaps unfairly, that when checking up on royalty accountings, you may get less assistance from the company's own publishing associate than from an entirely separate publisher.

What should I know about recording sessions?

You probably already know what goes on at a professional recording session even if you have never actually taken part in one yourself. The two vital people at a session, besides the artists themselves, are the producer and the engineer. The producer decides what sound he wants the instruments and vocals to have and whether anything needs to be re-recorded and at what point the recording has been satisfactorily completed. The engineer sits at the mixing desk in the control room and actually achieves the sounds that the producer wants. The two tasks overlap considerably. Most producers used to be engineers (or at least have their skills), and could do the whole thing themselves if they were familiar with the equipment of the studio being used. In fact, these days almost everyone sits in the control room, as most instruments are directly injected into the mixing desk. The live room is reserved for vocals, horns etc. and the occasional live drummer (something of a novelty for a lot of studios).

Thankfully, keyboards can be programmed in advance and put down from the computer, and other instruments can be recorded separately, though you should still expect to play through some tracks numerous times for the engineer to obtain the right sound before he even attempts to take it. Professional session musicians will expect to be given a copy of the music specially arranged for their instruments and will simply read this off, though if you're lucky and explain yourself well enough, they'll hopefully ad lib whatever you want them to play. (Careful though not to ask for too much by way of a contribution, or you may end up giving away part of your publishing at some point in the future, as occurred not so long ago with the song 'A Whiter Shade Of Pale'). Bands should have rehearsed the song sufficiently beforehand so that there is no question of them forgetting it if they can't read music or have no music to refer to.

Traditionally, a session lasted three hours, but other than in the worlds of film or classical music, sessions can take as long as needed (usually as long as you've got) and you can't get very much down in three hours, so you'd expect to hire a studio by the day. Ever since the days of The Beatles, it's been quite accepted that a band can record complete tracks without ever meeting each other in the studio. Professional session musicians will be expected to arrive with their instruments. For large instruments the musician should receive an additional fee called 'porterage'. A group should ask beforehand whether their instruments and equipment will be wanted on the session. The producer and engineer may think it necessary to hire better equipment or there may be some at the studio already.

What should I expect to pay for studio time?

If you're signed to a label with its own studios, check to see whether they can charge you a 'standard' hourly rate for your sessions and offset this against your royalties. A smaller independent studio will usually do a deal for a 10–12 hour day for perhaps as little as £200 for a 24-track session, or for 'downtime' when they're otherwise empty or for a 'lockout' where you hire the studio for 24 or 48 hours or more. If the desk is new and computerised, and there's plenty of outboard equipment that you otherwise might have to hire in, then the cost may be higher, but will probably be worth it to you, provided of course that you know what it can do. Because of this, it's as important to know what 'toys' they have as to know what the basic recording equipment is.

Some studios have their own programming suites that are compatible with the studio and can be hired at much lower rates. Of course, if you can do the programming at home then you can save even more.

If you're recording onto tape then the studio will supply the tape, but unless you've paid for it, expect them to retain the master tape (though not, of course, the right to exploit it without your permission). They can run off CDs and DATs or other copies for you, but if they let you bring your own CDs or DATs then they'll be a lot cheaper than 'buying' them from the studio. This applies to reels of 2″ tape as well, though it's harder just to lay your hands on a reel of 2″ tape these days. Even refreshments supplied supposedly gratis might be charged to you, especially by larger studios, so it's worth making enquiries, especially if you're paying the bills upfront (rather than just out of your royalties).

A smaller studio may do a deal whereby they don't charge you the full rate in return for an override royalty on your records, but don't expect it. They have to make a living and, if they wanted to gamble, they'd probably get better odds on the horses, no matter how great you try to persuade them you are.

The increasing accessibility of high quality home recording is certainly working to your advantage, since this means that studio costs are kept relatively stable, but it can also be to your disadvantage as fewer studios are economically viable because of lack of business.

What should I be paid if I'm asked to produce a record?

As we've said, name producers would expect around 4% royalty in the UK (maybe more) and around two-thirds of that for overseas earnings, together with fees, part upfront and part on delivery of the recordings. They may be able to choose the studio they work in, or this may already be decided (most producers have preferences for certain studios, sometimes as much for the ambience or the history as for the equipment). A producer with no track record may be offered around 2% royalty or even just a flat fee. If it's your own (or your own band's) record that you're producing, then don't necessarily expect anything extra, even though you're clearly saving the record company money.

The record company will generally do the negotiations and the paperwork and will sign you (the producer) directly. They will sometimes, but by no means always, only pay the producer royalty once they have recovered not only his advance but also the costs of the production of the record. Naturally, this is a very good incentive to you as the producer to keep the costs low.

Some freelance producers can earn large sums by way of fees plus royalties, and there are even companies acting as agencies for producers, finding them work and negotiating fees.

Of course, many producers of dance tracks and dance-orientated pop tracks are, in effect, the artists, just using a session singer on lead vocals and doing all the rest themselves. In the past, production teams such as Stock, Aitken & Waterman, The Bee Gees and the Motown and Memphis Soul teams used to produce records that would invariably come out under the name of the singer, though the producers would usually be using their own songs and playing some of the instruments. They might also either have a share in the ownership of the recordings or else be on a royalty. If you are a producer/artist then you should receive at the very least half the total artist royalty, and hopefully all of it (if you can get the featured vocalist to agree to a session fee). You wouldn't necessarily be signed by a label as an exclusive artist/producer, but some larger companies would want to do this (sign you under that artist name for anything up to a five-album deal) because this is their company policy, even though their A&R person signed you on the strength of just one rather good dance track! Some singers who feature on such records have a big enough name to command a high artist royalty in their own right. In such circumstances you, the producer, should try to decide in advance how much of the royalty you really want to give away on what is basically your record. If it was always envisaged that the track would be released as xxxxx (producer's name) featuring zzzzz (lead vocalist), then it will be easier to negotiate the lion's share of the royalty.

What should I be paid if I'm asked to remix a record?

Unless you have a big name as a DJ or remixer then you'll probably be offered (usually directly by the record company) a flat fee of a few hundred pounds and maybe a royalty of 0.5%–1%, which may come out of either the artists' royalties or the original producer's royalty. If you have a reputation, you could receive several thousand pounds per mix. You'd usually be expected to go away and do them yourself, but if studio costs are expected to be high then the record company might well pay these, too.

Is there any organisation representing record producers?

There is an organisation called MPG to which a large number of professional record producers belong. They even have a standard form of agreement for producers to use in respect of their services. (Generally, however, such agreements are similar in form to the agreement signed by the artist the producer is work-

ing with, though somewhat shorter and for a shorter term). MPG's contact details are in the 'Useful Addresses' section.

What might I get if I'm in a stage show that is recorded?

You will appreciate that a record company will not want to place the entire cast under contract. They probably would not be able to anyway, for many recording artists supplement their income by appearing in stage shows, even though they may otherwise be under contract to a record company other than the one that intends to record the show. What generally happens is that each member of the cast receives a session fee for the recording, and separately the record company pays an Artist Royalty at the going rate to the actors' union, Equity.

What might I get if my record is included in a film?

This is completely open to negotiation and varies enormously, but a hit record in a new film with a relatively small budget, say £4m or less, should bring in anywhere from £5,000–£15,000 in all. It's usually the top end of that for a full usage of, say, three minutes, and not a lot more even for a big budget epic, though it would be a great deal more for a really big song by a big artist. If it's a music film and you're guaranteed to be on the soundtrack album (which will bring in its own royalties), then it may be less, especially as there will be more songs and records for the film company to pay for.

The film company will usually want all media in perpetuity for the territory of the universe for this, or they just won't want to use your record (smaller budget and independent films can be a lot more flexible), though they will usually pay extra for 'out of context' trailers advertising the film. If you're actually asked to appear in the film, a new artist might get around £3,000 or substantially more, but as a part of a 'package' with his or her recording and song, while a top artist appearing in a film performing their record could be worth an all-in fee of tens of thousands.

It's such good exposure for you, or your record, for your song to be in a successful film that the fees are sometimes surprisingly low, unless you're already so big that you're helping to sell the film. Unless you started out as an actor then this could launch you on a whole new career (if you can act!). From Al Jolson and Bing Crosby in the Twenties and Thirties through to the likes of Elvis Presley, David Bowie, Gary and Martin Kemp from Spandau Ballet, Phil Collins and Madonna in more recent times, fame as a singer/musician can be a route into straight acting (though rarely to good reviews).

SONGWRITING

GETTING A PUBLISHING CONTRACT

You may be a songwriter or composer who is not looking to become a recording artist in your own right, or you may be a recording artist who writes or co-writes their own material. If it's the latter, then you may have signed a recording contract with a record company under which that company has asked for everything you write to go through their own music publishing outlet (most of the larger record companies have these). Our advice is that if at all possible you should try to give these valuable rights to a different company. Finally, you may be an artist and songwriter looking for both a publishing deal and a recording deal, but it is possible that getting the songwriting deal can lead to the recording contract (and of course vice versa).

Whichever it is, you need to know how to protect your rights and exploit them (to the extent that you want to). It is possible to go it alone, either in your home territory or across the world, but the vast majority of writers in the UK prefer to use a professional music publishing company. So how can you go about deciding which publisher and what sort of deal you should pursue?

Which publisher should I approach?

The first basic rule is to choose a publisher who is properly in the business of music publishing, and preferably has a track record of success in your style of music. The most obvious way to find this out is to check label copy on CDs, but you can also do some research online. Unfortunately, in the UK this rules out most but by no means all companies outside London (or Dublin in Eire), though cities as diverse as Manchester and Brighton do have their own thriving music scenes and at least one major publisher now has a presence in these cities. In most countries, the publishers and record companies are grouped fairly closely together in one area of the capital city, the US being a notable exception with New York, Los Angeles, Nashville and other cities all being music centres (Germany is another exception, with Hamburg, Munich and Berlin all being music centres). Most regional UK publishers are in fact record producers/managers/publishers, with the emphasis not usually being on the publishing side. For this reason, if you assigned your songs to even the largest and most reputable of these, the chances are that they would probably pass rights on to a publisher in the capital. So unless the local company is also doing other things for you, you might as well go direct to the 'dedicated' publisher yourself – you'll probably end up with a larger share of the earnings and will probably receive any royalties due to you more quickly. You'll probably also have better access to the people who are actually looking after your songs. Once you have a deal, don't be afraid to ring the Copyright Department with a query on how and when the songs were registered and any terms of the agreement you made. You can also contact the Royalty Department with a query on statements and cheques or electronic payments you receive, or talk to the Licensing Department about placing your songs in films or adverts. They may not be able to answer instantly, but you could probably expect a response within a week or so. A list of publishers with addresses is shown at the end of this section; the MPA (see 'Useful Addresses' below) also have a very helpful site listing publishers by name and by genre.

How can I get them to listen to my music?

Much of the advice we can give in this area overlaps with our advice in the

Getting A Record Contract section above, but there are specifics relating to Music Publishing. If at all possible, try to visit the publisher in person, but do make an appointment beforehand, even if you simply phone up asking to come in with your songs in a couple of hours. Sometimes they'll even agree to hear them straight away, but don't bank on it. Gone are the days when you'd turn up with a guitar or ask to sit at the piano and sing something to a man with a fat cigar who'd say, 'Don't call us, we'll call you'. They might well be prepared to listen to your demo in your presence, or they may ask you to send something to them first (though a good many publishers, for legal reasons, will not accept unsolicited material through the post). Chances are that if you send an unsolicited demo by post it will end up in a big box in someone's office with hundreds of others, with only the smallest chance of being heard. The same goes for email – we all get spam and we all delete it without even looking, so unless your email is expected, chances are it will never get opened. At least by ringing first you'll know the name of the person (usually in A&R) who will be responsible for assessing your demos, and you'll know

that you won't be completely wasting your time, as you might if you sent something out of the blue. If you do send something by post make sure you put your address/phone number on the CD itself rather than just on the case, and try to put together an attractive and eye-catching package, without being so gimmicky that you risk antagonising them.

How many songs should I include?

Whichever way you present the songs to a publisher, don't expect him to hear more than three at any one time and definitely put the best one (or one most likely to grab the listener's attention) first. If the first minute or so of the first song is poor, it's very possible that the others won't be heard at all. Always make a copy of your demo, in case a publisher wants to 'hang on to it' for someone else in the company to hear or in case it becomes lost or damaged. The few companies that accept postal submissions will not undertake to return them (and the few of those that do will expect you to include a stamped addressed envelope). If a publisher keeps your demo for a while, don't think that he's intending to steal your songs, but don't be afraid to find out when he'll be prepared to give you a decision on them. Incidentally, don't waste a publisher's time making excuses for the poor quality of your recording or your voice before playing the songs. Most writers do this, but there's really no need. If you're an aspiring singer, then the publisher might be interested in passing the demo on to his record company affiliate, or some friend of his at a record company. Many of the bigger publishers have contacts with particular record labels, even if they are not owned by the same conglomerate. Otherwise, don't worry – it's the songs the publisher is most interested in and, unless the demo is really rough, he'll see beyond any technical deficiencies.

Is a home-made demo really adequate?

Again, the advice in our Recordings section overlaps, but in general a studio-recorded demo, or one recorded at home and mixed down in a studio, is obviously preferable, but a clear home-recorded demo is often adequate for selling a song (much more so than for selling an artist to a record company). Try to use the best quality medium you can afford. It depends on the individual A&R manager but, obviously, it's worth considering sending in MP3 files by email, with accompanying materials in electronic form; or point them to your MySpace page or website. The best thing is to try to find out what the A&R manager prefers; remember, these people receive countless submissions daily and the easier it is for them to get to your music the better. In any event, make sure that there's no long silence before your demo starts and that there's nothing else immediately after it.

Is it worthwhile sending songs in?

If you can't get to the capital, don't despair. Plenty of songs sent in to publishers from around the country have found their way onto hit records. When you ring, ask for the name of the 'Creative Manager' or 'A&R Manager' (or possibly 'Professional Manager', which was the old title for such people), then send the demos to him or her with a list of the songs and, if you posted it, a stamped addressed envelope for the return of the CD (assuming you want it back if it's rejected). A copy of the lyrics could be helpful, depending upon the clarity of the recording and the type of songs. You could send a top-line or 'lead-sheet', which is the basic tune and lyrics, but there's not too much point these days. Certainly don't bother to send an accompanying full manuscript or a manuscript on its own, except in the concert/serious music field.

If you think the song is suitable for a particular artist, especially one who had a hit with one of that particular publisher's songs in the last couple of years, then there is no harm in suggesting this. Publishers like to have ideas set before them as well as the songs, but be sensible. It's generally best not to suggest that they send the songs to international megastars, especially non-UK based ones, unless you know that the publisher has connections with a particular star or that they're about to record in the UK.

There are magazines (tip-sheets) in the UK and other countries to which you can subscribe. These give details of which artists and their managers or producers are actively looking for new songs for a current or forthcoming recording project. These sources can seem expensive, but it's your career we're talking about, and they can be a very useful guide to who is recording a new album, who is producing it and for which label, as well as containing other useful background information about the local music scene. Check around to find out which magazines are current and reputable, and try to avoid a long commitment (just in case you judge that their content isn't up to scratch).

A LIST OF UK MUSIC PUBLISHERS

We have included here a list of some music publishers. As with record companies, some are more concerned with dance, garage, soul, country, folk, jazz, rock, 'MOR' (middle of the road) etc., than others, and the publisher credits on labels of records that you yourself may have will give you a guide. The publisher's name should be somewhere on the label of a vinyl 12" single and at the top or bottom of the lyric if it's printed on the insert of a CD. Better still, printed music will have the British publisher's name and address usually on the title page at the bottom.

Remember that the absence of a publisher's name from the list in this book doesn't necessarily mean you shouldn't deal with him, any more than the presence of a publisher's name here guarantees his complete competence and integrity etc.

As with record companies, many new independents pop up each year and many go out of business or become the subsidiary of a larger company. So once again, check those websites and industry sources for lists of subsidiaries.

A longer and constantly updated list – and more information on all aspects of music publishing – can be found at the Music Publisher's Association website (see Useful Addresses below).

Amphonic Music
20 The Green
Warlingham
Surrey CR6 9NA
www.amphonic.co.uk (01883 627 306)

Associated Music International Ltd
34 Salisbury Street
London NW8 8QE
www.amimedia.co.uk (020 7402 9111)

Amco Music Publishing
2 Gawsworth Road
Macclesfield
Cheshire SK11 8UE
www.cottagegroup.co.uk
(01625 420 163)

Associated Board of the Royal Schools of Music
24 Portland Place
London W1B 1LU
www.abrsmpublishing.co.uk
(020 7636 5400)

Barking Green Music
19 Ashford Carbonell
Ludlow
Shropshire SY8 4DB
(01584 831 475)

BBC Music Publishing
E107 Woodlands
80 Wood Lane
London W12 0TT
(020 8433 1723)

Belsize Music
29 Manor House
250 Marylebone Road
London NW1 5NP
(020 7724 6295)

Blue Mountain Music
8 Kensington Park Road
London W11 3BU
www.bluemountainmusic.tv
(020 7229 3000)

Bocu Music Ltd
1 Wyndham Yard
Wyndham Place
London W1H 1AR
(020 7402 7433)

Boosey & Hawkes Music
Aldwych House
71–91 Aldwych
London WC2B 4HN
www.boosey.com (020 7054 7200)

Bourne Music
2nd Floor, 207/209 Regent St
London W1B 4ND
(020 7734 3454)

Bucks Music Group
Onward House 11 Uxbridge St
London W8 7TQ
www.bucksmusicgroup.com
(020 7221 4275)

Bug Music
Long Island House
Unit GB 1–4 Warple Way
London W3 0RG
www.bugmusic.com (020 8735 1868)

Bugle Publishing
2nd Floor, 81 Rivingting Street
London EC2A 3AY
www.milescopeland.com
(020 7012 1416)

Campbell Connelly & Co Ltd
14–15 Berners Street
London W1T 3LJ
www.musicsales.com (020 7612 7400)

Carlin Music Corp
Iron Bridge House
3 Bridge Approach
Chalk Farm
London NW1 8BD
www.carlinmusic.com (020 7734 3251)

Carnaby Music
78 Portland Road
London W11 4LQ
(020 7727 2063)

Castle Hill Music
2 Laurel Bank
Huddersfield
W Yorks HD7 4ER
www.fimusic.co.uk (01484 846 333)

Catalyst Music Publishing
171 Southgate Road
London N1 3LE
(020 7704 8542)

Chelsea Music Pub.
124 Great Portland St
London W1W 6PP
www.chelseamusicpublishing.com
(020 7580 0044)

Cherry Red Songs
3a Long Island House
Warple Way
London W3 0RG
www.cherryred.co.uk (020 8740 4110)

Chester Music
14–15 Berners Street
London W1T 3LJ
www.chesternovello.com
(020 7612 7400)

Chrysalis Music
13 Bramley Road
London W10 6SP
www.chrysalis.com (020 7221 2213)

Congo Music
17a Craven Park Road
Harlesden
London NW10 8SE
www.congomusic.com (020 8961 5461)

Dejamus Ltd.
Suite 11, Accurist House
44 Baker Street
London W1U 7AZ
(020 7486 5838)

Digger Music
21 Bedford Sq
London WC1B 3HH
(020 7637 0848)

Eaton Music
39 Lower Richmond Road
Putney
London SW15 1ET
www.eatonmusic.com (020 8788 4557)

ELA Music
2 Queen Caroline Street
London W6 9DX
www.ela.co.uk (020 8323 8013)

EMI Music Publishing
27 Wrights Lane
London W8 5SW
www.emimusicpub.com
(020 3059 3059)

Essex Music Group
Suite 207
535 King's Road
London SW10 0SZ
(020 7823 3773)

Faber Music
3 Queen Square
London WC1N 3AU
www.fabermusic.com (020 7833 7900)

Fairwood Music
72 Marylebone Lane
London W1U 2PL
www.fairwoodmusic.com
(020 7487 5044)

Faith & Hope Publishing
PO Box 601
Stockport SK4 3XA
www.faithandhope.co.uk
(0161 839 4445)

Famous Music Publishing
20 Fulham Broadway
London SW6 1AH
www.famousmusic.com
(020 7385 9429)

4AD Music
17–19 Alma Road
London SW18 1AA
(020 8871 2121)

Gut Music
112a Shirland Road
London W9 2EQ
www.gutrecords.com
(020 7266 0777)

Hornall Bros Music
1 Northfields Prospect
Putney Bridge Road
London SW18 1PE
www.hobro.co.uk (020 8877 3366)

Independent Music Group
Unit 3 York House
Langston Road
Debden
Essex IG10 3TG
www.independentmusicgroup.com
(020 8523 9000)

IQ Music
52 Perrymount Road
Haywards Heath
W Sussex RH16 3DT
(01444 452 807)

Joustwise
Myrtle Cottage
Rye Road
Hawkhurst
Kent TN18 5DW
www.4realrecords.com (01580 754 771)

Kassner Associated Publishers
Units 6 & 7
11 Wyfold Road
Fulham
London SW6 6SE
www.kassnermusic.com (020 7385 7700)

Kingsway Music
Lottbridge Drive
Eastbourne
E. Sussex BN23 6NT
www.kingsway.co.uk (01323 437 700)

Leopard Music Publishing
PO Box 77
Liversedge WF15 7WT
www.leopardmusicgroup.com
(05601 480 068)

Maxwood Music
1 Pratt Mews
London NW1 0AD
www.maxwoodmusic.com
(020 7554 4840)

McGuinness Whelan
30–32 Sir John Rogersons Quay
Dublin 2
Eire
(00353 1 677 7330)

MCS Music
17–19 Bedford Street
London WC2E 9HP
www.mcsmusic.com (020 7868 5400)

Menace Music
2 Park Road
Radlett
Herts WD7 8EQ
(01923 853 789)

Minder Music
18 Pindock Mews
London W9 2PY
www.mindermusic.com (020 7289 7281)

Moncur Street Music
PO Box 16114
London SW3 4WG
www.moncurstreet.com
(020 7349 9909)

MPL Communications
1 Soho Square
London W1D 3BQ
www.mplcommunications.com
(020 7439 2001)

Music Exchange
Claverton Road
Wythenshawe
Greater Manchester M23 9ZA
www.music-exchange.co.uk
(0161 946 1234)

Music Sales
14–15 Berners St
London W1T 3LJ
www.musicsales.com
(020 7612 7400)

Mute Song
1 Albion Place
London W6 0QT
www.mutesong.com (020 3300 0000)

19 Music
33 Ransomes Dock
35–37 Parkgate Road
London SW11 4NP
www.19.co.uk (020 7801 1919)

Notting Hill Music
Bedford House
8B Berkeley Gardens
London W8 4AP
www.nottinghillmusic.com
(020 7243 2921)

Oxford University Press
Great Clarendon St
Oxford OX2 6DP
www.oup.com/uk/music (01865 556767)

Panama Music Library
12 Trewartha Road
Praa Sands
Penzance
Cornwall TR20 9ST
www.panamamusic.co.uk
(01736 762 826)

P&P Songs
40 St Peter's Road
London W6 9BD
www.pandpsongs.com (020 8237 8400)

Peermusic (UK)
23–24 George Street,
Richmond
Surrey TW9 1HY
www.peermusic.com (020 8939 1700)

Perfect Songs
8–10 Basing Street
London W11 1ET
www.spz.com (020 7229 1229)

Peters Edition
10–12 Baches Street
London N1 6DN
www.editionpeters.com (020 7553 4000)

Plangent Visions Music
27 Noel Street
London W1F 8GZ
(020 7734 6892)

Reliable Source Music
67 Upper Berkley Street
London W1H 7QX
www.reliable-source.co.uk
(020 7563 7028)

Reverb Music
Reverb House, Bennett Street
London W4 2AH
www.reverbxl.com (020 8747 0660)

Revolver Music
152 Goldthorn Hill
Penn
Wolverhampton
W. Midlands WV2 3JA
www.revolverrecords.com
(01902 345 345)

Right Bank Music
Home Park House
Hampton Court Road
Kingston-Upon-Thames
Surrey KT1 4AE
www.rightbankmusicuk.com
(020 8977 0666)

Rough Trade Publishing
81 Wallingford Road
Goring, Reading
Berks RG8 0HL
www.rough-trade.com (01491 873 612)

Schott Music
48 Gt. Marlborough Street
London W1F 7BB
www.schott-music.com
(020 7534 0700)

SGO Music Publishing
PO Box 2015
Salisbury SP2 7WU
www.sgomusic.com (01264 811 154)

Snapper Music Publishing
1 Star Street
London W2 1QD
(020 7706 7304)

Sony/ATV Music Publishing
30 Golden Square
London W1F 9LD
www.sonyatv.com (020 3206 2501)

Strongsongs Publishing
107 Mortlake High Street
London SW14 8HQ
(020 8392 6839)

United Music Publishers
33 Lea Road
Waltham Abbey
Essex EN9 1ES
www.ump.co.uk (01992 703110)

Universal Music Publishing
136–144 New Kings Road
London SW6 4LZ
www.umusicpub.com (020 8752 2600)

Valentine Music Group
26 Litchfield Street
London WC2H 9TZ
(020 7240 1628)

V2 Music Publishing
Unit 24, 101 Farm Lane
London SW6 1QJ
www.v2music.com (020 7471 3000)

Warner Chappell Music
28 Kensington Church Street
London W8 4EP
www.warnerchappell.com
(020 7938 0000)

Westbury Music
Suite B, 2 Tunstall Road
London SW9 8DA
www.westburymusic.net
(020 7733 5400)

MUSIC PUBLISHERS

Music publishers have existed for centuries, acquiring manuscripts from composers and printing them for performances at concerts or for sale to the public to sing around the piano at home. Over the last hundred years or so, 'publishing' has gradually come to mean finding and then exploiting songs, mainly through recordings, synchronisation and broadcast in TV, film or adverts, broadcast on radio and synch in video games (to name but a few media), as well as funding showcase gigs, making demos and master recordings and so on. Actual printing and publishing of music is nowadays almost a separate undertaking from most pop music publishers' business and is carried out for them by specialist print music publishers, the leading company in the UK being Music Sales Ltd. That said, the printing, sale and, especially, hire of musical scores is still very important to 'classical' publishers and those who control stage musicals.

What should the publisher do for a songwriter?

Generally, a publisher will not sign a song unless he intends to do some or all of the things mentioned in the introduction to this section to try to earn money for both of you. If you don't have a top quality demo, he'll pay for one, which should be noticeably better than one you could do yourself. If you are not an artist or producer yourself, he'll use his contacts with record companies to try to get one of their suitable artists to record your song. Bear in mind, though, that in the UK this is now relatively difficult unless you are also a producer, in which case the publisher may be able to get you the job of producing tracks for an artist (which will probably involve co-writing with the artist). Once a record is released, he might well help the record company to exploit it. This could take the form of getting his own promotion people, if he has them, to work on the record. Or he might contribute to the cost of tour support, independent promoters or an advertising campaign of some kind. He may also arrange for the printing of a 'single edition' of your song for sale in music shops, if it's the featured track on a single or is a top five single in the UK (don't expect this otherwise, except perhaps as part of a songbook to accompany a best-selling album).

If it is printed, he will then have to deposit copies of the music edition with the British Library. He should also ensure that royalties are collected on the song by notifying certain bodies (see later) and by having it sub-published abroad, so that no money is lost if the song is exploited abroad. Your publisher should not charge you a fee of any kind for any of this (other than his agreed share of royalties) and should not make any further deductions. They take all the financial risk, but that's what their share of royalties is for.

Beware of advertisements from people offering to publish or record your song for a fee, write music to your lyrics or the like. Only send a song to them as a last resort if no 'proper' music publisher is interested in it, and you're really desperate to see it on record or in print and you don't have the facilities to do this at home. There is nothing automatically bad or crooked about these people. They simply provide a service for a fee, but if you ever hope to make any real money writing songs you will sooner or later have to convince a 'real' publisher that your songs are worth spending money on. Remember, there are plenty of publishers around to choose from, none of whom will charge you to place your songs with them, nor will they recover any of their expenses from your royalties.

What should the publisher's song agreement include?

There are two principle types of agreement, an assignment (or licence) for a specific song or set of songs, usually known as a 'Single Song Assignment' (SSA), and an Exclusive Songwriter Agreement (ESA, or blanket songwriter agreement). We'll deal with the ESA in a separate chapter, and for now concentrate on the SSA.

In an SSA you'll often be actually selling the publisher all the rights in your song in return for some initial 'consideration' (in other words the price), which may include a substantial advance payment or a nominal sum, such as £1, but should always include a share of all royalties the publisher receives. The actual wording of agreements varies a lot, and these days it's quite common for a publisher to agree to a licence rather than an assignment (meaning that in theory you remain the owner of the song and just give the publisher exclusive rights to exploit it and collect the income on your behalf). While it may seem preferable for you to retain ownership (ie. to make a licence rather than an assignment), in reality the length of time that the publisher has exclusive rights to your song(s), and the rights that they have, are much more important. For example, an assignment that lasts five years may be preferable to a licence that lasts for the whole life of copyright. Conversely, it is probable that should problems arise with a contract, a licence will be easier to terminate early than an assignment. Ultimately of course, the royalty terms offered will have the most immediate effect on you and your finances (probably even more important than the amount the publisher is prepared to pay as an advance), so we'll start with those. Even if you are a complete unknown, you should never be offered less than the figures below.

Printed music royalties – what should the agreement say?

You can expect to get 10%–12.5% of the actual retail selling price of the printed single song edition of your music produced or distributed by your publisher, or a proportion of that if the song appears in a compilation songbook (or 'folio'). Some contracts allow the publisher to recover the cost of production before paying you anything. You could obviously miss out on income through this, so you should consider such clauses carefully. Certainly it is uncommon for such terms to be kept in a modern pop publishing agreement, but it is a significant and necessary cost for a classical publisher, so if that's relevant to you, it may be that such a clause remains, perhaps with costs and ownership of the materials suitably divided between the parties. Some contracts may offer no royalty to you at all on songbooks or orchestrations, or uses of lyrics without music; unless you negotiate such a term in exchange for a better rate on a source of income you believe will be more lucrative, you should not accept such terms.

On print sales overseas or by third parties licensed by your publisher, you will get a royalty similar to your standard rate (other or miscellaneous).

The single printed music edition of a number one in the UK record charts will generally sell no more than about 1,000 copies (even less for some dance tracks), as against hundreds of thousands many years ago, when sheet music royalties were a songwriter's main source of income. Even today, big ballads can occasionally sell tens of thousands over time, but this is quite exceptional. Overseas, sheet music tends to be more expensive and sales are often even lower. Sales of songbooks on the other hand are very healthy, and the best of these outsell even hit single editions many times over – hence the warning about making sure you get paid on sales of songbooks. Since most publishers now appoint a specialist agent to print and exploit printed music for them, this may mean that your royalties from printed music sales are not based on the retail price but are regarded by your publisher as miscellaneous income. However, this shouldn't affect your royalty rate unduly. You may actually get slightly more, as they will have negotiated a blanket rate for all their published songs from the agent.

Mechanical royalties – what should the agreement say?

These are royalties paid by record companies for including your songs on the recordings that they sell, either as physical product like CDs or as downloads. This includes everything from hit singles to CDs given away with magazines, from full-price albums to cheap compilations sold at garages or in supermarkets. Even an unknown pop writer should get from his publisher about 60–70% of these so-called 'mechanical royalties'. In the 'classical' world, royalties can still be as low as 50%, primarily as composer development and promotion costs are traditionally higher and it generally takes much longer for a classical composer to reach his or her commercial peak. If you are also a budding producer with a master-quality recording of the song, which perhaps just needs remixing, or are a member of a hot new band with record company interest (or a deal in place), you might get as much as 80%–90%, although if you expect a substantial advance then your actual royalty percentage is likely to be lower. You may well also get slightly

less on recordings secured by the publisher that you had nothing to do with; these are known as 'cover recordings' or 'covers', although the exact definition varies and is worth looking at closely. If possible, try to ensure that 'windfall' covers (ones that the publisher didn't actively go out and get) are excluded from any special covers rate.

For income earned overseas the rates should appear to be the same as for UK income, but whether it means you get the same proportion of the money earned depends upon whether you have what's known as an 'at source' or a 'receipts' deal. We'll explain further in the next question.

What is an 'at source' publishing deal?

A publisher will have, or will appoint, sub-publishers in many countries who will register your songs in their territory, try to maximise the income and try to make sure none goes astray. (Way back when, sub-publishers would be appointed on a song-by-song basis, but these days a UK publisher will almost always have a general agreement with one company for each territory.) In return for that, the sub-publisher takes between 10% and 25% of the total income generated in their territory.

With a 'receipts' deal, a sub-publisher commission of 25% would mean that they send 75% back to the UK publisher. If, for example, you as the writer have a 70/30 deal, then you get 70% of the 75% that your publisher gets from abroad (i.e. only 52.5% of the original sums collected). However, if your 'receipts' deal has a maximum sub-publisher commission clause, then this can increase the proportion of the original income that you receive (see the examples below).

With an 'at source' deal at the same rate, you would get 70% of the original sum collected by the sub-publisher, leaving your UK publisher and his foreign sub-publishers to share the 30% between them.

If we assume that the UK is only 10–15% of the total market for your song, if it's a worldwide hit, you will see that this can make an enormous difference to the amount you eventually earn. In general, you should always try to ask for an 'at-source' publishing deal or for a 'receipts' deal with a reasonable maximum on the sub-publisher's commission rate. Do the calculation and work out what you'll actually receive from foreign income and think about what proportion of the income you expect to come from the UK and what from abroad. 'At source' is not always better than 'receipts', as the examples below illustrate:

1) An 80/20 'receipts' deal with a maximum sub-publisher share of 10% nets you 72% of foreign and 80% of UK income
2) An 80/20 'at source' deal would net you 80% of foreign and 80% of UK income
3) A 75/25 'receipts' deal with a maximum sub-publisher share of 10% nets you 67.50% of foreign and 75% of UK income
4) A 75/25 'at source' deal would net you 75% of foreign and 75% of UK income.

So if you have a choice between deal 1 and deal 4 and if most of your income comes from abroad, then deal 4 would be to your benefit. If most of your income comes from the UK, then deal 1 would be to your benefit (and you never know, the publisher might be incentivised to increase your profile abroad by the slightly higher share they can keep from the income they generate).

How are mechanical royalties calculated and collected?

The amount UK record companies pay for the use of music is set by negotiations between the MCPS – Mechanical Copyright Protection Society (formed in 1911 at the time of the first really effective UK Copyright Act, which gave writers and publishers a specific right to 'record' royalties) – for the publishers, and the BPI (British Phonographic Industry) for the record companies (for more on the MCPS see 'General Q&A on Songwriting'). Similarly, the various online download retailers (like Apple's iTunes) negotiate a scheme with the MCPS (though not as yet through a collective body like the BPI). If they can't agree, then the record companies or online retailers can refer the licensing schemes that MCPS is offering to a body called the Copyright Tribunal, which ultimately decides what is fair.

The current record company rate is 8.5% of the published price to dealers (around 6% of the actual price in the shops), but the record companies have tried in the past to get this reduced on the grounds that, as is usually the case for major retail chains, the 'actual realised price' that the companies get after giving discounts or freebies to retailers is substantially lower than their official published dealer price. Obviously, with the decline in the physical market record, companies looking to reduce costs will continue to keep pressure up on this point.

The current online download rate is 8% of gross revenue (ie. the price to the consumer or the appropriate proportion of a service's subscription revenue where consumers pay a monthly fee). This is under a scheme known as the Joint Online Licence (JOL).

All record companies or online download retailers pay royalties to the MCPS, or to one of their sister societies around the world (not all UK record companies pay the MCPS, see details in the section on Central Licensing below). The societies then pay the publishers, who then pay you (unless you are a member of a society outside the English-speaking world, in which case it's possible that a share is paid directly to you by your society, as it would be for performance income). If MCPS have the exact timings of each track from the record company, then they will divide the royalty between the songs on each record strictly according to how long each one runs for, regardless of the fact that there may be just one track that is generating all the sales). If they don't have timings, then MCPS divide equally according to the number of tracks.

MCPS charge 6.25% to your publisher for collecting from the established record companies (other societies round the world charge more or less, but generally around the same figure), which operate under what's known as the AP1 scheme. This means they only pay on actual sales they've made. The smaller ones have to pay on the number of records they press (AP2 and AP2A schemes), regardless of whether they sell them, as it's just too costly for MCPS to enforce the licences for thousands of different albums, of which only 500 or 1,000 each may ever be pressed. MCPS charge the publishers 7.5% for collecting from the significant 'smaller independent labels' (AP2A) and around 12.5% for collecting from the rest of these companies (AP2), as it costs them a lot more to collect and process the money and also to monitor the activities of companies, especially small ones that sometimes, through ignorance, press and sell records with no consent whatever. Similarly, the commission MCPS takes on download income (JOL) is higher (currently 12%) because of the complexity of the administration involved and the costs borne by the MCPS in settling the long negotiation over the rate.

Plenty of AP2 companies have hit records. If you're trying to work out what will be due to you, it's worth remembering that if your hit is on an AP2 label or is predominently downloaded, then the MCPS commission will be that much higher (though it's worth noting that the actual income from downloads may itself be higher).

How much should I actually get from sales of records of my songs?

An album on a major label that sells at, say, £13 including VAT in the big chain stores (more in retail outlets that don't enjoy substantial discounts), will have a dealer price of about £8 before VAT. With an £8 PDP, the total 8.5% royalty would therefore work out at 68p (say around 63p after MCPS takes its commission). If the album contains 14 tracks, each track will get roughly 4.5p (depending on precisely how long it lasts compared to the other tracks). If your deal with your publisher is, let's say, a 70/30 split in your favour, you'll get around 3p per track for every record sold. So if you see that the album has been certified as having gone gold (100,000 UK sales), you should expect very roughly £30,000 for your one track.

A single on an independent dance label selling at around £4 will have a dealer price of around £2.60 before VAT. The 8.5% royalty will be about 22p, so about 5.5p per track (say 5.1p after MCPS commission). If you were on the same 70/30 split, you'd end up with about 3.6p per track, or, if you wrote 100% of all the tracks, then that's about 14p per single (but remember this won't necessarily apply to 'white label' copies). If, however, there is a remix on which someone else gets a writer credit (maybe because there's a sample on it) and that mix is the longest, your royalty would suffer (see 'A-side protection' in the Glossary). Again, if the record company gives away promo copies (not just to reviewers but also, for example, to retail chains) to encourage sales, they don't have to pay on the first 1,500 of these.

For downloads, the current price of a single track is around 79p with DRM and 99p without DRM, so the MCPS will receive around 6.3p (DRM) and 7.9p (non-DRM), the publisher 5.6p and 6.9p, and you on your 70/30 deal 3.9p and 4.9p.

It might be argued that a significant factor in the decline in physical sales of singles has been the trend towards the rapid inclusion of the latest hits on compilation albums. These sell so well (and at a relatively high price) that the royalties achieved make up in part at least for the decline in physical single sales. They are comparable to that achieved by tracks on the original album from which the single may have been taken. That said, the royalty is often split across many tracks, and a compilation of older tracks on a budget label can have a dealer price of as little as £1, which means a tiny royalty (since in the UK there is no minimum royalty per track). Compilations can make a big difference to your royalties, but don't necessarily expect more than a few hundred pounds from most best-selling budget compilations using one of your songs.

There can be substantial earnings from cover-mounted CDs on magazines or newspapers, whether or not they're actually advertising anything. (MCPS charge 6.5% of 50% of the price of the magazine under their AP7 licensing scheme for 'cover mounts', subject to a minimum, so the amount per song per record is very low but the sales figures can be huge.)

Record royalties for songs are paid in roughly the same way in most countries, though rates vary. In the rest of Europe, in principle it has long been the case that the mechanical rights society collective body (known as BIEM) negotiated with the record company collective body (the IFPI) and arrived at a royalty rate, but in reality the situation is not clear cut, with rates and deductions varying from country to country. The royalty rate is generally slightly above the UK one, but can be reduced by record company deductions for such things as packaging allowances, discounts and holdback provisions, and higher society commission rates (sometimes due to higher costs, sometimes due to society-led initiatives such as composer welfare funds). The amount that reaches you can also be reduced through the operation of Central European Licensing (see below). Finally, the European Commission and European Collecting Societies have introduced the concept of Pan-European Licensing (PEL), initially at least with the focus on online rights. This is the result of efforts by online download and streaming retailers to pressure collection societies into offering a 'one-stop-shop' for European rights (as opposed to the country by country rules currently in place). Ideally, this should benefit publishers, their writers and the retailers, but it remains to be seen whether PEL will ultimately operate to the benefit or detriment of publishers and songwriters.

How does Central European Licensing affect my mechanical royalties?

This started with a deal between PolyGram Records (which became part of Universal) and STEMRA, the Dutch equivalent of MCPS, in the Eighties, and now most major record companies have a deal with just one of the European collecting societies (there's generally one society in each country). It means that the record company pays some or all of its mechanical royalties to that one society for record sales throughout Europe, which, as per the principles of the European Union, is legally considered one 'market'. That society then pays the other local societies in the countries where the sales actually took place, at the appropriate royalty rate, and the local society then pays the local publisher.

So the money for a UK sale can go from the record company to, say, the German mechanical society (GEMA), then on to the MCPS and then to the publisher. By putting an extra step in the normal chain, this could mean that you get the money slightly later (though, as the system has bedded in, this problem has largely been eliminated). More worryingly, both the society collecting and the local society want a percentage of the royalties as an administration fee, so this cuts down the amount you get. Fortunately, under an agreement between the collecting societies and the publishers called the 'Cannes Agreement', the societies pledged to try to bring down the overall amount to no more than about 7% between them in the case of the bigger societies.

What are controlled composition clauses?

This is another phrase you are likely to hear in connection with royalties for sales of recordings of your songs, and is another reason why your mechanical royalties might be less than you were expecting. This has become increasingly complicated over the years, but as briefly as possible, this is how it works. In the US and Canada, the rate paid by the record company to the owner of the song is set by law at so many cents per track per record (or a certain amount per minute for tracks over five minutes long); this is known as the 'statutory rate'. This rate is increased regularly to allow for inflation – it has been set at 9.1 cents since 2006. However, this 'statutory rate' is higher than record companies had been used to paying in the past and many ask publishers to license songs at a proportion of the statutory rate (usually 75%). This is perfectly legal provided the publisher concerned agrees to accept it. For big songs the answer is usually 'no', but for a new song, publishers may often agree to it just to make sure their song is recorded and released.

The other way US record companies get a discount on the statutory rate is where the artist on the record is also the writer. Here they put a 'controlled compositions clause' in the artist's recording contract, obliging them to have their publisher accept a discount (again usually 75% of the statutory rate), or to accept that the difference will be deducted from their artist royalties. Over time, other such clauses have been added to artist agreements, such as that he mustn't put more than 12 songs on his album, or two songs on a single, that he must insist that the publisher grant a licence for promotional videos for nothing, or that the record company will only pay royalties to the publisher on sales of records on which the artist was being paid.

Without these so-called 'controlled composition clauses', the publishers would be able to collect the full royalty on the full price of all sales at the rate applying when the records were actually sold. This is instead of 75% of what the rate was when the record was first 'delivered' to the record company or else first released (only around half of the current rate for a record made 10 years ago), and maybe much less depending upon the terms of the artist agreement with the record company.

What's more, if you do decide (or the record company decides for you) to put someone else's song on your record and the publisher of that song insists on 100% of the statutory royalty, the record company will reduce the amount they pay on your own songs (or else your overall artist royalty) even further, to cover the cost to them of paying this full royalty.

Your publishing agreement may ask you to guarantee that your publisher's North American sub-publisher won't be obliged to accept controlled composition rates. If your publisher paid you a big advance partly on the strength of your potential in the USA, then this will be very important to him. If not, then you don't necessarily need to accept this clause, but you do need to tell him whether his American people should accept a reduced rate or not. If they don't accept it, and your artist agreement has a controlled compositions clause, then the difference will come out of your artist royalty. If you're both a recording artist and a songwriter, then deciding these issues may be difficult, and it will depend on your own circumstances. It's worth factoring into your decision that you usually start getting paid sooner under a publishing agreement than under a recording artist agreement.

Most US mechanical royalties are collected by a body called the Harry Fox Agency, but they don't have the power to overturn controlled composition clauses – they just collect at whatever rate the publisher and record company agree should apply for each track on each record. Despite these complications, the commission they charge is, like MCPS's commission from major record companies in the UK, roughly 7%.

Performing and broadcasting royalties: what should the agreement say?

In the UK, all of these are collected by a body called The Performing Right Society Ltd. (PRS). It was founded in 1914 by composers, songwriters and publishers to license the public performance of music and collect royalties for that use. If you are a PRS member, and you should be (or, if you are a foreign national, a member of the equivalent society in your home country), then royalties collected by the PRS for your songs in the UK are nearly always paid 50% to the publisher and 50% to the writer. Only in very exceptional circumstances would the PRS consider paying the so-called 'writer's share' to a publisher, and you are very unlikely to see an agreement that attempts to change this.

Your publishing contract therefore will discuss the division of the so-called 'publisher's share' of performing royalties. In the distant past, when publishers and writers generally divided all royalties equally between them, a publisher's share belonged to the publisher and the writer's share to the writer and that was that. Nowadays, it's quite usual for the writer to participate in the publisher's share (unless they're on 50/50 rates for other types of income, say if they compose classical or production or library music). Often, this rate will leave the publisher with the same share of the whole performance royalty as they keep of mechanical income. So, if your mechanical rate is 60%, you would expect your share of the publisher's share of performance to be 20% (you get 50% of the whole from the PRS and 10% of the whole from the publisher, ie. 20% of the publisher's share). You will see this expressed any number of different ways in a publishing contract, so if you don't follow

the relevant clause, make sure your lawyer takes you through it before you sign.

The PRS issues a licence to every place that wishes music to be publicly performed on its premises (be that live or recorded music). This includes everywhere from your local hairdresser to Wembley Stadium. Even if the music is just for the benefit of the staff in an office or factory, that's still a use of the writers' and publishers' property and they receive payment for it through the PRS, though there are a few exceptions, including performance of music at home for your own pleasure and that of your friends, and performances in services of religious worship. Think how many places you go to where you hear music playing – all these need a licence from the PRS!

On top of this, the PRS collects lump sums from the BBC, ITV, Channel 4 and Five as well as cable and satellite companies for broadcasting (or 'diffusing') music on television and radio and on the internet, based on their audience or income from licence fees, subscriptions or advertising. The PRS then shares out all the money collected that year from each of these licences among all the songs used. Generally, the money collected from the BBC is divided among all songs used by the BBC and so on, rather than all the income being put in one pot and then divided up.

Finally, the PRS collects the writer's share of all the performance and broadcast income collected by its sister societies around the world. These royalties are paid on 100% to the writer, as the publisher will have collected their share from the foreign societies directly through their sub-publisher. Of course, all of these royalties are subject to a society commission, which the PRS calls its Administration Rate (currently around 20% for UK income depending on the source and 8% or lower for foreign income).

In the US, the picture is a bit more confused as there are several further significant exceptions to the places that need a licence (such as cinemas, small and medium-sized bars and hairdressers for example), and several different bodies are able to collect licence fees (most notably ASCAP, BMI & SESAC).

How much will I actually get for a performance of my song?

The big money comes from television and radio broadcasts – less than £1 for a three-minute song on the smallest local radio stations to around £40 or so for national radio, up to around £150 on BBC TV and around £200 on the ITV network (though these payments are being banded by PRS, so that you'll get more from peak-time TV transmission than you would from off-peak). PRS has paid out slightly more if the song is 'featured' (apparently being heard by the people on the screen) than if it is 'background', but the amount has never been based on individual viewing figures for the programme, just for the general estimated reach of the channel as a whole. It would be so complex for PRS to 'weight' every single performance according to its audience that there would be no money left to distribute, which brings us to the question of 'sampling'.

Will I always get paid if my song is performed or broadcast?

The answer is no. Again, it would be so expensive for PRS to identify every single performance of every single song at every single venue or on every single radio station that there would be nothing left to distribute to the writers and publishers.

If your song is broadcast on terrestrial television, major satellite channels like Sky One or on BBC national radio stations, then you can definitely expect to be paid (even for short snatches of music in commercials, channel idents or trailers). The same applies to Capital, Virgin and other major radio stations. However with many local and Internet radio sta-

tions, PRS uses a sampling system. Generally, they identify exactly what was played in a given week by one station and have to assume that all other stations that week played the same. The major exclusion is locally originated music that was particular to one station. This should be analysed separately and you should receive payment, although remember it may be very small. Pirate radio stations, as the name suggests, don't pay PRS anything, so a play on one of these is guaranteed not to earn anything. PRS used to pay a small amount per year as a so-called 'unlogged performance allocation' to writers who did have some earnings but were thought to have missed out in the sampling process, but this has now been dropped. Unless you're very unlucky or the amounts you might have got are very small, then, on the basis of swings and roundabouts, you'll probably wind up with roughly what you are entitled to.

So when I'm starting out in small venues, will I never get paid for the songs I play?

If it's not viable for PRS to analyse every performance on radio, it's obviously even less so with so-called 'general' royalties from pubs, clubs, hotels etc. PRS get 'returns' from a selection of venues of varying sizes telling them what music was played there, and use these returns to pay out for all other uses in the same category. Of course, this will tend to discriminate against minority forms of music, but PRS know this and try to compensate by using samples from venues that play particular genres of music.

PRS also have a list of so-called 'significant venues' around Britain, which includes most of the major local concert halls. There are several hundred, so this doesn't just mean the NEC or Wembley. The county town of most counties has at least one hall and perhaps a university that would be on the list. PRS ask these venues to tell them what's been performed, so you or your manager should tell the venue your set list in detail, as it's their responsibility to report to the PRS. If you're at all worried that this hasn't happened, you can report your gig and set list yourself to the PRS. This is especially important with a tour (most tours by 'name' artists take place almost entirely in significant venues), where the set list was pretty much the same for each night. If you're only the support act, your songs will be worth as much as those of the main act (unless you had to agree otherwise in advance of the concert). Provided that PRS know what was performed at a concert at one of these venues, then you should definitely get paid if it included your songs.

Can I collect any of this money myself and cut out PRS?

As regards licensing of performances, PRS is effectively a monopoly, but this is not as bad as you may think since it has huge advantages for you as a writer in terms of the cost of collection, enforcement of licences in thousands of venues, and in collective bargaining with those venues. In fact, when you join the PRS you assign the performance right to them, in exchange for which you and your publisher are entitled to receive 50% each of the royalties the PRS collects on your behalf. This means that if you are a PRS member you have given them the exclusive right to license performances, and you can't legally grant those licences yourself. The principle criticism of this system, as pointed out by the band U2 in the Nineties, is that when a performer plays only their own songs it would be much simpler and

cheaper if they could just collect their performance royalties straight from the venue. That's undeniable, but consider for a moment that even U2 have been known to perform a cover of someone else's song. What happens then? Should U2 collect the performance income for that song and then pay the writer(s) and publisher(s), or should the venue seek them out? How do they know accurately who the writer(s) and publisher(s) are? If a band less scrupulous than U2 performs a cover, what's to stop them taking the money and saying they performed one of their own songs? Someone has to police the system, and while it may not be perfect, it's hard to see how the current method could be much improved upon.

In response to this, however, PRS did come up with provisions to cover the circumstance where an artist is performing entirely his own material; so if you think it might benefit you, or if want to know more, you should contact the PRS's Live Music team. Incidentally, the actual amount of the fees – the so-called 'concert tariff' – was originally set by a body called the Performing Rights Tribunal, and its successor, the Copyright Tribunal, remains responsible for setting these fees as it does for the mechanical rate for sales of records/downloads etc.

What if a payment I was expecting wasn't on my statement?

Remember that money does take a while to come through the system, so don't expect a broadcast one month to be paid out in the statement you get the next. By all means query your statement if you think something significant is missing or wrong, but try not to waste PRS or your publisher's time querying tiny uses; they're mostly very patient and conscientious people but they only have so much time, and the more of it you ask them to spend on little issues, the less time they'll have to look into something big you might raise later. This is especially so if you believe a use would have been subject to sampling or you're not sure whether the money would have come through yet anyway.

What about foreign broadcasting and performance fees?

Foreign performance societies will pay 50%, sometimes expressed as 6/12ths (all performing right societies used to calculate shares in twelfths, and some still do) as a 'writer share' to the PRS for UK writers, and divide the other 50% between your publisher and the local 'sub-publisher' (or, more likely, pay it all to the sub-publisher, who will pay your publisher his share under their agreement). Because of the time delays involved, it might take as much as two years for foreign performing fees to reach you. If you find foreign fees you were expecting are missing you can contact PRS or your publisher, who will ask his local sub-publisher to get the local performing right society to look into it. It's always worth checking your society and publisher statements against each other in case your writer share turns up but not your share of the publisher's share (or vice versa). Often there is an explanation and the money would have turned up in due course anyway, but where there's a significant amount of money involved, it's worth making sure

Should I join the PRS?

Provided the activity on your songs warrants it (see next question) then the answer is 'yes'! If you are not a member of the PRS then it may pay your writer shares to your publisher who may pay you, but it's possible that if your publishing contract doesn't deal with this properly, the publisher could end up keeping all of the money they collect or paying a share that is lower than you would have got if the PRS paid you directly. Ideally, your agreement with them will require them to pay your writer's share in full within 30 days of receiving it, but at the

very least he should pay it in full in his next schedule accounting, and he should not be able to recoup it from any advances he has paid you. The best way to avoid the problem is to join the PRS.

Can any writer join the PRS?

The rules vary from time to time but, basically, to apply for membership you must have at least one of your songs (whether co-written or written solely by you) recorded or broadcast or else printed and performed a set number of times, thus making it likely to earn significant performing royalties. It is clearly a waste of your time and theirs to apply to join the PRS if your songs are not being used, but if your songs are getting broadcast or generating other activity you should join without delay. There is a fee of around £100 to join and we would very strongly urge any British writer to do so. Not only will you be paid directly by them and therefore more quickly than if the money had to go via your publisher, but also you will be paid royalties from abroad that your publisher might not be able to collect for you so long as you remain a 'non-member'. (Many foreign societies just put non-member writers' shares back into the 'pot' to be shared out among their members, so once that money is gone, it may be gone for good.) To join the PRS, simply contact the Member Registrations Department (020 7306 4805) and ask for the relevant forms, or apply online on the MCPS/PRS website (see 'Useful Addresses' list below). To speed up the payment of royalties, some UK publishers join not only the PRS but other overseas societies too, and some UK writers are also members of one or more foreign societies for the same reason, usually including one of the US societies. Generally, however, a UK writer will join the PRS, an Irish writer will join IMRO (Irish Music Rights Organisation), an Australian writer APRA (Australian Performing Rights Association) and so on.

Should I register my share of songs at the PRS or leave it for my publisher to do?

As a member you will have access to the MCPS/PRS system, where you can check the records for your works and, if you wish, register your share directly (worth doing if you haven't got a publishing deal yet). Once you've got a deal there's no harm in keeping an eye on things, but it's best to leave registrations to your publisher, if only to prevent confusion. MCPS/PRS receive thousands of registrations every single week! Even if your song is not yet recorded, it's normal for your publisher to register it with MCPS/PRS as soon as possible after he's acquired it. Some agreements will actually stipulate that the publisher and his sub-publishers in all the major territories will definitely register the song regardless of earnings.

So should I join different collecting societies for different countries?

The vast majority of UK writers are happy for the PRS to collect for them from other performing right societies around the world. There are some established PRS writers who are direct members of one of the US performing right societies – ASCAP, BMI and SESAC (thus getting their US performing royalties quicker and with slightly less commission deducted) as well as other societies in major territories.

Although it is not always stated in songwriting agreements, many publishers will allow you to nominate which US society you'd like your songs to go through. SESAC is much the smallest, specialising in Latin, gospel and country music. ASCAP is slightly larger and longer established than BMI, and has traditionally been considered better for more MOR pop writers, while BMI was considered better for rock. In practice, however, both ASCAP and BMI represent writers of all types, and either could be better at any given time depending on

how their current distributions are structured and on their current commission rates. The US societies have helpful representatives in the UK who can explain to you how they work, and the relative benefits of their organisation.

As we have said, writer members of MCPS can collect foreign mechanicals through MCPS if they have no publisher or if they agree with the publisher to collect their own share (more common in classical music), but, in practice, very few UK writers are members of foreign mechanical collecting societies.

Can I get an advance or loan from the collecting societies?

The societies don't actually pay advances in the UK in the way that publishers do. The American performing right societies will do so, as they are in competition, and some other societies abroad will make loans to members. The PRS does have a so-called 'Members' Fund' into which a small part of its income is put, as well as the income from certain songs that some writers or their heirs have 'donated' to the Members Fund (one of the best-known being 'Get It On' by Marc Bolan). However, its purpose is to help writers (usually, but not always, older ones) who have genuine financial difficulties.

How much do I lose if foreign lyrics are put to my songs?

As regards foreign performance royalties, the publisher finds himself sharing his part of these with a foreign publisher, and sometimes, when a local cover is recorded and/or performed, the same applies to the writer, who has to share his part with the writer of the foreign lyric in each country, usually to the extent of dividing the writer's share 1/3rd to the foreign writer and 2/3rds to the original (or 2/12ths of the whole). This should only apply to actual uses of the foreign lyric and these days it usually does, but there was a time when the foreign lyricist would receive his share even when the original lyric was used. Ideally, your agreement with your publisher should guarantee that he won't permit foreign lyrics or translations without your permission, and certainly that he should not negotiate away any share of the work without your approval. You should note, however, that in some territories once you let someone make a local lyric, if he's a member of the local collecting society he will get paid automatically under the society's rules.

Having said all that, if your song is pretty well dormant in a particular country and a big artist there wants to do a local lyric version, it could completely revitalise the song, and then it would be worth letting the foreign lyricist get a bit of your money for that version only.

Can I ask my publisher if I can collect more than 50% PRS royalties directly?

Yes, and increasingly foreign societies are able to handle splits other than the standard 50/50 writer/publisher split (though in some cases any share over the standard 50% will be paid to a fictitious 'writer designee' in order to fool the society's systems). Just remember that if the publisher has offered you an advance it will be based on the expectation that he is collecting the full publisher share of performance. So if you want to collect part of that directly then you can expect the advance to go down (and since performance is generally worth more than mechanicals, you can expect it to go down substantially).

What else does the PRS do?

Once you are a member of the PRS you will receive regular bulletins and reports that are well worth taking the time to read, about the work of the PRS and its foreign affiliates, including the very readable '*M*' magazine, which they produce regularly, and access to the members area of their website (including the

works, cue sheets, products and uncollected royalties databases). Their work includes efforts to combat piracy, protect and increase the rights of British writers in many overseas countries and in new technology, supporting British musical institutions, organising additional benefits for its members and sponsoring competitions and showcases. They hold regular 'surgeries' around the country, not just in London, and you'll receive invitations to your local ones automatically.

How often do I get paid by the PRS?

The PRS make four distributions every year, in April, July, October and December, to writer and publisher members. The PRS will send you a statement and pay the money straight into your bank account (remember to tell the Member Services Department if your account changes.)

How much should I get if my song is used in a pub/club/concert etc.?

It's very hard to say what you'd get for small gigs as sampling is used and those works which appear in the samples get paid and those that don't, don't. This also applies to pubs and restaurants and other small venues, whether it's live or recorded music that's playing. The formula for samples is constantly changing and the amount of full reporting data is increasing, so even if you do get paid, it's hard to tell just how much it will be. For bigger concerts in the UK, the PRS's Concert Tariff, at 3% of the gross box office receipts, comes into play, and there's a higher tariff specifically for classical concerts and certain other specific types of music (check their website for details).

Synchronisation royalties – what should the agreement say?

Fees for use of your songs in films, commercials and other audio-visual media (including some uses on the Internet) are called synchronisation fees and are usually licensed directly by your publisher, though, in practice, some publishers may ask MCPS to do this, and most such fees for television in the UK are covered by society blanket agreements. The definition of synchronisation fees tends to be stretched to cover radio commercials too, even though no actual synchronisation of your music with visual images takes place. The country where the production company is based should really be the country where the licence is issued.

You should usually receive the same share of synchronisation income as you do of mechanical royalties. Or, perhaps to encourage the publisher and their sub-publishers to put extra effort into pitching your songs, you might concede that they get to keep 5–10% more (in the same way as with 'covers' that the publisher specifically 'procured').

Often, publishing agreements give the writer 'prior approval' over synchronisation rights, and this means that the publisher has to ask your permission and provide details of the proposed synch before agreeing with the licensee. That said, the same clause will often state that your permission should not be unreasonably withheld. You may also negotiate clauses forbidding synchronisation that promotes certain products (eg. meat if you're a vegan), political stances or contexts (such as sex or violence). The more restrictions you put on synchronisation, however, the likelihood is the worse the royalty rate your publisher will be prepared to offer, so strike a balance if you want to get reasonable income in this area.

How much synchronisation income should I get if my song is used in a film or TV production?

Fees for the use of the whole of a hit song or standard that is used in a major film are often around £10,000 to £20,000 (usually more if it's over the opening or closing credits, and substantially more if the film is named after the song). If the song is to be used 'out of context' in a trailer or commercial for the film then there should be an additional fee, but for all other uses the film company will want to 'buy out' all the rights now existing or to be created in the future, in perpetuity, so don't expect any more income except for money from the PRS and its affiliates worldwide when the film is shown or broadcast.

There are no fees for the showing of films in US cinemas, so this is taken into account when setting the synchronisation fee. Remember that if the song is unknown it's possible that the film will make it a hit. In this case the fees will be much, much lower, although your publisher will never actually pay anyone to put it in a film. The fees could be slightly lower if the film company agrees that your song will definitely be on a soundtrack album, or if the film is a low budget independent production and you negotiate a mechanical royalty from DVD or download sales.

Competition is increasingly stiff and pressure on fees is always downwards (especially in the US), so unless you're lucky enough to write one of the few really classic works that get used time and time again, you shouldn't really have high expectations for synch income; think of it as a nice occasional bonus rather than a staple of your income.

How much should I get if my song is used in a commercial?

Your publisher could usually get £20,000 to £50,000 or upwards for a nationwide (networked) television commercial using a hit song, maybe another £10,000 or more for a networked radio commercial, another £10,000 or so for a nationwide cinema commercial and another £12,000 or so if the television campaign extends to Ireland. Unlike record royalties or PRS royalties, where only the duration of the use counts, here the importance of the song and how badly the film company or advertising agency want to use it affect the fees enormously. A few really big songs could be worth well over double the above figures, whereas for unknown songs or old ones that haven't seen the light of day for years, you and your publisher might be happy to let them be used for a fraction of these fees, just to create fresh interest in the song. Then again, your publisher can get more money for a song if they offer exclusivity for a certain period of time (the problem being that if the song gets really associated with the brand, it may not be used again by others for quite a while afterwards).

As with other types of synch, competition is stiff, so downward pressure on fees at present is especially fierce and, with so many different media to advertise on, licensees are often looking for a discounted all-media package to keep their options open.

Incidentally, remember that in addition to synchronisation fees you will still get your share of broadcasting royalties through the PRS every time the film, TV programme or commercial is shown or broadcast.

Are there any other sources of income that I should receive a share of, and what should I expect to see in the agreement?

There should be clauses in your agreement covering 'miscellaneous' or 'other' income. The rate will nearly always be the same as your standard mechanical rate. If your song is used in stage shows (see also under Q & A 'films, musicals and plays'), your publisher will also extract performance fees for the use. The same applies to printed music or lyrics in books, newspapers and magazines. A use of the lyric in a best-selling pop music magazine is worth in the region of £500 depending on the circulation of the magazine (your publisher, or their print rights agent, should collect this direct from the magazine publishers). There are royalties to be had from

such obscure sources as music chips in mugs, birthday cards or even items of clothing. MCPS normally collects these for publishers under their Greetings Card or Novelty Product (NP) licensing schemes, though sometimes they're licensed in the Far East, where most of the chips are produced, and at much lower royalties. There are also royalties for karaoke, whether for performances in venues or mechanicals for home-use CDs (or video games like SingStar), and the use of the lyrics on sheets or on the screen is normally licensed at 2% of the published dealer price on top of the mechanical royalty. For use of your song on the Internet and for information on mobile phone ringtones, see the Internet section.

How often should the publisher pay me?

Normally you'll be paid twice a year, usually 90 days after June 30 and December 31 every year. If you've already got a track record you may get the publisher to agree to pay within 45 or 60 days, or even quarterly rather than half-yearly. Not all publishers are geared up to do this and, unless you're a really big act, the extra effort and expense will end up being reflected in a lower royalty rate. Generally, if no money is due to you but you had an advance then a statement should be sent, but often is not. No advance and no income usually means no statement. If there if money to be paid then normally it will be paid either by cheque or straight into your bank account (publishers generally prefer the latter), and if you're VAT registered you'll need to send an invoice for this to the publishers (this applies also to royalties from record companies).

What if I only write lyrics or only write music?

There are plenty of examples from the distant and not so distant past of successful writing teams – Gilbert & Sullivan, Burt Bacharach & Hal David, Elton John & Bernie Taupin, Andrew Lloyd Webber & Tim Rice – where one member of the team wrote music and the other wrote lyrics. Obviously, there is still plenty of work for a composer of music working alone, but these days it's much less common (but still possible) to be a successful lyricist.

There is an unwritten rule in pop music that the music counts for 50% of the song and the lyric for the other 50%, but this is by no means set in stone, and some words-and-music teams choose to identify themselves as both composers and authors of works, and there are significant copyright implications depending on how you choose to identify your creative roles. Briefly, if you choose to be identified solely as the lyricist then you may not get royalties from the use of the music alone, almost certainly not when different lyrics are used, and a foreign lyricist's share will often come out of your part of the royalties alone. If you choose to be identified solely as the composer then you may get 100% of the royalties for instrumentals and not suffer a reduction in royalties for foreign lyric versions; then again, you won't get paid for lyric-only uses.

Societies and publishers have trouble distinguishing 'music only' or 'words only' uses, and it makes life much easier for them if you're both treated as having written both, and there is a general assumption that this is the case. Works where all parties are identified as composer-author are known as 'joint works' (or legally, 'works of joint authorship'), which means that the contributions of the creators (legally 'authors') are not divisible, and whatever parts of the work are used, you will receive your share of royalties.

The final implication of choosing whether or not a song is a 'joint work' lies in the distant future, but will be very important for your children and grandchildren. A 'joint work' remains in copyright in its entirety until 70 years after the death of the last surviving creator, whereas songs with defined composer(s) and lyricist(s) are effectively two copyrights, and each has its own lifespan (70 years after the death of the last surviving composer and 70 years after the death of the last surviving lyricist).

Could I get to write English lyrics to foreign songs?

There used to be far more demand for this, but it's still another possible source of work and income for a good lyric writer. These days, the original writer or the publisher will usually insist that at least the meaning is the same as the original even if it isn't a straight translation. Many of the songs we think of as 'standards' today originated in South America or in Continental Europe, and it is the work of the US or British lyric writer that has made some of them successful here. In many cases, however, the lyric-writing job will go to a writer-producer who is able to secure a recording here with a big artist.

As we said earlier, a UK writer of a complete song would lose one third of his writer's share of performing fees earned abroad to a foreign lyric writer. Thus, this one-third is what you should get for writing an English lyric to a foreign song. The usual percentage of mechanical royalties offered is 12.5%, while as much as half of the total writer's share can be paid to top lyric writers.

Avoid giving your lyric the same title as the original song, as that will make it difficult for bodies collecting and accounting royalties to differentiate between uses of the song with or without your lyric. You might occasionally collect on performances of the original version accidentally, but you're more likely to lose out. UK sheet music royalties will usually be 2.5% of the retail selling price, as against around 12.5% if you wrote the whole song. This sounds terribly low when converted into cash, but is quite normal.

Will I collect on all uses of my lyric to a foreign song?

Sadly, probably not, even if you changed the title. In a few countries, your lyric will still be disregarded when it comes to making mechanical and performing royalty distributions. Unlike the PRS and MCPS, most foreign societies are governed almost entirely by local authors and composers, who for many years have defended their vested interest in maximising the income for local lyrics at the expense of the original writers. As a consequence, even if you know and can prove that records reproducing your lyric have sold in a particular country, the person actually receiving the 'lyric writer share' may be the author of the local language version. Within Europe, such preferential treatment for local songwriters is technically outlawed, and hence this situation has improved significantly in recent years.

A final consideration will be exactly who owns or publishes the new lyric version. Very often that will be the owner and publisher of the original work, and even if your publisher is able to obtain local or wider sub-publishing rights for your share, you may be paid by the original foreign publisher for many uses, so expect to have an ongoing relationship with that publisher.

How long will the publisher keep the rights to my songs?

Until around the mid-Seventies it was quite normal for writers to assign songs to publishers for the life of copyright (see 'Copyright For Songwriters' below), and this is still not entirely unknown, especially in the classical world. There are many writers of hits from that time who are still getting honest and regular statements from their publisher. They may or may not want to change publishers, but what they would definitely like to be able to do is renegotiate the rates. Some artists who are still active are able

to actually do this using the carrot of the newer material that they own, but they have no clear and definite right to reclaim their songs or negotiate better terms.

These days, a new writer would probably be asked to assign a song for maybe 10–15 years. If the publisher wants it badly, he may accept as little as three years. Hit songs tend to come back into favour every 10 or so years, so the publisher will want to try to benefit from this almost inevitable revival and, if he's paying a big advance and high royalty rate, then it's not unreasonable. If not, try to get the song back within 10 years, so you can re-negotiate better terms with your publisher or give it to another one, who will be paying you a better rate if and when the song is hot again. Remember that depending on your contract, there will usually be a 'post-term collection period' of one year, but this could be unlimited (see Glossary of terms).

Will the publisher want the rights for the whole world?

Actually, he'll probably want the whole universe, or at least the Solar System. This may seem ridiculous, but satellite broadcasting and space travel do mean that there is a possibility that a contract just for the world won't always mean 'everywhere'. It's very rarely worth asking your publisher to accept a smaller overall territory than the whole world/universe. It might be possible for a writer to collect all his UK fees by joining the PRS and MCPS and acting as his own publisher (it's relatively common practice for established writers in the US). Elsewhere, however, the benefits of having someone on the spot exploiting your songs or simply checking the accuracy and completeness of local royalties that come in are sufficient that even successful writers usually don't think twice about passing on all the rights to a publisher.

What if someone else claims to have written my song?

There will be a clause in your agreement in which you guarantee that the song is 'all your own work', or to the best of your knowledge and belief it is. As you are technically selling the song (if it's an assignment) to the publisher in exchange for a sum of money (however nominal) and ongoing royalties, the publisher has the right to take you to court if he ends up out of pocket because the song was in fact not all your original work. In practice of course, the publisher is on your side, and is unlikely to take the matter to court (unless it's clear that you intended to deceive), but it's a good reason to make quite sure that your songs really are original and that you tell your publisher if they contain any samples (see 'Sampling' in 'General Q & A').

If faced with a counterclaim from another writer or publisher, your publisher would normally be perfectly entitled to suspend payment of royalties to you until the matter was sorted out, though ideally he shouldn't be able to do this unless he's actually being faced with legal proceedings. Even then, as soon as the counterclaim is settled he should pay you your share (preferably with interest). The agreement will also state that the publisher is appointed to act for you should someone else try to claim your song, infringe upon it, or use it unlawfully. It should be at his expense initially, but he may be entitled to reclaim all his legal fees (but not a fee for his own time or in-house expertise) from any damages before paying your royalties if the case is successful. It's also possible that in exchange for the risk he's taking by outlaying for those legal fees that your share of royalties from any legal settlement may be reduced (often split 50/50). For this reason you will want to make sure that he has to consult you before and during any action he decides to bring against someone else for infringement of your song.

Can the publisher make alterations to my song?

The publisher usually has the right to have new lyrics made in foreign languages. There are good reasons why you might not want this, so even this should be subject to your prior written approval. He should certainly need your approval to make any substantial changes to your English lyric (or whatever language you wrote the song in) and to the music (see also 'Moral Rights' in the next section). Changing the beat or the vocal or instrumental arrangement is generally less contentious than changing the words or music, however small the changes.

If a publisher really thinks your song needs a bit of reworking at the start, then he should tell you before you even assign the song to him. He would normally ask you to rewrite any parts he felt needed improvement before resorting to anyone else, but he may suggest that you get together with another writer signed to him. This could be a way of getting you to give up part of your song, but it's more likely to be a completely genuine attempt to convert a song that may not be quite good enough into one that will earn everyone some money, and if the co-writer he suggests has had hits before, or else is a hit artist (even if his songwriting is awful!), that's all the more reason to agree to it.

Can I stop an individual making alterations to my song?

Of course, in practice, anyone can do what they like to your song in private and the same is pretty much true if they perform it live in public. If they record a changed version (for example, with lyric changes that you haven't approved) and release it to the public, then firstly they will not be entitled to a share of the publishing royalties (unless you agree it) and, if the changes are substantial, you may be able to prevent release.

If your song is used in software, interactive devices or on a website where sounds and images can be manipulated by the user, then of course you have no control over this once you've said yes to your song being included in the product or on the site. At present there is no set guideline for fees for such uses, but it shouldn't matter provided that the user doesn't try to release on record or otherwise exploit what he's done to your song, and if he does, then again you have the right to stop the release.

Should I ever give up part of my song to anyone other than a co-writer?

There is no reason why an artist, producer or remixer should necessarily get a piece of your song unless you agree, in good faith, that they really have made a noticeable improvement to it. If you do feel that you are being pressured into cutting someone else in on a song for no good reason, create a fuss and, if necessary, consult your lawyer, as this could be very important if the song becomes a hit. Don't just leave it and hope the problem goes away!

Your publisher may tell you that he can get a major artist to record your song on condition that you give up part of the writing credits and royalties. It's quite likely that your publisher would have to give up part of his share as well, since the artist will probably be signed to another publisher who will want to control his share. Another possible scenario would see you keeping the full writing credit but the artist would participate in royalties arising from their recording. Whichever it is, if

the artist insists, then so long as your contract gives you the necessary prior approval, it's ultimately up to you to tell your publisher if you're prepared to allow it. As we said earlier in this section, someone who simply makes an arrangement of your song can't claim a share automatically.

What about the other small print in the publisher's agreement?

There are a few points you should ask for:

a) Your publisher won't be allowed to do a sub-publishing deal overseas just for your songs as distinct from the rest of his catalogue. He's not obliged to tell you what sub-publishing deals he has, though they should be 'arm's length', meaning that if they're with his own companies, then they should be on the terms that are normal in the business.

b) He should use his best endeavours or 'best commercial endeavours' to collect money from his sub-publishers, whoever they are ('best endeavours' is quite a strong phrase, and means he really should do almost whatever it takes to get the money).

c) He should use at least reasonable endeavours to promote your songs (see also 'Reversion Clauses'), unless your agreement with him is what's known as an 'administration deal', where you've already got the activity and exploitation and you just want the publisher, in return for a small percentage (say 10–20% 'at source' worldwide), to collect the money.

d) There should also be an audit clause (see 'General Q & A on Songwriting') and a clause covering moral rights (again see 'General Q & A on Songwriting').

COPYRIGHT FOR SONGWRITERS

This began centuries ago as simply the right to make copies for a limited period (hence the name). Since that time it has been expanded to include the right to perform a song in public, grant permission for its use in films etc., make recordings of it for sale to the public and so on, right up to the use of it on the Internet. Basically, most of these rights fall into one of two categories, either mechanical (like making and selling CDs, downloads or copies of DVDs) or performing (like playing live, on the TV, over the Internet or on the radio). In the UK, the Copyright Acts, in 1911, 1956 and 1988, form the basis on which most of a songwriter's rights rest. By various international agreements, notably the Berne Convention and the Universal Copyright Convention, your song, whether written in the UK or elsewhere, is protected to a greater or lesser extent in almost every other country of the world (and increasingly to pretty much the same extent). In Europe, the EU Commission and Parliament have attempted over the years to bring most of the laws concerning copyright into line in all countries of the European Economic Area and the European Union. Most countries have, like the UK, also passed various Copyright Acts over the last hundred years or so, updating the law to try to cover the new technologies as they have come about.

How do I copyright a song?

In Britain you don't have to do anything to 'copyright' a song. As soon as it actually exists outside your mind in some 'tangible form', that is, once you have written it down or made a recording, whether amateur or professional, then technically copyright begins from that moment. The same is true in most other countries. In the US it used to be necessary to 'register' songs with the copyright office of the Library of Congress, and many songwriters or composers still choose to do this for important works and to firmly establish the date on which copyright begins. Your publisher should ideally agree to register, at his expense, any song that has been commercially released in the USA; the current cost is $35 online and $45 for a paper registration, so it's unlikely they'll commit to registering every song you write.

The international symbol of copyright is a 'c' in a circle (©) and if you are sending or taking around manuscripts or lyrics with tapes of your songs you should write, at the foot of the first page of any manuscript or lyric, '© Copyright YYYY by XXXX' (where YYYY is the year you created the work and XXXX is your name and address).

In the UK, even if you sell or assign your song to a publisher, you are the first owner of the copyright. In some Continental-European countries you always remain the owner, while in others you assign the copyright to the collecting society when you join (just as UK writers do to the PRS with their performing and broadcasting right). In effect, you then only license the publisher to do certain things for you, i.e. print, license uses, collect royalties etc. The only exception in the UK is if you were actually employed by someone else to create the song, as a newspaper reporter would be when writing an article. In that case, the employer is the first owner, and the song is known as a 'work for hire'. Most film music over the years has been written under such agreements, though it is much less often the case these days. Instead, the film companies insist that you enter into a writer/publisher relationship with their associated publishing company.

If you want to make an arrangement of someone else's song then you may be asked to assign the copyright on a 'work for hire' basis, meaning that you effectively agree that you were employed to do it and therefore have no rights in the new material you've added. This sounds tough, but if you've used someone else's recording/song and it's given you a hit recording as an artist, it's a small price to pay.

Technically, for a 'work for hire' you're not even entitled to the writer's share of performing income, but often in practice you will still collect those royalties, and your terms of 'employment' may even grant the right to other royalties. The other serious consequences are that 'works for hire' are usually exempt from laws that force publishers to return copyrights to their original creator (most notably termination rights in the US, which used to be known as renewal rights), and that they will usually be assigned to your 'employer' for life of copyright.

How long does copyright last?

In the UK, copyright lasts for the whole of your lifetime and for 70 years from the end of the year of your death. If two of you wrote the words and music of the song together then, as we have said, copyright continues for 70 years after the death of whoever dies last. This is not too likely to worry you, but might concern your heirs. Thanks to the international agreements we mentioned earlier, this applies in the UK to foreign songs as well, and your song will in turn be protected for the same or roughly the same length of time in most other countries too. Copyright in the US used to last for two periods of 28 years then an extra 19, making 75 in all, and then only if you 'registered' and 'renewed' it. However, from 1978 new songs received life + 50 years' protection, since extended to life + 70 so that US works would get the same protection as European works in Europe, where life + 70 is granted and it became no longer necessary to register works. US copyright law allows you to terminate

any assignment of your US rights 35 years after the assignment was made, even if you made a life-of-copyright deal.

What if someone steals my song?

If you heard a song in the charts that sounded exactly like one you wrote say a year ago and you discovered that it was written after you wrote yours, then you would have to prove that the writer of the hit 'had had access' to your song (i.e., he'd had the opportunity to hear it, and then copy it) if you wished to make a claim against him. If you kept your song to yourself and the only copy was in a sealed, self-addressed registered envelope, or in a solicitor's or bank manager's safe keeping (two processes often suggested to new composers), then 'access' would be impossible and the similarity in songs would be regarded by the courts as coincidence.

By sending a copy of your song to yourself in a registered envelope left unopened and intact, you could at least prove that you hadn't stolen the hit, but now no publisher is likely to be interested in it and you'll have to write it off as very bad luck.

If, however, you think a song of yours (or part of it) that has had 'exposure' has been copied without permission, and (perhaps surprisingly) it happens very rarely, then your publisher would take up the matter for you.

Do remember that virtually everything you write has been written before in some form or other, no matter how original you think it is. If you use a classic blues chord progression or a reggae beat, you obviously aren't the first to use it, and there are only so many tunes. It's your choice of course, but if you pursue every little similarity you open yourself up to similar claims. So you should only ask your publisher to pursue those works that very strongly resemble yours and that your publisher thinks are worth pursuing.

If someone claims that you have infringed their song, then you either have to prove that yours was created first, that you couldn't have heard their song, or try to find another earlier song that sounds like both theirs and yours (this is known as 'prior art').

It's often quite obvious, listening to a new song, where the writers got the idea or the sound or the instrumentation, and even some of the words or tune. However, once a musicologist (an expert musician who will compare one song with another) gets hold of it, then, unless a substantial part of the actual tune is identical, the chances are that his report will declare it not to be a plagiarism and no one will consider that you have a case. Musicologists can charge several hundred pounds for an initial report and several thousand pounds for a full report, but it's worth getting a report from a good one if you seriously think your song has been 'ripped off', and you'll need one if it goes to court.

Is even the shortest musical work protected?

It's been argued from time to time that some pieces of 'music' (eg. one long note, a drum pattern etc.) are not really 'copyright musical works', but length is not really the issue; rather, it's how distinctive the bit of music is. Take the example of the well-known Christmas song 'The Twelve Days Of Christmas' – it may surprise you to learn that most versions of this song performed in the UK are protected by copyright. Though the original song is very old and well and truly out of copyright, the distinctive bit of tune where you sing 'five gold(en) rings' is in fact a much newer addition and is in copyright (listen to a US recording of this work and you'll notice the different tune they tend to sing on this line – that's the original).

EXCLUSIVE SONGWRITER AGREEMENTS

Most publishers who think your songs have any promise will want to give you a 'blanket' songwriting contract for a period of years, usually know as an ESA (Exclusive Songwriter Agreement), so that if they've spent a lot of time, trouble and money trying to promote your earlier efforts, they're guaranteed your entire output at least for a while once you've started writing hits. The UK courts don't look too kindly on 'exclusive' agreements for long periods, especially if they appear heavily loaded in favour of the publisher. They tend to hold that they restrict the development of your career, and for this reason any British publisher trying to sign you up for more than five years, or giving himself options to do so without paying you a reasonable advance for each option, is probably making his contract unenforceable, should you wish to challenge that contract in the future. That said, you should never sign a contract with the express intention of challenging it in the future – not only is it a bit dishonest, but you may find yourself stuck with it if a court doesn't think it as unreasonable as you do.

Why sign a blanket agreement anyway?

You may well ask what is the benefit to you in agreeing to write exclusively for one publisher – why not leave your options open to write for whoever offers you the best deal on a song by song or album by album basis? Well, some established writers and composers do this, especially in the classical world, and it may be a route you decide to take, especially early in your career when the deals on offer are not so tempting and involve longer retentions by the publisher. On the other hand, the usual inducement is money. The publisher may offer an advance payment, which they can recover from your future royalties but can never make you pay back, even if none of your songs has earned a penny during the time they control them (or even if those songs earn money after they revert to you). Another reason to sign is that it may encourage your publisher to make much greater effort in promoting and developing your career, looking to place new songs with other (perhaps more successful) artists, get exclusive new tracks into films (if you're a record-

ing artist too) or find exciting opportunities to collaborate with other songwriters and artists. If your publisher is guaranteed for a certain period that they have exclusive rights to your new songs, they have a vested interest in a part of your future. Then again, if they simply suggest that it's standard practice and that they're not interested in you if you don't sign exclusively, then you should think carefully about just how interested in helping you develop your career they really are.

These days, many publishers have recording studios or access to them, and can use their contacts and their money to try to get you a recording deal; once again, the incentive for them to do this is that they will benefit from the new material you create under your new record deal. Remember, there's no particular benefit to you in being able to say, 'I've been signed up by a music publisher' unless you're all agreed on what they're going to try to do for your career, or unless you simply want them to collect royalties for you (for a small percentage), while you, your manager or even your lawyer do the legwork developing your career.

Should the royalties be higher under a blanket agreement?

Not necessarily, as it depends very much on the size of the advance(s) you want and how long the publisher wants to keep the songs. Rates, advances and retention period – these considerations are the three basic 'commercial terms' that have to be offset against each other in any publishing contract negotiation, be it for an ESA or a single song assignment.

You can certainly ask for a higher royalty as part of your publisher's options to extend the contract into a second or third period, but, unless you're already a major success and they're really keen, don't expect them to agree to increase the royalty on 'first period songs' during the second period. Again, you may be able to get them to escalate the rates once they have recouped the advance (unless they've also got to pay you another advance). Any 'royalty escalation' is a bit of a nightmare for a publisher's administration staff, so often the publisher is more prepared to negotiate on the initial royalty rate than complicate matters by having the rates change partway through the contract.

How long should I sign to a publisher for?

The most common ESA will be for one year with two options for the publisher to renew it, each for one year or until you've had a certain number of songs released (usually, if you're also a recording artist, the 'year' will last until your next album is released). If the agreement extends till the albums are released, then there should be a so-called 'long-stop' date (usually after one or two extra years), which will be the date on which the agreement terminates (or he has to exercise his option) regardless. Without this, it's possible you could be signed to the publisher forever!

By signing an ESA you will be giving, or agreeing to give, the publisher all the songs that you write during the term of the agreement. Obviously, not all your songs will be included on your albums or 'covered', and any that aren't should come back to you within a period defined in the contract. (Usually you ask for the song back and the publisher has a set further amount of time to get some activity on the song; if they fail then the song reverts to you automatically.)

What advances can I expect?

The publisher will usually pay an advance on signing. For a typical new band with no record company interest yet, you might get, say, £10,000 'upfront' and up to £500 towards your lawyer's bill for negotiating the deal, also paid as an advance by the publisher. You could try to get them to swallow this as a non-recoupable expense, but most publishers won't. The actual cost to you of a lawyer negotiating your deal will be anywhere from £500–£700 up to £3,000 (or more if you're a big writer and the negotiation is stretched out), but £1,000 is not untypical, particularly if your lawyer is the one who recommended you to the publisher in the first place.

You could ask for 'development money' by way of, say, another £2,000 to £5,000 for travelling, recording equipment or demo costs during the first year. Other points at which further advances may be payable are when you actually sign a recording agreement, when the recording is completed or when the first album is released in the UK, US or another major territory (for an out-and-out dance act, this is more likely to be linked to the release of singles). On release of the album the publisher might pay perhaps another £10,000 to £20,000. That brings you to the end of the first 'year', although if the album is not released in that year then the first period of the agreement will probably continue until the 'long-stop' date or until the album is released.

Around four to six months after the album is released, the publisher may have to pay, let's say, another £20,000 to take up his option to sign you for the second contract period, in which you undertake to try to ensure that another album is released. The four to six months is to give him time to see how well the first album does, and is quite normal. When and if the second album comes out, the publisher would, in this instance, probably pay another £20,000 or so. The same would apply to the third period and the third album, but with the figures increased yet again.

You could also ask for chart bonuses. The normal definition of a 'bonus' in the music business is a sum of money that is not recoupable by the publisher, record company or whoever, but here the sums will probably be recoupable from your royalties. You might ask, for instance, for an extra £10,000–£20,000 if your album makes the UK Top 10, or if any singles make number one.

Suppose I already have a record deal?

The above figures are based on a brand new writer/producer/act with no record deal as yet, where the publisher is risking that you won't even get a record deal, never mind have a hit. If, however, you're already signed to a recognised and respected record company, then you may be able to put a nought on the end of most of the figures above. A lot depends on whether or not you can induce a 'bidding war' between interested publishers. If you can, then you will need to be careful; if you leave it too late to sign with either before the release of your first single or album and sales are only mediocre, then you could lose all the interest. Then again, if it turns out to be wildly successful, then the heat of the bidding war may only intensify (though you don't want to wait too long after that, because the people with really big offers for synch uses and the like will only wait so long for a publisher to talk to before they go elsewhere or to the next big thing).

Is the publisher bound to pay the advances in the agreement?

Yes, so long as the condition for that advance is met. So you'll get the advance 'on

signature' when you sign, the advance on the option when it's exercised and so on.

The most complex condition to meet will be if you have a 'minimum commitment' to deliver (ie. get a commercial release of) a target percentage of songs in a given period. Say, for example, that your contract states that you must deliver a minimum of 90% of 10 songs in the first period. If you deliver less than that, then your next advance will probably be reduced accordingly (the same may apply to chart bonuses and to the payments on release of the second and third albums). The target will probably be the aggregate of your shares of songs delivered in the period; so if your target is 90% and you actually write 10 songs on an album equally with another writer, your aggregate will only be 50%, and therefore you may only get 55.55% of the advance(s) specified in the agreement.

Can I give any rights at all to another publisher during the term of the agreement?

Generally the answer is no, certainly not without the publisher's prior written consent. You might be able to exclude upfront any music you're commissioned to write for films or other audio-visual productions. These days, often you won't get such a commission if your publishing rights are not free for the commissioner to place in their own publishing affiliate; and if the commissioner doesn't want the publishing, you could assign to your existing publisher on a 'single song' basis. If you're in a fairly strong bargaining position and you want to get into commissioned film or TV music then you should consider asking for such an exception in your contract. Obviously, however, it's a concession by the publisher and he will expect a quid pro quo in the form of lower rates, retention longer or lower advances.

You should make sure that the works assigned under your music publishing agreement are limited to musical works; for example, if you write a book, article or play in the future, you'll want that to be unencumbered when you come to negotiate with literary publishers.

How would I get out of a blanket writing agreement?

The first thing you do is simply to write to the publisher asking for a release. They'll probably be quite prepared to do this if they're having no success with your songs, or if you have any justifiable grounds for being discontented with them, or if you really have stopped writing. If they paid you an advance that shows no sign of being recouped, they may offer to release you from the contract provided that you refund all or part of it. This is perfectly reasonable provided that in return you get back the rights to the songs you wrote under the agreement. If they won't release you, check through your royalty statements for accuracy and regularity. As we have said, the contract will normally provide for these to be sent every six months, within so many days of June 30 and December 31. If they are not being sent on time, write to the publisher demanding that he keep to the terms of the contract. If he continues not to comply with the agreement, then you may have grounds for termination. If the publisher has given you any other undertakings in your contract that haven't been fulfilled, then, again, if you give appropriate notice, you may have grounds to terminate.

Also check any option clauses – if your publisher hasn't exercised an option on time, then you're almost certainly free (unless the agreement contained a provision that obliges you to write to them asking if they want to renew). Then again, if you continued to act as if the option had been taken (delivering songs, accepting royalties, corresponding about synch clearances on new works or, worst of all, accepting the option advance), you may fatally weaken your case.

If you feel you need to start writing formal letters, then get your lawyer to do it, but

Oh please release me,

always start with the friendly, reasonable approach. Your lawyer may also be able to advise you on possible get-out clauses. No matter who writes, keep copies of all correspondence (emails and letters carry almost equal weight these days in court), fax transmission acknowledgements, receipts for registered letters and email "read receipts" and "delivery receipts".

Also remember that one default in sending royalty statements on time may not be enough to get you out of the deal; the default must be "persistent" and "material". Incidentally, there's no point in attempting to deceive him by writing for another publisher under a pseudonym. First of all, you'd be getting dangerously close to committing criminal fraud (since you obtained your advance and your publisher's services by promising to write exclusively for him) and, secondly, if they find out (and they almost certainly will), not only will your first publisher claim the song but your new publisher will probably want some recompense. While they sort that out, the money will be in suspense; lawyers' fees and the compensation to the second publisher will probably take all the royalties and the second publisher may want his advance back.

Finally, remember that your agreement probably says that the publisher will have 30–60 days from the date of your letter in which to correct your complaint.

GENERAL QUESTIONS AND ANSWERS ON SONGWRITING

How can I get to write for TV and films?

The producers of many films, TV and radio programmes are always looking for new songs and music for use in their shows, and you can send in demos and ask for a meeting just as you would with a music publisher. Inevitably though, unless you already have a reputation, it's largely a question of who you know. Some publishers, including some with 'production music' libraries, specialise in supplying music for audio-visual productions, and they will have the contacts you don't, if you can convince them that you can take on a commission (which means being able to produce a broadcast-quality recording of the music as well as writing it, and doing it to a deadline).

Much of television in this country is now produced by independent production companies, who are commissioned to make programmes by the broadcasters, though the BBC and ITV (Carlton-Granada) still have substantial in-house production departments. Sky, Channel 4 and Five are almost entirely "publisher-broadcasters" rather than "producer-broadcasters", but even they may need music for idents and trailers. You'll find a good many of the major production com-

panies in our 'Useful Addresses' list below, but others can be found easily by checking the end credits of programmes.

Film is an even more difficult area. Again there is a multitude of producers of all sizes, and the reputation and "who you know" principles very much come into play. Many film composers start out in TV or writing for commercials, and then their work gets known or the director they usually work with graduates to film.

What will film and television companies pay and what rights will they want?

This depends very much on what instrumentation is required. If they expect a full orchestra they'll pay a lot more than a track composed on a synth, albeit using sampled sounds from an orchestra. Even a new writer should get a three-figure sum per minute of music, but there really are no hard and fast rules. The broadcast performance fees amount to much more than the commissioning fee, so this is the main consideration. If you are successful in interesting television or production companies in your music, they will wish to acquire world broadcasting rights in all media (including cable, terrestrial, satellite, subscription, pay-per-view and online time-shift streaming), and probably a buy-out of your mechanical rights (though you may get a royalty at society rates or a proportion thereof). This is so they can sell the programme all round the world without prior reference to, or permission from, you, although you would of course still get broadcast performance fees in all the places where the programme was shown or heard. Some will want you to assign all the rights to their own publish-

72

ing company, but others will be content to accept just broadcasting rights from you, leaving you free to assign all the remaining rights, performing, recording, printing etc., to a publisher. A film company will probably have its own affiliated record company, and will expect you to agree to license the recording for a soundtrack album and to accept controlled composition provisions when it's released in North America, and they are less likely to allow you to assign your rights to another publisher.

Can I or my publisher stop anyone recording my song?

As a preface to this answer, remember that if you have assigned the copyright in your song to a publisher, the song is legally his property; if you only licensed the rights, you remain the legal owner. Prior to the 1988 Copyright Act, only the copyright owner had the right to try to stop a new recording, and then only the first recording. Once one version had been 'published' it was technically a free-for-all. As a result, you can ask MCPS not to issue a first licence without you or your publisher giving approval (the "first licence refusal" or FLR process), so that you can choose the first recording to hit the market.

The 1988 Act changed the position somewhat and, since then, in theory, the copyright owner's permission is required before anyone records and releases a song unless it's almost a carbon copy of a previous release. So if there are substantial differences between the original recording and the new, then in theory you or your publisher can injunct to prevent its release; and obviously a sample use falls into this category. Your publisher can advise as to the likely chances of success in a particular case.

Can I or my publisher stop anyone else performing my song?

As regards performances, it is virtually impossible to prevent people performing your song once they have been able to get hold of some material (sheet music, demos or recordings) from which to learn it. Once the song is well-known then a performance can only be prevented if, for instance, it is a parody or is included in a film or show without having been properly licensed. In most cases an unwanted performance is of no great consequence.

'Ere.. thats my song You're singing! Give us a swig and we'll call it quits!

Can I or my publisher stop anyone else printing my song?

Anyone wishing to print the song in any form will have to apply for permission from the publisher and, if your contract provides for prior approval, your publisher will have to ask your permission before granting their own.

Can I or my publisher stop anyone making a parody of my song?

Yes. If your original music or lyrics are used, a parody should be cleared specially with your publisher by the user before it is used, and the parody writer should never receive a written credit or part of the royalties (unless you agree that they do). A 'parody' is not necessarily a comic version of your song (that's subjective anyway), but rather a version where the lyric has been substantially altered. You shouldn't confuse this with a 'pastiche' where the song "sounds like" (and is intended to sound like) but is not the same as your song, and about which you can do very little.

In the US, however, the Supreme Court ruled that rap artists 2 Live Crew's 'parody' version of Roy Orbison's song 'Pretty Woman' was encompassed by the concept of 'fair use' and, so long as royalties were paid, then publisher's consent was not needed. To stop a parody in the US it is now necessary to have it considered a 'derogatory treatment' of the song itself.

What happens if my songs are included in musicals and plays?

The living stage rights ('dramatic performance') in a musical are termed 'Grand Rights'. Unlike almost all other performing rights, these are usually licensed directly by the publishers to the producers of the show, in return for a percentage of the box office receipts, and the PRS are not involved.

If a producer commissions music for his show, he may want the Grand Rights (so that he can license future productions of the show without reference to another party), but all other rights (so-called 'small rights') may remain with the writer and then be assigned to a publisher.

A musical show that contains songs that already existed and weren't written specially for it is known as a 'compilation show'. The PRS claim the right to license these, but in practice the amount they can charge under their Tariff T (theatres) is laid down by the Copyright Tribunal and generally works out at only about 1% –3% of box-office receipts. So, at the publisher's request (a '7(f) notice'), they will stand aside and allow the publisher to negotiate a higher rate and collect the money directly, and generally the publisher can achieve 3% to 6% of box office (pro-rated across the songs in the show) depending on the total percentage of the running time of the show that is music. Most publishers would regard it as petty and uncharitable to exact a fee for the use of a song or two in a local primary school Christmas show, but the fee for their use in a big West End production could be hundreds of pounds per song every week, and some shows run for several years, go on to a provincial tour and then are revived in the West End, so the income can mount up. Oddly, the only exception to the 7(f) notice process is a traditional pantomime, which is fair enough ('oh no it's not', 'oh yes it is' etc.).

If I write a song with someone else, how is the money divided?

It is hard to overemphasise how important it is to agree as soon as a song is in its final state exactly who the writers are, what their roles are (arranger, composer, lyricist or composer-author) and the percentage splits between them, and preferably to agree in writing. Two writers of the Fifties hit 'Why Do Fools Fall In Love' who had never been paid and credited at all won a case nearly 40 years later in the US. (Only to have it overturned on appeal because it took them so long to bring the case, the time limit being stated to be just three years.) Then again, in late 2006 in the UK, despite the usual time limitation on such claims (generally held to be six years), the originally credited writers of 'A Whiter Shade Of Pale' lost 40% of all future publishing royalties to another band member. These are extreme cases, but in recent years there have been more and more legal battles, sometimes years after the song was a hit, over exactly who wrote the song. Legal and other costs can be astronomical, disputes can take years (or decades) to resolve, and often royalties can be held in suspense for just as long. Worst of all, if the song isn't big enough it may never be economically viable to resolve the problem through the courts and, if neither side is willing to compromise, nobody will ever get paid.

You may not want to be seen to mistrust your co-writer by asking for something in writing, but how much worse will it be decades later to face them in court after years of bitter wrangling? If all the writers are signed to the same publisher, then by signing an agreement/confirmation letter with the publisher you are putting in writing your agreement to the split.

Beware of studio musicians, producers, remixers and artists who seem to expect a share of the song. If you think they've done a great job in turning your song into a hit (which they frequently do) or if you'd agreed on a split from the start then fine, but make it crystal clear what you think they should get, and avoid saying anything on impulse.

Most songwriting 'teams' divide songs equally, even where one wrote all the music and two others wrote the words, for example. Just as with Lennon & McCartney or U2, an equal credit and split is agreed even where a song is largely written solely by one person. In the UK, the music and lyrics are regarded as separate copyright works, which is why it makes life easier to credit all the writers with words and music (see our discussion of 'joint' works in the 'Copyright for Songwriters' section). Make sure your publisher knows if the splits are not equal, or they may well assume that they are. Also, if you think you might have trouble from a co-writer, make sure to let your publisher know, so he can keep an eye out for any conflicting claim. If you have it, let him have a copy of your written agreement of splits.

Incidentally, under an ESA you will probably be asked to try to persuade your co-writer to sign his share of the song to your publisher. There's no harm in agreeing to use 'reasonable' endeavours to do so, but it shouldn't be worded any more strongly than that, especially as your co-writer may be bound by similar obligations.

What do I get when my music is rented or hired out?

This may come under the 'miscellaneous' or 'other' section of the contract or, if your music is of a classical bent, you may

have a separate rate. If it's under miscellaneous you will usually get the same share as for mechanicals of whatever the hire fees amount to on printed editions or manuscript copies of your music. (Generally, only serious music, symphonic works, classical pieces or the scores of musicals are hired out, and for these this is very big business.)

With regard to the songs used in videos and recordings that are hired or rented out, the MCPS generally administers these rental rights on behalf of publishers and writers (where they have not been bought out by a catch-all synch fee).

Can I use bits of other people's songs in mine?

Not without permission of the copyright owner, unless the song you use is out of copyright (see 'Sampling' in General Q & A).

Will I be paid on my versions or arrangements of existing songs?

If the existing song is in copyright, then no; if it's 'traditional' or out of copyright (described as being in the public domain or PD), then possibly yes. If the song you've arranged really is PD then your new arrangement of it, even if you've hardly changed it at all, becomes a new copyright expiring 70 years after your own death, and you'll be paid on it just as if it were all your own work (of course, unless you add something really distinctive then you're unlikely to be able to claim royalties on recordings other than your own). That said, even if you think the work is PD, as we've said elsewhere, if you're 'arranging' a song that someone else has arranged and recorded in the last 70 years or so, it's quite possible you're infringing the copyright of someone else and you need to be very (very) careful to make sure that your 'arrangement' doesn't include any part of theirs. This means you need to go right back to the original song or else you may have to credit the act whose arrangement you've adapted and let them collect the royalties.

A few foreign performing rights societies grade the level of originality in an arrangement and pay royalties accordingly on a sliding scale. If your song is 'based' on a PD work and it's not crucial that you keep the original title, then change it. The other reason for doing this is that when it's performed or broadcast, the societies won't have the problem of identifying whose arrangement of the PD work was used, and you're more likely to get paid.

How many old songs are actually traditional?

Quite a large number of songs, including the likes of 'Greensleeves', 'Camptown Races' etc., are widely known to be traditional, but our advice is to check up if you are at all uncertain about the copyright status of a piece of music. If someone wrote a song at the age of 16 and died at the age of 90, it will be 144 years before that song becomes 'PD' in the UK and most of the rest of the world. Some songs that never saw the light of day during the writer's lifetime get a further period of copyright from the date they were published, regardless of when they were written. Even more confusingly, because in the US works written before 1978 only attract 95 years of copyright from first publication, it's quite possible that a work regarded as PD in the US is still in copyright in the rest of the world.

This inevitably means that there are even old Victorian music hall songs that are still copyright. The children's songs 'Happy Birthday To You' and 'I Know An Old Lady Who Swallowed A Fly' and several well-known Christmas carols are still copyright. Most spirituals are PD, as are many well-known folk songs, but others, like the Steeleye Span song 'All Around My Hat', contain so much new material that anyone using them today would be almost certain to be including someone's copyright work.

How can I find out whether a song is traditional?

The MCPS and PRS will be prepared to answer queries on whether a song or piece of music is copyright. You can contact them (see the list of 'Useful Addresses') but remember that they are extremely busy, so try not to query more than a title or two at a time, and try to give them the original composer's name if you can find it. This is a help to them as they have many different songs by different composers but all with the same title, including around 500 different songs all called 'I Love You'! Your publisher can also advise as to whether or not certain songs really are traditional in the UK. Finally, the Internet, though it can't always be entirely relied upon, is full of helpful material and will at least alert you if the PD status of a work is the subject of controversy.

If I record a brand new arrangement of someone else's recent hit, can I claim a share?

If you wish for any reason to record a song that you know very well to be a recent work then, as we've said earlier, if you're going to make substantial changes to the original, you should send a copy to the publisher and ask if they have any objection (and they'll check with the writer if they are obliged to do so). They may well allow it but subject to you not making a claim to any of the royalties. Also, as we've said, they may ask you to assign any new material you add to it as a 'work for hire'. If you ask for a share they may be willing to let you have one, either because you have added substantially to the work and they think it may be successful, or because you are a proven artist (or have one lined up). But if it's substantially different from their original, then they're fully entitled to say, "No – don't release it".

Are there any subjects to avoid in song lyrics?

A tricky subject. 'Explicit lyrics', 'offensive lyrics' and 'bad taste' are in the end your subjective and artistic choice. Anything too extreme and your publisher or record company may not want to be associated with the song. Broadcasters in the UK and abroad will have different standards for what they'll broadcast (and at what times of day), and you'll have to choose a balance between your artistic decision and getting a wider audience for your music. Some artists record 'clean' and 'explicit' versions of songs to get round this problem, though obviously this will cost money.

What you certainly shouldn't do is make statements about specific people, brands or companies that are libellous (ie. you can't prove in court to be true), or criminally incite hatred or violence.

There are no real titles to avoid (though certain words will end up often being *****ed out, and this has been known to cause problems with income flow if your publisher doesn't register them as an alternate title). Out of interest, however, of all the songs that have been hit singles in the UK, the following are the commonest titles: 'Crazy' 13 + 'Crazy For You' 4; 'Tonight' 11; 'Star' 10 + 'Stars' 5 ; 'Stay' 11 + 'Stay With Me' 9; 'Heaven' 10; 'Heartbeat' 10; 'Freedom' 9; 'Don't Stop' 9; 'Everyday' 9.

Is there any formal body looking after the interests of songwriters?

Yes. These exist in many countries. The society in the UK is called the British

Academy of Composers and Songwriters. There is a yearly subscription, which you can arrange to be deducted directly by the PRS from your royalties. They have for a long time produced standard publishing contracts for the use of members and can give valuable advice generally on songwriting and the music business. They also produce a regular newsletter for members, a members' only area on their website with news and updates on upcoming events, and writers' workshops where new writers have the chance to have their work assessed by hit writers. This is also the body that has for many years presented the annual Ivor Novello Awards to the best or most successful British songs and songwriters, as well as the Gold Badge Awards for long-term achievers in the business, and the British Composer Awards. They also run the Songwriter's Academy, which offers chances to upcoming songwriters to work with more established ones. You don't have to have achieved any particular level of income or activity to join, so contact them or check their website for further details (details in the list of 'Useful Addresses').

The writers' organisations work together with the publishing fraternity to promote and protect music copyright in the UK and abroad under the umbrella of an organisation called British Music Rights (details also in our 'Useful Addresses' section).

Can I use as many pseudonyms as I like?

There is nothing to stop you, though you always run the risk that royalties will go astray if someone doesn't make the connection between you and your pseudonym. The PRS does ask, however, that you use not more than two different pennames, as it can become highly confusing, so if in doubt stick to two. Always tell your publisher and the societies your full real name and all your pseudonyms or you'll almost certainly miss out on royalties due to you. The society will arrange for an IPI (formerly but often still called CAE) number for each pseudonym and for your original name, and will ensure that on the worldwide IPI database those numbers are linked (though the link is only visible to societies).

Can I write a song with the same title as an existing song?

Yes, as there is no copyright in titles. The only note of caution is that if your title is the same as the title of a very big song, and your song is not as successful, it's possible that some of your royalties will accidentally end up going to that song.

What are reversion clauses?

These days, all songwriting agreements, even single song assignments, should provide that if nothing happens to your song within, say, two years (or a year or two from the end of an ESA), you can ask for it back. The publisher usually has three months to prove that a record was released or was used in a film or commercial or (sometimes) printed. If not, then it reverts to you.

Try to ensure your agreement clearly states that when the agreement ends, and the songs revert to you, you get them back for the whole world. If you can't, then at best you should continue to receive your foreign royalties from the original publisher, or at worst they will continue to recoup against your advance.

Can I get my song back if the earnings have dried up?

If a song has ever earned money, however long ago, then the chances are there will be nothing in the agreement to say you can have it back, and your publisher is highly unlikely to let it go. Any song that's ever been released, especially a single that had airplay, stands a chance of being 'picked up' and reactivated. If it's been inactive for many years, and has never been active, then a publisher may be happy to give it back, but he might well ask for all or part of your advance and/or demo costs back (and you should get to own the demo).

How do co-publishing and administration deals for writers work?

If you are in a strong position you may be able to ask for one of these deals, rather than just assign or license your songs to your publisher.

Co-publishing usually means one or two things – either that the publisher will form a new jointly owned company with you that owns the rights to your songs (and which the publisher administers worldwide), or you might form a company yourself, then assign half the rights to that company and half to your publisher, with your publisher administering the whole world for a set period of time (after which your company gets its half back and the publisher may well retain his share). In the latter case it's also quite common for your company to own the domestic rights entirely and administer them directly. This is a relatively common arrangement with established writers in the US, but is not as popular in the UK, primarily because in the long run it generally leads to your song being administered by several different companies and makes any clearances a bit of a nightmare.

In an administration deal, you generally adopt a trading name or actually form a company that is assigned your works, and the publisher then makes an agreement with your company to administer its catalogue for a set period of time. This has the advantage that you keep ownership of the works, potentially has certain tax advantages, and allows you to parcel up sets of songs in separate companies and deals, easily monitor their performance or, if you want, place them with appropriate specialist publishers.

The splits between your company and the publisher would be roughly similar to an ESA, but established writers could command 80/20 at source or better, especially if they don't want an advance.

What are Moral Rights?

These are rights that a UK writer has under the 1988 Copyright Act (Continental-European writers have had a stronger version of these rights for many years). They are a right of 'paternity' and a right of 'integrity'. Paternity is the right to be identified as the writer of a song. You have to 'exercise' this by informing your publisher – the assignment usually covers it. Obviously, you'll be aware that writers of jingles for commercials are never 'identified', though film credits increasingly credit songwriters.

Integrity is the right not to have your work 'messed about with'. It's not clear where a 'cover version' becomes a 'derogatory treatment' (the legal term), but you should be approached before anything more than minor changes are made to your song, regardless of the precise wording of your assignment to your publisher.

Who owns the demos my publisher makes?

Generally they do, unless, as is advisable, your agreement with them says otherwise (probably in exchange for them being able to recoup their costs from your royalties).

These days, demos and full-blown master recordings are often indistinguishable, and a demo can usually be remixed and improved on to make a commercial track. Some publishers will actually issue white labels of your recordings as a promotional tool to try to secure you a record deal, though if these are sold rather than just given to DJs etc., then you should have a separate form of 'artist' agreement with the publisher, saying who will get what (frequently a 50/50 split of any profits).

When should I renegotiate a publishing deal?

The usual way to get a renegotiation, as with record deals, is to offer another album's worth of material in return for better rates on the songs on your current, successful album, and maybe bigger advances from now on. If your single or album is high in the charts or about to break in the US, you'll obviously get a better deal than if you wait too long and the record begins to drop. Also, remember (and a lot of people don't) that you can also negotiate downwards if you think a publisher is basically doing a good job but your first album flopped, and by accepting a smaller advance for the next option period you can perhaps avoid being dropped by the publisher.

THE INTERNET

DOWNLOADS, STREAMING, PODCASTS AND WEBSITES

The Internet is not only the fastest-growing source of music for consumers, but is also the most contentious. In 2002 the Oxford Union debating society voted, perhaps not unsurprisingly, hugely in favour of music being free on the Internet. As a listener to other people's music, especially if you can't afford to buy all the CDs you'd like to, you might think this is great. However, you're also someone who will hopefully be earning your living from your songs and recordings, and you don't need us to tell you that free downloads and streaming are bad news for you. World record sales have recently dropped by between 5% and 10% a year, and a lot of that is down to Internet piracy. As broadband spreads into more and more homes, as things stand we can only expect to see this process accelerate (certainly that's the pattern we've seen in the US, where broadband really took off a few years before it did in the UK).

Why has it taken so long for the record companies to put their music on the Internet?

There's little doubt that if the majors, who control around three-quarters of all music (songs and recordings), had responded more quickly and collectively to the threat of Internet piracy, with a simple and attractive way for people to stream and download music legally, then at least some of the pain they're now facing could have been avoided. But hindsight is a wonderful thing and it's never wrong.

The truth is that various people in the music industry reacted differently in the early days. Some saw the potential for digital delivery very early on, some saw the Internet before broadband and believed that it was just a fad (speeds were so slow, no one would ever want to use it) and, as the thing snowballed, some just stood there transfixed as the world as they'd known it for nearly 100 years turned upside down. By the time it was agreed that something must be done, piracy was rife through services like Napster and Gnutella, and everyone's focus shifted to fighting the pirates (rather than offering a better alternative). Once Napster was shut down, peer-to-peer services sprang up everywhere, and some record companies and organisations (in the US mainly) decided to start suing end users (including private individuals) to make an example of them. Finally, the record companies could not agree among themselves on a united approach to legal online music services (see the discussion of file formats below), so, unlike illegal services, no one service offered tracks from all companies; there was no legal one-stop shop for music.

In the meantime – Apple packaged existing digital music player technology with their characteristic style and a dedicated online music service and the iPod and iTunes became market leaders, largely leaving rival legal services, including those belatedly set up by the record companies, in their wake.

What's with all these file formats, and what is DRM?

iTunes uses a specific file format called AAC (Advanced Audio Coding), which includes DRM (digital rights management) technology to prevent files from being copied more than a few times. Many record companies and rival online music services partnered with Microsoft to use their file format WMA (Windows Media Audio), which also includes DRM.

DRM has, however, not proved popular with music consumers for a number of reasons. First among these is the limit on the number of times the file can be copied – one change of computer and one change of digital music player and your uses are up, and after that the file is locked unplayable.

MP3 is the oldest format (in fact and AAC, was designed as its successor) and by far the most popular. Because it's the oldest, the size-to-quality ratio for the files is much worse than the other formats but it has several advantages in the eyes of consumers. Primary among these is no DRM, plus the fact that not all players will work with AAC or WMA but nearly all work with MP3 files. In fact, MP3 is so popular and DRM so unpopular that several record companies have given permission for legal download services to begin to sell tracks (at a premium price) as non-DRM MP3s.

So what are the record companies doing about illegal download services?

Action continues on several fronts. As mentioned above, companies have recognised the need to offer superior legitimate services to consumers; somewhere a consumer can go and know that they're getting the track they asked for (free of viruses and the like) and, for those that care, they can pay a little extra to be able to copy it hassle free to their many music-playing devices. As for companies that make money from piracy, record companies and industry bodies continue to pursue them wherever they are (be it BitTorrent-related sites like PirateBay or pushing the Russian government into action over AllofMP3.com). Lastly, the BPI is discussing with the government and ISPs (internet service providers) ways in which they can work together to target frequent users of illegal services and encourage them towards legal ones (the ultimate sanction being denial of Internet service on a three strikes and you're out basis).

So what do I actually get if my song or recording is downloaded from a legal site?

The record companies, which, in the early days of the Internet, offered ridiculously low rates or took large deductions from your royalties, have now, by and large, agreed that you will be paid for downloads at the full album royalty rate (which is usually about 25% higher than the physical singles rate), and without the packaging deductions of up to 25%. The actual amount you receive for each download depends on the retail price to the consumer (in the UK for example 79p for a DRM track and 99p for a non-DRM track on iTunes) and the share of that the service paid to your record company.

The MCPS-PRS operates a joint scheme for mechanical and performance rights known as Joint Online Licence (JOL), under which the current online download rate is 8% of gross revenue (ie. the price to the consumer or the appropriate proportion of a service's subscription revenue where consumers pay a monthly fee). So for a 99p track, less MCPS commission that's about 7p to your publisher, if your mechanical royalty rate is 75% you should get around 5p.

So what do I actually get if my song is streamed from a legal site?

For a clip of 30 seconds or less the current convention is for websites to be allowed to play this music royalty free (though there is no legal basis for this); with the proviso that the service is not charged for, the music is not streamed in conjunction with visual images or obviously promoting goods or services. Sites making money directly from their service (directly or through advertising revenue) have to be licensed by the PRS, either under the JOL or the Limited Online Exploitation Licence (LOEL) (aimed at services with annual revenue of less than £3,000). Under the LOEL the site pays a flat fee, under the JOL the PRS will collect 5.75% of revenues for non-interactive services (you can't influence which track is playing) and 6.5% for interactive services (where you can select the tracks or influence their selection). What this translates to on a 'per track per play' basis is impossible to calculate, as it depends on how much the service itself is making.

In the US, the Digital Millennium Copyright Act specified your right to be compensated for uses of your music and the Library of Congress subsequently set a rate of \$.08 per track for Internet radio streaming. There is much controversy surrounding this rate, and moves are afoot by Internet radio stations to get it reduced either to a proportion of revenue or to a rate per hour (something like 33 cents per hour).

The PPL also have a scheme for Internet radio and streaming (banded into small and other broadcasters by revenue), and collect a small fee (a fraction of a penny) for each track broadcast, which they divide between the artist and the record company. If authorised by you, they will collect from their sister societies around the world. You should also receive at least 50% of what your record company receives when your recordings are 'simulcast' (i.e. as well as a concert being heard live on UK radio, it can be listened to on the Internet).

So what do I actually get if my song is part of a 'podcast'?

Music in 'podcasts', be they audio only or audio-visual, music shows, drama or factual, must be licensed by the rights owners, as a mechanical reproduction takes place when you download the podcast or put it on your music player. In addition, depending on the context, there may be synch rights to be taken into consideration, especially where sponsorship or

direct advertising is involved. As you can tell, this is a complex area, and the societies are working on a permanent scheme. At present, however, licences are negotiated on a case by case basis. So it's hard to say at present exactly how much you will get for a particular podcast, and the complexity explains why so many have music stripped out of them.

What would I get for a ringtone download of my song or recording?

In the UK, the MCPS offers licences to operators of sites for downloading of ringtones at 10p per download or 10% of gross revenue of the site, whichever is higher, and the PRS licenses at 5p per download or 5% of gross revenue (again whichever is higher), subject to an annual minimum of just over £900. Rates differ in other countries, and in Europe ringtones form part of the various PEL initiatives (Nokia, for example, obtained a licence from the Finnish collecting society to cover ringtones throughout Europe).

On the recording side, until recently nothing like a 'master' in effect existed, but the advent of more sophisticated phones and the 'Realtone' has increased the market for ringtone masters. Many publishers are creating their own library of specially created masters that they can license to providers, and record companies are actively negotiating blanket deals with the same providers (an example is Sony BMG's deal with Vodaphone, under which some users could download 30-second soundbites of as-yet unreleased tracks to their mobiles as an incentive to buy Vodaphone's products and as exposure for Sony BMG's records). There is at present no set rate for the use of an existing commercial recording as a download.

Downloads are big business, as you can imagine – especially as many people will change their ringtone after only a few weeks and download a new one. If you buy a phone with commercial ringtones on it, then the manufacturer will have had to pay the equivalent of the download royalty upfront on the number of phones with those ringtones already included. In Japan, ringtones are such big business that as long ago as 2000 the Japanese equivalent of the MCPS collected around £20million in just one year.

What about mobile phone music services?

The MCPS/PRS administer these services as with any other online music service under the JOL (or LOEL for smaller value services).

The picture for recordings is once again more piecemeal, with individual services, mobile phone networks and record companies coming to a variety of exclusive and non-exclusive deals. But what's certain is that you should not see a significant reduction in your royalty rate (though it's probable in such a competitive environment that, initially at least, the actual cash will be lower than for a physical sale).

What about mobile phone TV & video services?

The MCPS/PRS licenses music broadcast and reproduction element of the use of music in TV and video mobile phone services under the General Entertainment On-Demand scheme (GEOD). This assumes that, if the material was originally created for another medium (eg. TV or film), the synch licence has already been granted by the publisher or under a society blanket licence. For recordings, the same goes as for mobile music services (see above). Fees vary from service to service, so it's impossible to estimate exactly how much you'll get if your music is used.

What actual rights do I have over use of my songs/recordings on the Internet?

As long ago as 1996 the World Intellectual Property Organisation (WIPO) agreed a 'protocol' recognising your right to prevent other people from digitally distributing your music. It basically said that companies and individuals have to have your permission, or the permission of someone you've given your rights to, to use your song/recording on the Internet. This subsequently became law in the US under the Digital Millennium Copyright Act and, in 2002, became law in the European Union too.

What about my song/recording getting changed in some way or put with video or other material?

If your song or recording is changed or synched with video by the website then they should seek your approval (just as with a conventional recorded adaptation) or that of your publisher and record company. If the website offers tools for the user to change your music, then this comes under the JOL definition of interactive services and the site will have to pay a higher rate (there's no practical way to get your approval every time such a service is used). If the service offers tools to synch your music to video online then your approval must also be sought.

Is it illegal to send a music file to someone else?

If it's your own song and your own recording (made entirely by you), you're not a PRS member (as a songwriter) and you're not signed to a record deal, then probably not! Otherwise, somebody somewhere will have the right to expect some payment. In practice, within the music business itself people send MP3s all over the world to their colleagues or potential customers to listen to, and no one tries to prevent this as it's part of the business (just like music publishers or record companies sending sampler CDs to advertising agencies, film companies and others who might use their song/record). Most people/companies don't own the song or the record but more publicity is in everyone's interest, so no one usually objects.

However, if you've 'ripped' a CD and sent it as an MP3 to one of your friends, this is illegal. If you download music files from a legal music service (either for a fee or as part of a monthly subscription service), it's still illegal to send it to someone else.

The EU directive to member countries to amend their Copyright Acts included a requirement to make any kind of attempt to get around 'encryption' (DRM or electronic devices to prevent duplication of recordings) illegal.

If I'm signed to a record company, will they want to control my domain name and website?

You might already have a good website up and running, possibly run by a friend, relative or long-standing fan in conjunction with your fan club. There have been moves by some record companies to try to take control of artist websites (or, more probably, relaunch them and close down the existing one) because they know that they can sell records and publicise themselves, as a company, through your site. If you haven't got a presence on the Internet, or you're not happy with the one you've got, then it may be worth considering allowing your record company to take control, so long as they agree to keep it up to date and perhaps give you approval over the content and/or the look and feel. Most importantly, you should own the domain name (the address of the site in words, eg. www.yourname.com) and they should agree to surrender control of the site when your agreement comes to an end. You may also want to put some limits in the contract on the type and amount of cross-promotion on your website (be that advertising or links to other artists).

Suppose someone else has used my name as part of the name of their website or in their domain name?

You won't be able to protect every variation of your domain name, not only because there are now so many suffixes (.com/.co.uk/.net/.org/.tv/.xxx etc.), but because of the almost infinite variation possible in the name itself (your-name, yourname, yournameshrine, yourname-fans and so on). That said, any implication that the site is your 'official' site or approved by you means you may have a chance to set your lawyer on them (or your record company's lawyer). If someone has taken your preferred site name or one of the more obvious variations that you'd like to use to redirect to your site, then you may be able to evict the 'cybersquatter'. Obviously, the more original your name, the more likely it is that no one else has used it yet, and the sooner you get your name registered the better. Domain names cost no more than a few pounds to register annually if you do it yourself, or you can pay any number of online companies, who will charge more but offer to renew the registration annually so you don't have to remember.

How can I make a site take my music down?

There is an organisation called 'Rightswatch', which was set up on behalf of the owners of songs and recordings to make it easier to remove offending sites from the Internet. The idea is that if it is quite clear that such a site is making available unlicensed songs or recordings, then the Internet service provider will co-operate with the rights owners to have the site or the songs/recordings removed as soon as possible without anyone having to go to court, with all the expense that involves. The project is in its infancy, so for the immediate future, if you have a deal then contact your publisher or record company; if not, your lawyer will act for you. Obviously, the Internet is huge and lawyers' letters (let alone legal action) cost money, so you should judge carefully if the site in question is worth the effort and cost.

Is there a big market for live concerts over the Internet?

It's one more way of getting to and expanding your public. Someone on the other side of the world may never get to see a conventional broadcast of your concert (or even to get to see you live), but by streaming it over the Internet you can reach them. Of course, they'll need to know that it's going to happen, which costs time and/or money for the publicity/advertising. In some cases, concerts are recorded solely for webcasting or simulcasting (broadcasting and diffusion on the Internet at the same time), either to an invited 'live' audience or no audience at all. But it's unlikely that you'll 'sell tickets' for a webcast concert (unless you're a really big artist), though you may be able to attract sponsorship. It's likely to be just a promotional tool rather than profitable in its own right.

Is it possible to control in which countries my music is available on the Internet?

If the use is legal, then yes, it's possible and in some cases it's practical (if it's not legal then this is the least of your problems). Current web technology is able to identify where most users are physically located and to restrict access to an entire site or to certain content; though it is possible for the more technically minded Internet user to circumvent this, most can't.

Who actually owns the design of my website?

If it's really all your own work then you own it. If you asked someone else to do the work for you and you pay them you should have a contract that makes clear who owns what, and if you don't, then it's quite likely that any original work by that person will belong to them. So if there's artwork or other material that was designed for your website that winds up on posters or sweatshirts or other merchandising, you should either make sure you own it or be prepared to pay royalties (either way, before you use the material make sure that a contract is in place).

Is it possible to sell my music from my own site?

Yes, but you would need to have all the rights – performing and mechanical and the right of distribution, and if you're a PRS or MCPS member, then you may need either to get a licence or at least pay them the commission they would otherwise have received from licensing the music.

Can I use the site in any other way to make money?

Obviously you can sell merchandise, put links through to online stores (and pick up the incentive often on offer from them), sell downloads and the like, so long as your agreement with your record company allows it. Indirectly of course, you can use it to get responses from visiting fans who, if you offer them something in return, might leave you their names and contact details (see 'Fan Club' question in the 'Recording section').

If you are, or would like to become, a session musician, or to get work touring with solo artists as part of their band, then you can use your site as a sort of online CV, to list your qualifications/records you've played on, with some 30-second samples to try to attract work.

MANAGEMENT

MANAGEMENT CONTRACTS

Public entertainers of all types have long been reliant for guidance in their careers upon professional managers. There comes a time in most semi-professional singers' and musicians' careers, and even those of non-performing songwriters and producers when they are simply too busy to worry about the business side of things, or when they feel that they are not busy enough and would like somebody to be hustling on their behalf.

Do I need a manager anyway?

This depends upon how busy you are as a performer, how much money you are making, and above all how much money you *want* to make. It is possible to exist as a semi-professional or even a professional singer or musician for years without a manager, but if you really want to succeed then you should get a good manager (you'll find that most people without a professional manager have a friend or relative who is effectively their manager and happens to have a talent for the role). In the meantime, you can get by with an agent to secure engagements for you, an accountant to balance your books and minimise your tax liability, and a lawyer to write the odd letter to any agency or venue that failed to pay you or review agreements you're asked to sign.

You can even employ your own publicist and secure your own recording and publishing contracts, particularly if you enlist the help of your lawyer or accountant. Nevertheless, a manager worth his salt should be able to secure better royalty rates and terms than you could get on your own or, even more importantly, a deal with a more suitable company. Indeed, he might be able to get you a deal, purely on the strength of his reputation, with a company that would otherwise have turned you down. Bear in mind that some managers who are wizards at securing good live work for high fees may be a lot less well connected and knowledge-able when it comes to recording and publishing.

Record companies and publishers will expect you to have a manager, and some, especially record companies, won't sign you without one.

Should I have a manager if I'm not a performer?

There are still quite a number of songwriters with no serious aspirations towards being recording or performing artists, and of course any number of classical or film and TV composers for whom that's not really an option. Pop songwriters, with the aid of their lawyers, usually negotiate with publishers themselves and would have no other immediate need of a manager. This is why the songwriting section of this book is somewhat longer than the others. Recording artists, on the other hand, are usually also primarily performers, and thus their managers who look after the 'live performance' side of their careers usually deal on their behalf with record companies too.

However, there are people who act in the same sort of way for songwriters as literary agents do for novelists. They try to set up publishing deals, monitor the income, look for work such as film and television commissions etc. in return for a manager's commission. There are also managers working almost exclusively or primarily for record producers and remixers, again using their contacts and knowledge to secure work at good rates for their clients.

How much control of my career will a manager want?

You should thrash this out with him as precisely as you can before signing anything, and as far as possible it should be enshrined in your contract, so that it is clearly understood what you both want. These days, even if the contract doesn't actually say so, you are in effect employing him, and the position of a music manager can be almost as precarious as that of a football manager. For this reason, although a successful management company who already have agreements with other artists will probably have a sort of 'standard' contract, agreements with managers vary enormously. A form of management contract is included in the Contracts Section, with the sort of provisions you might expect to see, but yours may be very different. You should definitely get legal advice before signing anything with a manager. While a simple one-page agreement may seem attractive, it is probably worse for you, as many important issues will not be properly covered, and what is may be too vague. Some acts have been so badly burned by management agreements that they've just given up on otherwise really promising careers, so be warned. If you don't get legal advice before signing, you may be able to overturn an unreasonable agreement by taking legal action against the manager, but if the agreement contains a warranty that you did take legal advice beforehand, you'll be on thin ice.

What should I look for in a manager?

The first essential is commitment and genuine interest in you and your music. It's harder to sell something you wouldn't buy yourself, and even if the manager believes in you, if he or she doesn't also like your image and your music then you may be better off elsewhere. Then again, if he or she has constructive suggestions on how to adapt what you have to the market, that may be better than someone who tells you that you're perfect as you are (after all, you're paying them partly for their experience and advice).

You may be approached by a big-time management company who will ask you to sign a contract that puts you and your career completely in their hands for a number of years. As with choice of publisher (and to a lesser extent record company), size isn't everything. A big company carries a lot of weight in negotiations and, in theory at least, will be the most professional with the most contracts, but they also have more clients to divide their attention and those contacts between. On the other hand, you may find a decent smaller company or individual with a few good contacts to 'manage' you, for whom you will be a high priority and are less likely to put forward another client if they're knocked back first time. The smaller or less experienced manager may, however, have fewer contacts and have more trouble getting heard where he doesn't have contacts.

If you already have an agreement, even a verbal one or a scrap of paper, with a small-time manager or just a friend whereby they're supposed to get a cut of your earnings, make sure that you write to them making it clear that you consider it terminated (if it hasn't already lapsed), before signing with a professional manager. It's worth showing your old agreement to your prospective new manager and discussing with him the best way to make sure the old one is out of the picture. If you're remotely unsure, take legal advice.

Will all my income go through the manager?

A proper manager will usually collect all booking fees, record royalties and songwriting royalties from publishers (though he may not collect PRS royalties, if you're a member of the PRS), plus royalties for you from the merchandising of goods bearing your name, image or likeness, fees for television appearances, even for opening fêtes and supermarkets. What he shouldn't get is a percentage of your income from any source outside the entertainment business. If you get to a position where you have money to invest elsewhere, your manager should not be entitled to benefit from any profits you make. Your contract should be very clear as to which kinds of income are subject to management fees and which aren't; it's quite possible that money you collect directly (such as PRS writer shares) will be subject to fees and you may have to submit figures to your manager to ensure that they can deduct the appropriate fees from money they have collected for you. Once again, if you're unsure what's covered and what isn't, talk to your lawyer, especially if there are types of income you're already getting, or think you'll be getting in the future, and which you don't feel should be covered by your management deal. In general if your manager negotiates (or renegotiates) an agreement for you, whether for live work, publishing, recording, filming or whatever, then he will expect, and should get, a cut of all the income that results. If you already had a particular deal before you

signed to him, he'll probably still expect a share of your income under that deal but should only get income that's earned while he's your manager and after any residual period with your previous manager has expired.

How long will the management contract be for?

The usual period these days is three years, though five years wouldn't be unreasonable. Any agreement that runs for more than five years is unreasonable, especially if it extends until any money advanced by the manager has been recouped by him. In some cases, especially with bands, the term of the agreement might be expressed as 'until x months after the release of the third (or fourth) album', which might well be a lot longer than three years. This wouldn't necessarily be unreasonable, if the manager got you the album deal, and there's a long-stop date when the recording agreement ends whether all the albums are released or not (this might be expressed as the management deal being 'co-terminus' with the record deal). Of course, some managers develop a close

relationship with their client and often work with them throughout their entire career.

What percentage will the manager take?

The manager will probably take 20% of your earnings from the music or entertainment business. With some streams of income this might be 20% of the gross amounts, with others of the net (ie. the profit).

You may never, for instance, make any actual profit from touring (when you're small you have to pay to get on tour, when you're big the massive costs can outweigh the income). So some management agreements give the manager a share of the gross income from touring fees as compensation for the effort he put it setting it up, though his percentage may be lower (say, 10%). His commission on individual live gigs should be at the full rate, but only on net income, not gross, and most managers should be perfectly happy with this

His commission could be on a sliding scale, so that once you're earning £100,000 a year, he isn't still getting as high a percentage as he was when you were earning £1,000 a year. If you are in the 'big time' he will probably collect all your earnings himself and pay you your share at regular intervals. Similarly, potential agents, record companies and so forth will know that they must approach him if they wish to make a deal with you. Until you reach that stage you will often be approached by these people directly, and your contract will require you to put them on to the manager, even though you may be tempted to deal with them personally. If any money that is covered by your management agreement is paid directly to you, you'll be obliged either to pass it over to the manager or send him the figures, so that he can calculate his fees and deduct them from your next payment. He should put all the income he receives on your behalf into an account controlled by him but in your name, out of which his commission and agreed expenses should then be paid at regular intervals.

What about record company advances that include recording costs?

Your manager will normally be entitled to his commission on any advance paid to you by a record label. However, if the recording expenses for the album are supposed to come out of that advance, then you should agree with your manager what proportion of the advance is for that purpose and he should only charge commission on the remainder (ie. your money, not the record company's money).

Will he ever want more than 20%?

Some management companies are effectively publishing companies and independent production companies as well, and in that case they may take anything up to 50% of your overall income from these sources quite legitimately. You may be OK with this so long as you're satisfied that the company has all the contacts they need to make the higher rate worthwhile. Obviously, they shouldn't then take their management fee off the top of your 50% share.

How would this work in practice?

Effectively, the management company, or subsidiaries of it, would acquire your exclusive songwriting and recording services and then 'license' them on to 'proper' publishers and record companies. In some cases, especially if the manager is acting as an independent production company, he may make your records and then license them to a record company on the basis that he can get better deal than you would as an artist signing direct. Remember, however, that he'll be taking a higher cut of these earnings, and also that he will probably own those songs or recordings he makes (unless there are provisions either for the works to revert to you sometime after the agreement ends or to co-own them with him).

Isn't 50% a rip-off?

If the agreements are all reasonable and you were properly advised when you signed them, then no – the rate is not the problem. Of greater concern is that any manager with this much control of your career, even through separate companies that he has a hand in, is in danger of falling foul of the law in the UK. The danger is that he has conflicting interests under his control, those of you as his client and those of his companies that have rights to exploit your works. If he breaks his 'fiduciary trust' and acts in his own interests rather than yours, you will be able to take him to court, but you probably shouldn't have got yourself into that position in the first place.

However, if the recording and publishing deals are for a clearly limited duration and on 'arm's length' terms (in other words, the record company and the publishing company specifically agree to treat each other as they would any other company, and not give each other advantageous rates or the like), you should not be overly concerned.

Who pays for what?

If you're signing with a professional management company the chances are that they'll initially pay for everything, although the contract will make it clear that ultimately it will be you who pays. They'll pay all your travelling expenses, plus a weekly allowance for living expenses while you're struggling. Until you start bringing money in, you will be effectively building up an advance to be recouped against future earnings, so while their basic office expenses won't

add to this balance, things like having a personal manager on tour will. They may wish to keep you on a low 'spending allowance' for some time after you've started to be worth big money, just to make sure that the advance is recouped and doesn't start to build up again.

All this is fine, and it's nice to know they have such faith in you. Obviously, management companies lose a lot of money this way as the 'advance' is only recoupable against earnings under your management agreement, and, if you don't succeed, they can't get the money back from you.

If all my money comes to me through one person or firm, how can I check up on their honesty?

Even with regular statements from your management, and even though you know what they're paying you each week in allowances, it could become almost impossible for you to work out just what they've spent on you, for you are very much in their hands. You could have hit after hit – the management may give you the money to go out and buy a Rolls or a new house, but are they still advancing you *their* money or actually paying you what *you've* earned? Keep asking questions and try not to let success go to your head (easier said than done). If they're honest, then regular statements (say monthly or quarterly) should be sent to you showing exactly how much you've earned and how much they've spent on you and taken in commission. As we said, they should be arranging for all your income to be paid into a separate account in your name so that you can see at any point what's going on, but, regrettably, you'll still probably lose track of just how much you are owed if you become very successful, if only because you'll be too busy to monitor it. So you need a good accountant unconnected to your manager who can monitor these matters for you (see 'Do I need an accountant?' in 'General Q & A').

Will the manager pay me an advance?

The manager will generally see it as part of his job to get advances from other people – record companies, publishers etc. – to enable you to survive comfortably without a 'proper job' until you're earning big money. Until he's got you these deals, he'll probably – as we've said – pay for anything you need out of his own pocket, which means that effectively he'll be paying you an advance.

Note that he will take his commission on advances as well as royalties that you get, so he might be tempted to do a deal with the company offering the most money upfront, even if it's not the best deal on offer over all. He should, however, tell you of any alternative deals on offer, even if he does attempt to influence you towards the one with the biggest advance.

How long will he go on getting his commission?

As we mentioned earlier, some management agreements will give him a share on everything you ever get from a deal that he negotiated, even years after he's ceased to be your manager. Say he got you a record deal that lasted five years, but you split with him after two. You'd be happy for him to get his share on records made and sold during those

first two years, but does he also get a share of records made during those years and sold for ever after, and what about records made during the other three years? He got you the deal, remember. Does he get a share of royalties from sales of those records too? The answer should be to try to limit his share to the period of your agreement, with perhaps a diminishing commission for up to 10 years on income from deals made during his time as manager. Then again, you might agree to pay him commission on, say, one more album (and the songs on it) after you split with him (preferably at a lower rate), to leave some margin for you to pay a new manager.

A new manager who renegotiated these deals after your contract with the first manager ended might expect his 20% on songs or records from then on (though they might accept less initially, if they're keen to represent you). So you can see that if you're not careful, an increasingly large share of your income will be deducted by managers old and new. Therefore it's really vital to get proper legal advice on your particular case. Especially so if you sign to a small-time manager before you've signed to a publisher or record label. If he wants commission to be payable for ever, then you should say 'no' or (if he insists and you're really anxious to sign) agree to a very low rate of commission.

Do I really need to read through contracts secured for me by my manager?

You might like to think that your manager couldn't possibly make a bad deal, and he will certainly let you think that he's an expert in everything to do with the music business. Alternatively, your contract with him might say that he has the sole right to negotiate the deals on your behalf and on terms that he considers to be advantageous to you (it shouldn't state this, but sometimes does). Nonetheless you should have your own lawyer, who should not also represent the manager, to negotiate all the finer points of any major deal, even if the manager has already agreed the main 'commercial' points, and your lawyer should read through the agreement with you in advance of any signing 'ceremony'. It may be a terrible deal that the manager had done mainly to impress you, or he may have been given a big advance payment for your services, and doesn't want you to know about it (though you'd be exceptionally unlucky to wind up with quite such a 'dodgy' manager). If he's also relatively new to the business he may simply not know enough about publishing or recording. Even the most professional of managers can still agree to a 'lousy' deal because of inexperience in a particular field, and some really top managers of big name acts admit that they learned about the job as they went along! If you and your lawyer think a major deal is awful you should make it plain to your manager in plenty of time, and even if he has the exclusive right to negotiate on your behalf he will have to take note. In any case, he should not be able to sign on your behalf in anything other than minor matters (see 'Power of Attorney' in the Glossary).

If we're a group, does he have to consult all of us?

It's normal in such cases for the manager to expect the group to nominate one member to be the 'contact' whom he can consult in the case of relatively minor decisions that often need to be made quickly. Any decision that would result in contracts the whole group would have to sign anyway, such as an ESA, a recording agreement, an agreement with an agency or with a merchandising company, should always be discussed at some length by all of you and the manager sitting down together.

If an artist is signed to a professional management company, why does he need a personal manager too?

You could be signed to a large management company but still have your own separate personal manager. He would generally be employed by the company though, if he works solely for you, his salary and expenses would be deducted from your earnings. Then again, he could be employed entirely separately by you, but this would very likely cause friction. He's there to look after you, especially on tour etc., and to be at your beck and call and to liaise with the other staff at the management, record and publishing companies. He's the one who should make sure you get from A to B on time and that the caviar sandwiches in your dressing room are always fresh, and generally act as a sort of high-powered PA.

How would I get out of a management contract?

This is the most important of our three 'how to get out of' sections, since if your manager is collecting all your money and turns out to be greedy, dishonest or simply lazy, then no matter how honest and hard-working your record company and publisher may be, you may not get a penny.

The advice given under publishing and recording contracts also applies here. First try the friendly approach, offering if necessary to pay back part or all of any advance sums or expenses paid by him on your behalf. Then check renewals and royalty statements to see that these have all arrived on time. If you haven't become successful the manager will probably let you go, possibly subject to his retaining some interest in your future in the form of a very small percentage for the rest of the duration of his contract. If you have become successful then he won't want to let you go and you will need to go straight to a lawyer to assess the case on its merits. He'll tell you as quickly as possible if he thinks you have a good case. If you succeed in getting out, then the lawyer's fees will be money well spent.

One suggestion your lawyer might make is that you write to your record company, publisher etc. asking that royalties be paid directly to you in future. Unless your manager is a signatory to the agreement, or there is an exceptional clause, they should comply; the agreement is between you and them after all, and they are obligated to pay you or whoever you nominate (up to now it was your manager). If your manager notices this, or is tipped off (perhaps by accident), then he may contact the record company or publisher and restate his claim, and it's quite possible that faced with two 'claimants' to royalties, the company will suspend payments until the dispute is settled (especially if lawyers get involved). Whether or not this happens, the manager will probably threaten to sue you for breach of contract, and negotiations, possibly leading to a court case, will begin.

AGENTS, AGENCIES, PROMOTERS, TOURING, MERCHANDISING AND SPONSORSHIP

Agents are the people to whom artists (or their managers) turn to find work, fix up concert tours and engagements and handle the work involved. It is a specialised field and, at the top end (in view of the high costs of travel and hotel bills, plus hire and transportation of amplification, lighting and sets) this can be very big business indeed, especially in the case of a top band touring the US or Europe.

Who are booking agents and how do they operate?

The principle function of an agent is to obtain work for you as a live performer. The agency will normally collect your fees for these events, deduct their share and account to you or you manager. However, you should note that on a semi-professional basis you will normally collect most of the fee in cash on the night from the venue, and then it will be your responsibility to pay the agent his commission (+VAT).

Can I have more than one agent?

In theory there is nothing to stop you using more than one agency if you wish, assuming that you have not agreed, even verbally, to be exclusive to one agency. However, most people have just one agent, and frequently appoint them exclusively for a period of time. The agent will liaise with others who need acts like you for venues that your agent doesn't have direct contact with. To start with, you'll generally have an agreement directly with the venue, which, as we've said, will pay you directly, usually in cash (though if you want to make sure it's in cash, you should ensure the agreement says so).

If you have just one agent, and he knows that, then he'll also be aware that he needs to keep you busy and will probably get you more work than if you're not exclusive to him. He'll probably prepare cards for you to hand out to interested enquirers at your gigs, which will direct them to approach him rather than you. He may ask for a list of free dates in a year and then try to secure bookings for those dates, although he should let you know before confirming them and always give you plenty of notice of when and where the gigs are (you're not obliged to take them, but you wouldn't want to refuse too many or the relationship may sour). So he will check with you beforehand whether you are free and wish, at the price, to play at certain venues. Once it is verbally agreed, he'll send you a form of agreement to complete. An example of this is included later in this book under 'Examples of Contracts', together with some notes about the terms.

As you wouldn't be looking to an agent to pay an advance, there's no reason not to make your exclusive agreement terminable by you at relatively short notice. You would have to fulfil any commitment you'd already made and pay the agent's commission on any gigs, so you may not want the agent to be booking you too far ahead. They'll also want you to agree not to take bookings yourself, although for a semi-pro act it'll probably be much more ad hoc. If that's the case, and you gave the agent a date you'd be free but get yourself a booking in the meantime, remember to tell him.

If the agent collects the money from a gig he should pay your share over to you within days (unlike royalties from publishing and recording, where you would expect to get paid half-yearly or quarterly).

There's not usually a huge amount of choice of agencies in any particular part of the country, and even if you live in London you'll probably want a local one to start with. At a higher level, a club DJ won't want an agency that books mainly rock bands, but most local agencies will find work for anyone, from function bands and DJs to fire-eaters and knife-throwing tightrope walkers. Agents will deal with individual venues and also, once you're big enough (which usually means you've had at least one album out on a successful label), with promoters, whose business it is to hire or buy venues and then find acts to fill them. Concert venues, even small ones, don't come cheap, as you can imagine, so promoting concerts can be very big business and very risky.

How much commission should a booking agent take?

The agent's commission is almost always 15% (or maybe slightly less on top of your manager's commission, if, as sometimes happens, he's also your agent). Be aware at the lower end of the scale that if you're collecting the cash on the night and paying him 15% of it, there is a probability that he will already have asked for a deposit from the venue or person booking you, particularly with one-off gigs like weddings, parties and functions, and he might well not tell you about this. Thus, a £400 gig might be costing the organiser £500–£600. Of course, the commission the agent charges you will only be on your £400.

If you have a manager, then of course he will deal with the agency or agencies on your behalf. Otherwise you can deal directly with an agency, or directly with the venues themselves quite satisfactorily. Most agents will, for a set period (usually about two years), expect you not to deal directly with venues you were first introduced to by them. A form of simple agreement between artist and

venue is also included in the 'Examples of Contracts' section.

Naturally, if you are contacted directly by venues, you will see no point in paying either a manager or an agent a percentage of this money unless you firmly believe that the agent can negotiate a much better fee. For this reason there is no necessity to tie yourself either to a manager or to an agency if, as a semi-professional, you have as much work as you want already. If you are a member of the Musicians Union, check that you're being offered at least the MU rates for gigs.

Should I pay a fee to the agent to 'sign on?'

The general answer is 'no'. An agent can't actually guarantee to get any work for you. As a semi-pro act or an act without a recording contract, you probably won't initially want to work entirely through the agent (i.e. you might not want more than one agent but, if you get offered a gig directly, you won't want to have to refer it to the agent and pay commission on it). If the agent is offering to do something very specific, such as undertaking to put a certain number of minutes' worth of your demo recordings on a general demo CD, which the agent makes (at his expense) and sends out to a certain number (at least several hundred) of prospective clients, then he might ask you for a small contribution to costs. Generally, however, getting you work is his business and this is how he makes his commission, and he should do it at his expense.

Do I really need an agent if I'm only semi-pro?

Most semi-professional acts who are working regularly do have an agent, though they'll probably also get work for themselves. If you're prepared to do a lot of ringing around visiting pubs, hotels, social clubs, golf clubs (or whatever your intended 'market' is) with a demo CD, cards and posters, then you'd be unlucky if nothing came of it. However, remember some venues, especially social clubs and the like, book all their acts for the year, as a package, for an all-in fee from one agent. If you have a good website this can help, and be sure to have prominent reviews and testimonials. There are also any number of directory sites that can help, such as www.partysounds.co.uk (which contains details, county by county, of acts playing for parties, dances and the like).

Do I need an agent as a session musician?

It's quite likely that if you're a session musician you'll have an agent getting you work, although you may also be getting it yourself. It's possible these days to get work for sessions or tours that might suit you from your website (provided that you include samples of your playing and details of your previous performances and recording sessions). Although getting tours and sessions is very much a case of who you know (or who you knew, for older musicians), it is still possible to get work this way if you fit the bill, rather than just relying on your contacts with a session 'fixer' who knows you and would recommend you.

How much per appearance should I be worth?

This really is the hardest question of all to answer, because there are so many factors to take into account. It's where managers and agents really earn their money, as they should know exactly how much they can get for your services in every situation.

You'll know roughly what a PA system and backline equipment will cost, but it's worth splashing out on a decent PA and microphones, or else hiring these on a regular basis. You'll obviously start out as your own roadie, but even if you're not being mixed from the back of the hall it

pays to have a friend who knows what you're supposed to sound like telling you what volume and frequencies to turn up or down. Do a sound check if at all possible, but you won't need us to tell you that it'll all sound quite different once the place is (you hope) full.

If you're a semi-pro band and are prepared to play music to dance to and can get bookings at working men's clubs, parties, wedding receptions etc., the minimum going rate for these should be about £100 for a solo act with backing tapes, £150–200 for a duo and £300–400 for a four or five-piece band. (At this point the law of diminishing returns comes into play, so a 10-piece band won't be offered much more than a five-piece one to play at a small function.) A really competent, self-contained five-piece band (with own PA, lights and interval music) playing a major function, a big corporate party or a residency at a big hotel, ought to be able to get between £500 and £1,000. You'd expect to play a minimum of two 45-minute sets, but could wind up playing up to four hours, with only a half-hour break in the middle, without much variation in the fees. If they do ask you to carry on beyond the stated finishing time, then you should get at least an additional payment in line with the amount per hour you're getting for the rest of the gig.

Music pubs are another source of bookings. At the right pub you're likely to be able to play whatever you want to, as you don't have to worry about whether people can dance to it. The audience will expect a much higher standard of musicianship than for 'functions', and the venue will probably pay a lot less because there are so many ex-professional musicians doing this for fun, especially in 'rockbroker belt' parts of the Home Counties. They might pass the 'hat' around, though, which will add to your take-home money. The downside of all these bookings is that you're very unlikely to be heard by anyone in the music business who might be able to further your career, and the gigs that could lead to better things frequently don't pay anything at all. You have to make the decision at some point which road to go down.

If you do succeed in getting a record deal, live work of course becomes enormously more lucrative. A straight 'pop' group with a recent hit (even a small one) should immediately be able to command £5,000 a night for a full gig, much more if they consolidate their success, and even more if (as has been the trend of late) they manage to fit into one night several mimed 'performances' of the hit on the club circuit. If they stay together, they can still be worth that amount long after the hit if they remain crowd-pullers. Major tours, however, which are discussed in 'General Q & A', frequently don't make any money as the expenses are so high, even when a major act can gross as much as $1m or so a night on US tours.

At the lower end of the scale, it is worth bearing in mind that as long as the instruments and voice are in tune, then sheer reliability – always turning up on time, having the voice clearly audible, avoiding technical hitches, feedback etc. – can be more important to the securing of regular well-paying engagements than real musical talent!

A group playing at social clubs, parties and the like, who are prepared to play and take their breaks when asked, to turn the volume up or down when asked, to look presentable, to set up and pack up quickly and to vary the programme to suit the age or taste of the audience, are certainly more likely to be re-booked than a bunch of brilliant but unruly musicians. For most functions, it's also important to try to play songs that the audiences already know and are more likely to dance to. (Though you might get away with a few of your own numbers or songs you particularly like, eg. blues, jazz, folk etc., and if you play these sorts of gigs you don't need us to tell you that it's up to you to assess on the night what you can 'get away with'.)

It is another plus for the group if they have their own stage lights and taped music to play during intervals – some small venues lack these facilities, though the club or whatever might draw the line at strobe lights, dry ice and pyro flashes.

What happens if a venue cancels a gig?

Generally, where an agent has dealt with the venue, the agent will have put into the contract a clause to the effect that a cancellation fee of perhaps 50% is payable if the engagement is cancelled by the venue less than a week before it was due to take place. If you are dealing directly with the management of the venue yourself and have made no mention of cancellation fees, then you will have to regard it as bad luck and avoid making any further bookings with that venue or management (or at least try in future to agree a cancellation fee).

What happens if the management of a venue don't pay me as agreed once I've played?

Like any other cash business, confrontations can arise, and most on-the-road veterans can recount stories of 'difficult situations'. Chuck Berry is famous for refusing to play a note until he'd been paid, in cash, in full. However, provided that you arrived on time and played, or made it clear that you were prepared to play during the time stated, then start by writing polite letters, followed by a strong letter from a lawyer if it's worth it. Unfortunately, this isn't always the case, but you can always ask a lawyer what his approximate charge would be for a letter like this, and what it would cost to pursue it through the small claims courts. If you were late or unable to perform for the length of time expected once you'd arrived, then the management of the venue, if they were bloody-minded, might deduct a portion of your fee for this, provided it was in proportion to the time during which you failed to perform.

What happens if I agree to perform somewhere and am unable to turn up?

If there is a good reason, then apologise to the management of the venue absolutely as soon as you know; they're unlikely to take any negative action with the exception of not booking you again. They could ask you to send a replacement, and some bands can provide 'deps' with no problem. However, only an agency can reasonably be expected to supply a whole substitute band. Your only alternative would be to offer to perform on another date, perhaps for a reduced fee.

Do I need to know if the venue I'm performing at is licensed for live music?

The basic answer is 'no'. It's the venue's responsibility. They will need an entertainment licence from the local council and a licence from the PRS. For years, the 'two in a bar' rule has been in force, meaning that a pub, for example, could allow a duo to perform without a licence but the moment a third person came up to join them for a guest spot, then the venue would be breaking the law. However, a change in UK legislation meant that any number of musicians could play provided that the venue had told the local council in advance and had had this provision added to the terms of their general licence.

Again, this sort of thing is the venue's responsibility, not yours.

Do I have to pay to perform or record other people's songs?

Singers or groups should never be charged for performing a song in public (even on television). The venue where the performance is taking place should be licensed by the PRS, as we have discussed earlier, and if it's not, then that isn't the fault of the performer who, having been booked to appear, can reasonably assume that the place was properly licensed for live music.

If you wish to put on an open air concert yourself, then for any performance to which the public has access in a place that is obviously not regularly licensed for the playing of music, permission should be sought from the PRS's general licensing department. This could cover everything from a tea party on the vicar's lawn to Fat Boy Slim on Brighton beach, as well as raves in the middle of someone's field (though these, in their heyday, were famously 'unlicensed'). You will probably also need the permission of the police and/or the local council for any such gigs. As we've said, religious services do not require a licence, although if a song of yours were to be broadcast on television or radio as part of a religious service, then this would be no different from any other broadcast as far as the payment of performing fees is concerned.

If you wish to record the performance then you do need to ask the publisher of the songs through the MCPS, and if you're releasing your own records you will have to pay a licence fee to make copies (for sale or giveaway). If you have a recording deal, then the record company will do this. Whoever applies for the licence, it'll cost the same in royalty payments whether you've recorded huge international hits or songs hardly anyone's ever heard of.

What do I need to know about touring?

Lots of medium-sized bands who've been in the business for years, who maybe haven't had a hit record for years (or even decades), but who still have a sizeable following, have got touring down to a fine art and can actually make money at it. This is by being as 'self-contained' as possible. They'll have the minimum road crew, and a tour manager who also drives a truck and sells the merchandise. If the act is no longer big enough to make money on its own, there are an increasing number of 'package concerts' in which several acts that are similar or are from the same era each play a shortened set and attract people who wouldn't have bothered to go and see any one of them individually, even for a lower ticket price.

A rock band on tour playing a different venue virtually every night will probably need at least 30 people with them – tour manager, road crew, lighting crew, caterers etc. On a really big tour like this there will even be a separate tour accountant, usually employed by your own or the manager's accountants, who will have worked out in advance how much everything should cost (and how much you might need from sponsors or your record company to break even). They will also collect the money from the venues/promoter,

check up on ticket sales if you're on a percentage of the take, and generally make sure everything is financially in order. Nevertheless, if an act can sell 10,000 tickets at £25 a time, on average they should make a gross profit of 50% of the £250,000 takings. Out of this the agent will expect to be able to make 15% and the promoter will expect to make at least 10–15% (depending on whether the act is on a percentage of 'box office'), as he's taking the risk of putting the whole thing on. What's more, it'll probably have to be organised around a year in advance or the venues simply won't be available. A webcast of one or more of the concerts, a 'live' DVD or even a 'rockumentary', which can be sold to television in the various countries where you're well known, may make the difference to the possibility of breaking even. At the very top end, the figures are huge (as of course is the potential risk).

How could I get a sponsor for a tour?

As major tours are frequently loss-makers and are primarily to improve your profile with the music-buying public, your record company will usually liaise with your manager in finding a suitable sponsor. You should have the right to say no to a particular sponsor, especially if it's inappropriate and possibly damaging to your image. But remember that if the record company is underwriting the tour up to an agreed figure, then the money they pay will eventually come out of your record royalties, so in general, it definitely pays to agree to sponsorship. If it comes as part of a general endorsement of the product or company, including press or television commercials etc., then of course you should be paid handsomely for the deal, though there are no hard and fast figures. If the sponsor wants to be involved in merchandising sold on the tour then your manager will need to work this out in advance.

The sponsors will probably want you to put their logo on your website, concert tickets, programmes, posters or anywhere where the venue itself will let you, bearing in mind that they probably have their own sponsor too! It's possible to approach sponsors directly but there are agents who, for around 10% of what you get from the sponsor (including a calculation of the value of any goods you receive), will try to find a suitable sponsor for you. If you actually like the product and are happy to talk about it and be seen eating it/drinking it/wearing it, even singing about it, then you can expect a better deal.

Like a Formula One racing car and driver with brand names plastered all over them, there's nothing to stop you having more than one sponsor, as long as it doesn't all look so blatant that your fans think you've 'sold out'. Your deals could be for one tour or could last for years; there are no hard and fast rules. For a lot more money you could even agree to appear in commercials for the product, but you have to be very wary of looking greedy or blowing your credibility.

It's worth remembering that your record company may have sponsorship deals with companies too, and you may have to balance that with your own sponsorship deals.

Can I get some money/free instruments by endorsing them?

On a smaller scale, even session players on tours as well as 'name' acts should be able to secure free instruments and amplification from a particular manufacturer, provided that they can be seen using the equipment on the tour (write to them and ask). Any additional endorsements, such as you appearing in commercials, posters etc., may be worth a substantial fee, depending on the size of the act and the likely impact that their use of it would have on sales of the product. This is particularly true of guitars and guitarists – companies like Gibson and Fender have, between them, produced models named after a host of famous guitarists – it's one of the ways to tell that you've really made it!

Can I get to tour as a support act?

This would usually be organised by your record company pulling strings and arranging for you to tour with a bigger act, either somebody on their label or handled by the same management/agency. Although the bigger act won't want any adverse comparisons with you, you should at least be playing roughly the same sort of music. If a major act really likes you, they may take you under their wing and let you tour for nothing, i.e. they don't pay you, you don't pay them, but you do get to share their audience (or at least the percentage of the audience who don't stay in the bar till the headline act comes on) and to use their PA. Otherwise you would expect to pay to join a major tour, maybe several hundred pounds a night, sometimes more. If it seems tough, remember that once you make it big you can get the same deal from support acts yourself. As we said earlier, touring is big business, especially in the US. With ticket sales of $1million plus for some individual gigs, you'd think it would be impossible not to make a profit, but touring is also very, very expensive.

What does a tour manager do?

A tour manager is usually employed by your management. Many fairly modest tours are 'run' by the manager himself with an assistant or two but, for big tours, there should be someone who is solely focused on the tour and, of course, the bigger the tour the more important he is. He's the one who will make sure that the whole 'show' stays 'on the road' and that you don't end up like Spinal Tap! He'll see to it that the trucks, the PA and the lighting rig all work and are replaced if they don't, and above all will smooth out any problems with the road crew or the staff at the venues, the hotel and so on. Unless it's dealt with by a separate company, he may also be the one who sees to it that the merchandise is there and that stocks are replenished if necessary.

What should I know about merchandising?

We've included this subject in this section because the most obvious place to sell merchandise is at live concerts, but actually this subject almost deserves a section in itself as there is so much money to be made from music merchandising (as well as from sport and other 'personality' products). As we said in the Recording section, unless you have specifically agreed some sort of 360-deal, you should ensure that your record company don't expect to control merchandising rights under your agreement with them. For megastars and cult acts, merchandising can gross millions of pounds a year! It helps if you're photogenic, but luckily you don't have to be good-looking, legendary and dead, like Kurt Cobain or Jim Morrison, to sell a lot of merchandise.

Can I do my own merchandising?

Most people do, to start with, and it makes good commercial sense. As soon as you (you, in this case, usually means a band) have enough of a reputation, it's worth organising the making of T-shirts and posters, which you then autograph (it may seem daft but it's probably best to have an easy version of your signature for autographs and the real one for contracts and cheques). If you or a friend can come up with something so eye-catching and of the moment that people might wear it even if they don't know who you are, then you're really winning. Back in the Eighties, Frankie Say T-shirts, as used to promote the band Frankie Goes To Hollywood, were briefly everywhere in the UK and, though the rip-off merchants made a fortune, the publicity certainly helped the band to sustain their initial success. Make sure that you do your best to protect your designs and logos and be clear exactly who owns them (if you use someone else's design). If the brand is successful then a specialist lawyer should be brought in to protect your trademarks

and copyrights in this area. You can start by giving copies to your girlfriend/boyfriend and all their friends if they agree to wear them (though maybe not to your mother). Someone walking around with your T-shirt on is a great piece of free publicity, especially if most of their friends and acquaintances haven't heard of you yet. If you've got as far as having your own fan club, they can sell them or give them away as prizes in competitions etc.

What can I expect to make per item from merchandising?

If you're doing it yourself then the profit margins will probably be high for the ones you manage to sell, but once you've actually got a record deal this starts to be big business, and there are experts who can make you more money in the long run than you could yourself. Obviously, the amounts and margins vary greatly according to the type and quality of the product you're selling. Aside from the cost of production, you should take into account that for merchandise sold at a live concert, the venue or the promoter will expect to take 25% of your revenue, or more like 35–40% in the USA.

There are specialised merchandising companies that will organise both the making and selling of your products. They may only expect to make less than £1 profit from a £20+ sweatshirt, but will be prepared to take the risk, especially with a well-known act, provided they can estimate pretty well the likely number of ticket sales and can be reasonably sure of at least some protection from pirated goods (see later). They'll hope for a total 'spend' of up to about £8 a head at the average rock concert.

Whatever deal you do, try to make sure you have some input on quality control, and, if at all possible, on pricing; better to get slightly less from a merchandiser than have your fans think you're ripping them off. On that subject, it must be said that one reason why pirates on the street corner outside the venue are so successful is that the official merchandise often seems very expensive in relation to similar quality, non-branded goods in the high street.

Suppose we pay to have the goods made?

If the act are effectively paying to have the merchandise manufactured and employing a separate company to sell it, they could hope to wind up with a higher percentage of the gross. Most artists could hope to get about 25% of the selling price of the merchandise (after tax and the venue's 25% have been taken off). You could reasonably expect your manager to know exactly how much he could negotiate for you. With sales in normal retail outlets, a deal is sometimes done whereby you will simply let someone else do the whole thing for a royalty to you of 10–15% of the retail price.

Can I get an advance royalty payment on merchandising?

You can expect substantial advances against royalties or profits from merchandising companies under deals where they make and sell them – as much as £50,000 or so for a big, but not huge, act touring over the course of a year. There are seven-figure sums to be made by really big acts from merchandising alone. These companies will be much less inclined to pay a big advance for a relatively unproven pop act with only a hit or two under their belts than they would for a larger, more established act, unless it's an emerging act who have already developed a brand in the way that The Spice Girls did. Specialised merchandising companies will hopefully bid for the right to make and sell your merchandise as soon as they know a tour is imminent. They'll know what's likely to sell, but you won't need reminding that merchandising can be far more than T-shirts. Back in the Seventies *Abba – The Film* was accompanied by everything from *Abba – The Album* down to Abba – The Soap! (literally a bar of soap).

It's worth bearing in mind that under some deals, if the tour is cancelled, or even if they don't recoup the advance, the merchandising company will have the right to carry on selling your goods, either at live gigs or at retail outlets, until they have got their money back, which may hinder your negotiations for a lucrative new deal for your next tour.

What rights do I have to give the merchandiser?

First of all, they will want the exclusive right to use your name/logo on their particular merchandise. The first question they will ask is, 'is your name/logo a registered trademark?' For any artist these days it's worth trying to design and register a good logo almost from the start; try for something relatively original and fitting to your musical style. If it's not distinct enough, or too like someone else's logo, you may have trouble getting a trademark registered. Without a trademark, you will have little protection against pirates, and merchandising companies will want the protection of a trademark too.

So can I actually make my name or my band's name a 'registered trademark'?

Yes, you can. It's expensive, but if you seriously expect to be successful then it's worth doing it sooner rather than later. It will cost several hundred pounds just to register it in the UK, and you will have to define the circumstances in which the trademark in your name will apply. In your case you'll want to cover recordings and probably also clothing and posters in the first instance. It will take months before it comes into effect, but at least it'll then be backdated to the time when you applied for the registration. To protect your name completely you will need to do the same thing in the US and the rest the major countries of Europe too, at perhaps the same sort of cost in each country. However, if you're successful, it will be worth it many times over! In the UK, if you have a registered trademark you can ask the Trading Standards Authority to prosecute anyone you find selling 'bootleg' merchandise using your name. As we've said, if your record/ management company, and their merchandising licensees, know that you're registered, they'll almost certainly be prepared to put a lot more money behind you. If your manager/record company help with this, it is vital for you that the registration is made in *your* name/logo, not the manager's name or the record company's (i.e. that you own the name/ logo and not them).

How else can I protect my stage name or group name?

Unless you are already successful then you are probably not in a position to prevent another artist from using your name. If you haven't achieved national recognition at any level, and another artist or group appears and becomes successful with an identical or very similar name to yours, then there is really not a great deal of point in sticking to your name. Members of the public hearing the name will immediately think of the other, already successful, act. If you persevere with the name, the other act may feel sooner or later that it's necessary to settle the matter and threaten legal action. You might think that having used the name for longer would count in your favour but, in fact, who registered the trademark first or whom the larger part of the general public would recognise from that name count much more. Of course, if you have had some success then you should stick to your guns and, if necessary, issue legal proceedings to stop the new band, even if they are suddenly (and perhaps briefly) more successful.

The more unusual your stage name, the less likely it is that anyone else will already be using it, and possibly the more memorable it will be (though try to keep it short). Furthermore, by registering at www.bandname.com you may discour-

age (though it won't actually stop) anyone else from using your name. There is a small annual charge that again is well worth it, and we would urge any band to join. There are, of course, examples of artists who have actually decided to legally change their name to their stage name. It's not enormously expensive to do this, but there's really no point unless you particularly want to.

What can I do if my real name is the same as someone famous like Paul McCartney or Diana Ross?

I'm afraid this is, as you'd probably expect, simply bad luck. Obviously, if your famous namesake is still alive (especially if they're still performing/recording) then you'd be silly to try to use it, as no one would dare book you or record you under that name for fear of audiences and record buyers thinking they were going to hear the star. (In fact, the manager of the well-known artist would probably take you to court over it anyway.) A name like Elvis Costello, on the other hand, was fine as there was really no likelihood of anyone confusing him with Elvis Presley. A songwriter with a 'famous name' would be well advised to use a pseudonym because of the possibility of their royalties going astray. Remember however, in that case, that you must tell your publisher and PRS your real name in any event and, as we said, all names and pseudonyms have a unique 'CAE number', so these days there's less scope for confusion.

If a group splits up, who owns the name?

Regrettably there is no straightforward answer to this question. It may be that the members will work something out between them. It may be that they themselves do not actually 'own' the name at all. If the record company or manager suggested it in the first place, then there may be something in the contract whereby they reserve the right to the name. In that case, if all the members of the group leave together or one by one, they can be replaced by an entirely new group with the same name. This perhaps chilling prospect is something to question managers or record companies about when signing with them.

In your contract you will almost certainly be asked to guarantee that you have the right to use the name, but not necessarily that you're the only person or band in the world using that name at that point in time. If your band name is a registered trademark then there's even more reason to decide in advance, and to put something in writing as to what will happen to the name if the band breaks up.

If you, as a band, formed a limited company, or agreed to work as a legal partnership, then that will at least have prompted you to think what happens to the name if you disband or split. If you had a company you could agree to split the profits equally if you disband, but you ought to think about some 'formula' for calculating how much the name of the band might be worth to any member who might want to carry on using it, if it's successful (even remotely successful). If just one member leaves then the others could agree to 'pay him off', and he probably wouldn't expect to have the right to use the name if it was well-known. But you need to think what you'd do if a four piece band split in two, for example.

Can I stop anyone else recording or performing in my style or manner?

Unfortunately not, unless they are actually deceiving the public into thinking that they're really you, which is known as 'passing off'. In that case, your manager or record company, if you have them, will take action against the other artist. If you come up with a 'great new sound' then the chances are that all sorts of people will copy it, and unfortunately there's nothing you can do to stop this either, unless people are actually sampling your records.

There's nothing to stop you looking like someone else as long as you're not actually pretending to be them or deliberately trying to put doubt in peoples' minds.

The press and public can be quite cynical about record companies jumping on the bandwagon of the latest big success with their version of that act. While sometimes they are deliberately remoulding an act to the latest trend, just as often the act was there all along, but it took the first act's success to open doors for them. Don't be too churlish if you're the trend setter – other people deserve a living too, and your music will live or die on its merits in any case.

Is there anything to stop me forming a 'tribute band'?

A 'tribute band' can play someone else's songs and call themselves a name similar to that of the stars without any authorisation. Again, as long as there's no likelihood of anyone seriously thinking you are the star, or that when they buy your records or go to your gigs they're actually going to hear or see the star, then it's fine. If the original band are no longer gigging, then so much the better.

The grey area is with bands, mostly from the Sixties and Seventies, who may have one member left out of five and still perform under the same name. Provided no one else owns the name and wishes to stop them, then even a band with no members left from the original line-up can pretend to be the real act, although there should be some sort of tenuous link. Authentic line-ups are a subject of some controversy (take a look at Pete Frame's excellent *Rock Family Trees* for more on that topic).

Tribute or semi-authentic, it's still big business. Many tribute bands are amazingly good copies of the original act in their heyday, and offer younger fans a chance to experience at least a flavour of what a real gig would have been like. As such, it's hard to begrudge them the excellent living they make in return.

GENERAL QUESTIONS AND ANSWERS

GENERAL QUESTIONS AND ANSWERS ON THE MUSIC BUSINESS

Is it illegal to record TV programmes or films onto PVRs, DVD or video recorder?

No, so long as it is for personal use (ie. to 'timeshift' the programme as you would with a PVR or Sky+). But it is illegal if you were to make further copies and either give them away or sell them, even to friends. This would be 'piracy', unless the TV programme was released over 50 years ago and the writers of every piece of music have all been dead for at least 70 years (as is everyone else whose contribution attracts a copyright that wasn't bought-out) – which rules out most of the TV or film created in the modern era. Remember, even if the programme or film was created more than 50 years ago, it's very possible that a songwriter or composer lived for a long time after that, and then you have to add 70 years. For example, the music in the films of Laurel & Hardy made in the Thirties may be out of copyright in their original form, but the music itself is well and truly still in copyright.

Is it illegal to copy music onto CD or rip to MP3?

Yes, especially if you were to make copies and give them away or sell them, even to friends. Again, the only exception would be if the recording was released over 50 years ago and the writers of the song have all been dead for at least 70 years – still a very small proportion of music ever recorded. Although manufacturers of CD and DVD recorders might seem to be inviting people to do this merely by making their products available, it is illegal to record any copyright material without the permission of the copyright owners. The only legitimate audio copying use for such devices is for reproducing audio in which you own the copyright (and remember, your recording of someone else's song includes not only your copyright but also theirs).

Even copying or ripping for 'home use', like putting your CD collection onto your iPod or onto a hard drive for sharing across your home network, is technically illegal. However, a proposal is in train to legalise the practice of ripping to a portable digital music player such as an iPod for personal use, but at present it remains illegal.

In some countries (but not the UK) there is a levy on the price of recording equipment and blank audio and video cassettes, DVDs and CDs to compensate rights owners for part of their losses through home taping. It doesn't amount to much actual income and the UK industry has always preferred not to have a levy. It reasons that the levy may seem to legitimise an activity that remains completely illegal; without it, the industry can legitimately campaign for better protection and use copy-protection software such as DRM to prevent music being copied, without being accused of trying to have their cake and eat it too. A levy would also penalise the people who genuinely do only ever use recording devices and media for legitimate purposes. Remember that a publisher can't usually give permission for the use of a recording, and a record company can't usually give permission for the use of a song.

Is it always illegal to make copies of printed music without permission?

Assuming that we are not talking about your own unpublished compositions, then there are a few circumstances under which it is acceptable to make copies of music. Some publishers (but by no means all) subscribe to a 'code of fair practice' for individuals or educational establishments to make a few copies for study purposes. However, any copy materials used for performance will need permission from the rights owner. Most publishers will permit small numbers of copies to be made of single sheets or smaller pieces on request if copies are not sold or used for other purposes, usually for a nominal fee. But if you require many copies and the music is in print, they may require you to purchase original printed copies (or a licence to print your own copies through a website such as Sheetmusicdirect.com).

In the past, the publishers have had to resort to suing schools that flagrantly photocopied music without permission. It's not great PR for publishers, but the schools should really have known better.

Remember, even if the underlying piece of music is out of copyright, it's quite possible that the layout of the sheet music you are copying or the particular arrangement is still in copyright, so it's always best to check first.

How long must I wait for my royalties?

Royalties can take a very long time to reach you from the time when they are first earned. Using the example of overseas publishing royalties on record sales, if a song you write is a hit in, say, the US in the autumn of one year, the American record company waits until the end of the next accounting period under which they have to pay mechanical royalties to the Harry Fox Agency (the US mechanical collection agency). At the end of HFA's accounting period, they account to the US publisher, who waits until the end of his next accounting period to pay the UK publisher. At your publisher's next accounting period, he pays you or, if you have a manager, he'll receive the payment and then, maybe a few months later, he pays you.

Most, though not all, accountings are half-yearly (though the PRS account quarterly and MCPS monthly), but in many cases, for every single link in the chain you might be waiting up to another six months for your royalties. It could easily be at least two years after the records were actually sold or the performance took place. Some collection societies outside the UK have processing and registration backlogs that can extend this time period by a year or two more. Some publishers account (and have their sub-publishing network account) quarterly, or even more frequently. It is undoubtedly true that the industry in the digital age is moving towards faster accounting practices, but a great deal of work remains to be done for systems to be in place. It might also be argued that the industry has little financial incentive to stop hanging on to your money until the end of their long-established accounting period.

Artist royalties should be accounted slightly quicker (especially those relating to downloads, where record companies have made substantial investment in new systems). The problem with these, however, is that until all your advances/ unrecouped balances are recouped, you won't get anything at all in cash money (you'll only get any additional advances the record companies undertook to pay you). The moral of this is: don't go out and buy your Ferrari or 1959 Les Paul Standard the moment you learn that you have a hit song in the US or another foreign country, as you may be waiting years for the money. It would be wrong to assume also that your publisher, record company or manager is being dishonest. Just try to keep track of where your biggest earnings should be coming from, what stage they've reached in the process, and be patient. This is one reason why publishers and record companies pay advances and artists and songwriters accept them. They can afford to wait longer than you can for the money to come trickling in; the price you pay of course is that the bigger the advance (in effect a loan) the lower your royalty rate (ie. the higher the interest rate you pay).

111

Where will my biggest earnings come from?

In terms of straightforward UK earnings for a UK artist/songwriter (unless the songs become standards, in which case they will go on earning year after year), artist royalties on hits will bring in more money than songwriting ones, but only once you've recouped the advances, which will almost always be much bigger (but take much longer to recoup) under your record deal than your songwriting deal. Over the period when you have the hits, your earnings from live appearances, provided you were capitalising on your popularity, will be even greater, though not usually for a really big 'stadium' act, who may well make relatively little money from gigs because of the sheer expense of staging them.

The best place in the world in which to have a big hit moneywise is, as you can imagine, the US, though as an artist you'll almost certainly have to spend months there touring, doing interviews, possibly writing with local songwriters or guesting with local acts, supporting local acts on tour etc. before you take off. Next comes Japan, where some unlikely foreign acts are really big, whereas other huge international acts strangely fail to make it at all. After this comes GAS (Germany, Austria and Switzerland – again, a market with its own particular tastes and peculiarities), then the UK, followed by France (another unpredictable market), Italy, Brazil and other 'markets' such as Spain and Portugal, Benelux (Belgium, Luxembourg and the Netherlands), Australasia, Canada (almost always lumped in with the US), the Nordic Countries (including Scandinavia) and South Africa. Owing to ineffective copyright protection and consequent lack of exploitation, large areas like the rest of Africa, India, non-EU Eastern European countries and Russia, the Middle East, parts of the Far East and parts of South and Central America can be almost ruled out when working out where money will be coming from. It is possible to generate some

income in South America, where legitimate sales are huge by volume of units, but exchange rates, currency movement controls, inflation and other economic factors substantially reduce the actual value of money taken out of the countries involved.

In most of these places there is copyright protection of sorts, but generally it's not properly enforced. In some, many foreign recordings are imported and sold (in which case, publishing royalties will be collected by the appropriate society in the exporting country and your artist royalties should come in from the sale). But they compete on a less than level playing field with 'bootleg' and 'pirate' recordings and thus the prices achievable are quite low. In the Far East and Middle East things are often even worse, as there is little in the way of a 'culture of copyright'. There are places in the world, mainly in the developing world, where money may have been collected for you and put into a bank account in your name. Contracts with publishers and record companies sometimes specify this where 'Exchange Control' regulations prevent money being sent out of the country. This means that if you ever want to spend that money you will have to go there to do so, and no matter how tempting the amount sitting there for you, we certainly wouldn't recommend any attempt to avoid these controls as the consequences for you could be dire.

Isn't Anglo-American music still dominant worldwide?

In the main, yes, English and American pop music, in the English language, still commands a large share of the world market in terms of music sold and commercially exploited. In part this is because places such as India or China, which do have their own flourishing music scenes (and certainly in the case of India, substantial markets for that music outside their home territories), don't necessarily have the culture or infrastructure of copyright protection in place to fully exploit that music. The biggest exception is

Japan, where millions of Japanese do rush out to buy largely Japanese artists singing Japanese songs. To some extent the same is true the world over; for every international (Anglo-American) act there is an artist producing local covers of Anglo-American material and another producing wholly home-grown material. It's true to say that there are non-English language acts who are international, albeit only in the Latin countries, but the majority of truly global acts are of Anglo-American origin or sing primarily in English. In some countries, state-owned radio and television stations are obliged to broadcast a minimum proportion of local language recordings (eg. France), in an effort to arrest the spread of Anglo-American culture through rock and pop music (similar to the way that the BBC or Channel 4 are limited in the amount of US-produced television that they can show).

The US has been prepared in the past to put on their trade 'blacklist' countries that don't have or don't enforce copyright. This was mainly aimed at software piracy and protecting other forms of industrial intellectual copyrights, but that obviously includes artistic intellectual property such as music.

Since its absolute pinnacle of dominance in the mid-Sixties, the market for UK music in the US has had many highs and lows, and predictions of the end of UK success in the US have been as frequent as its comebacks. It's certainly an attainable goal for any UK artist to 'break the USA', but equally it's as difficult as ever to predict just who will and who won't.

Can I assume that a printed contract will be 'standard' and therefore reasonable?

These days, very few contracts are signed using pre-printed standard forms. Even if the words 'standard contract' are used, you can bet that the rates and other key terms will vary depending on your negotiation skills and those of your manager and/or lawyer. It is worth noting,

however, that if you are offered a printed contract the company offering it is less likely to let you have anything altered in your favour, as the terms are indeed probably pretty standard. That's not to say that the standard terms are the ones you'd want or the only ones you could get. So obviously the only real answer is to read it. A 'standard' contract may have attached to it a 'schedule' setting out the royalties and the duration as well as other important details, or these may be in the main body of the document. Either way, the main body will contain a number of clauses, terms and conditions known as 'boilerplate clauses', which are fairly standard legal terms for any contract, but also in the main body may be special terms and clauses that modify the meaning of the schedule. So an apparently high royalty and short duration may be totally different once the small print is applied, or a 'contract year' can turn out to be a whole lot longer than a calendar year. Our advice as always is to read the whole document carefully, however boring it looks, to ask questions and don't sign anything until you've had a lawyer look over it.

If the contract is altered by hand the alterations should be initialled by both parties, and make doubly sure that all the copies are identical and that the meaning of any added wording is completely clear, especially if it relates to how long you're signed for or the royalty rates. Usually there'll only be two copies, but the publisher/record company etc. may want an extra one and may prepare an extra one for you to leave with your manager or lawyer.

If the copies are not all exactly the same, then even if the difference seems trivial and you believe the meaning to be substantially the same, you should make sure that the copies are altered (or best of all retyped) to be identical. Even the smallest difference could in the future lead to a dispute that you will regret for years to come, and have very real financial and legal consequences.

What should I know about insurance?

It's perfectly possible for you to insure your voice, fingers or whatever you fear might be lost if something happened to you. It's just a question of balancing the cost against the possible risk. If you've been paid a big advance by a record company, they may want to insure you at their expense and may ask you to undergo a medical examination. It may not be a 'deal-breaker' if you say no, but you should be prepared for this.

Some semi-pro bands do insure their equipment, though the cost can be high for decent cover, but once you're making your living from music you can't afford not to have some sort of protection. People in the music business don't have a great reputation for 'stability', be it The Who smashing guitars on stage, bands trashing hotel rooms or 'gangsta' rappers involved with guns and drugs, and this reputation problem can add to the cost of insurance.

It is also possible to get third party insurance (public liability insurance) in case, for example, your PA speaker falls on someone's head. If you're a Musicians Union member, you can get public liability insurance free of charge up to a certain amount, and also a certain amount of insurance for your equipment. Major acts have to have third party insurance to cover themselves against accidents to road crew, lighting technicians and others who are effectively employed by them to run big concerts and tours. Venues will have their own third party insurance, but will look to pass on the liability to you if an accident appears to have been caused by you or your entourage.

What happens if I lose my copy of the contract?

Just a general cautionary word about being methodical where contracts or any other important pieces of documentation

are concerned. Even if your manager has secured the contracts for you and has copies himself, always try to keep a copy of every contract you sign. You should also try to keep a copy of every letter or email you write or receive on the subject of contracts, or relating to any dispute that arises later. Put the relevant letters with the relevant contracts – you never know when you might need to produce them. If you lose a contract, you can ask the other party (publisher, record company or whoever) for a copy to be made of the one they have, and most companies will do this quite readily. A crooked company could then always take the opportunity to alter the terms in its favour; this is highly illegal and isn't at all likely to happen, but it has been known. Much more common (though still fairly rare) is that over time the ownership of the company with which you have a contract changes several times. In the process of taking over that company, the new owner may be given or may mislay their copy of your contract, and it's quite possible then that your terms may be set up wrongly in their systems. If such an issue arises you should be in a position to provide your copy of the contract to ensure that any administrative errors can be quickly corrected.

Should I join the Musicians' Union?

The MU has been active for decades in ensuring an increasing supply of work for musicians and at reasonable fees. They have constantly campaigned to ensure that radio stations do not play recorded music all day, so that a proportion of the airtime is devoted to live music. They have at various times required that all musicians appearing on television programmes must either play live or, if they wish to mime, must mime to a re-recording of their record, thereby making more work for musicians and singers.

The union lays down certain minimum rates for all session musicians, at a specific rate for a three-hour session plus extra for doubling on another instrument, extra for porterage (bringing a heavy instrument to the session), overtime, etc. If a session musician records for a commercial record, there's a separate fee payable if that recording also gets used in a television programme etc. The record companies have agreements with the MU whereby they agree to pay MU rates for all their sessions, and you should certainly be a member if you wish to start doing sessions regularly – the union is in any case working in your interests. This would mean agreeing not to play for less than union rates, but this is unlikely to worry a good working musician whose interests the MU is safeguarding.

Membership also brings such benefits as a certain amount of free legal advice (the MU lawyers will check over any agreements you may have been offered), plus public liability insurance. Each branch sends out a regular newsletter to members in its area full of useful information. Annual membership of the MU costs £60 for students, £144 for those earning less than £15,000 from music, and £264 for those earning more than £15,000 from music. A professional musician should be a member of the MU anyway but, if you're not, and you're tempted to think 'that's 150 quid I could save', or that it's only for orchestral or jazz musicians, think again. If you seriously want to make money as a per-

former then you need all the help you can get, and the MU could help a lot. Check their website for more details, and for the latest subscription rates (see the 'Useful Addresses' list below).

What do publicists, PR and marketing people do?

Some managers, record companies, artists, venues or publishers make use of independent publicists (PR companies), either to generate publicity for themselves or their artists or to release statements to the press about new artists signed, forthcoming tours arranged and suchlike. Other larger organisations have their own internal PR or marketing departments. In short, PR (public relations), like the old 'press office', deals with communications with the outside world (the public and journalists), responding to events or making announcements about upcoming events in your personal or professional life. Marketing is a closely related area, whose practitioners seek to expand the market for your music. This can involve either helping you to start, become part of, or mould your music or image to current trends.

What can I do personally to get publicity?

If you are just a local artist and want to get some publicity, then the possibility of getting a record deal (for a 'proper' record company, rather than making your own to sell at gigs or through your website) is usually enough to interest the local press. Of course, the Internet, as we discussed in the Getting A Recording

Deal section, is a powerful tool, and a MySpace page, a website and a mailing list are key. But don't be afraid to contact other popular music-related sites and blogs and try to get some coverage – they have a voracious appetite for new material and are much more approachable that the conventional press. The most basic piece of publicity is to have cards printed with your name (and artist name if it's different) and what you do plus your address, website and phone number to give to enquirers or to leave at venues where you have played. A few hundred of these will cost no more than a few pounds or so and are an absolute must. As we've said, if you have a manager or agent, he will provide you with cards showing himself as the contact instead of you. Advertisements in local papers are not too expensive, though the 'entertainers' heading will mostly list children's magicians and mobile discos. The other obvious means of attracting publicity is through posters, but you need to be very careful that you don't fall foul of the local authority by putting these up where you shouldn't. If you're doing pub gigs, they'll probably expect you to produce your own posters and do a bit of local PR.

PR is obviously a lot cheaper than advertising, although a lot of PR comes at a price (sometimes for example a magazine will do an article on you but only if you take out a full-page advert). As regards PR, you are more likely to get this if you look good and are good at, or very amenable to doing, interviews. It's only beneficial to be really antisocial and unhelpful if you're already well-known and that forms part of your public image.

Can anyone start up their own fan club?

Principally as a result of scams based around fake fan clubs for established acts, there have been moves to try to regulate the running of these but the basic answer is yes, and even an unsigned new band would benefit from doing so. Obviously, this is all the easier with the help of a good online presence, and you can either dedicate a part of your official website as a 'members only' area with exclusive forums, news items, merchandise, wallpapers, photos and advance warning of upcoming gigs, or establish a separate presence offering the same. When you're starting out, if at all possible you need to find some friend, relative or fan who is prepared, more or less unpaid, to be the secretary. While this person is not likely to be a legal employee of yours, and especially if you are planning to charge for membership (even just to cover costs), then you need to be very sure that whoever's organising it for you can literally deliver the goods. The last thing you want, even if you're only well-known locally as yet, is a minor scandal caused by fans paying out, however little, and getting nothing or next to nothing in return.

Once you are more successful, you can afford to pay to have your fan club organised on a large scale if you wish. Incidentally, if someone you don't know or don't approve of wishes to start a fan club, fan website or even an Internet 'shrine', you're in no position to stop them, though you can prevent them from implying that they have 'official' status, that they are endorsed by you or if they use your logo (if you have one copyrighted); they can even try to charge for their 'services' if they want.

Beware of record companies wanting to get involved in your fan club in order to sell not only your records/merchandising but also material by their other artists. The same pressure exists to take control of your website. In both cases, only in carefully negotiated circumstances should you consider their involvement, and you should try to retain as much control and ownership as you can; ultimately it's about your public image, and you don't want to lose control of that. It's also worth bearing in mind that, under the UK's Data Protection Act, you can't (not that you may necessarily want to) go selling lists of the members of your fan club to other people, unless you specifically tell your members when they sign up and give them the chance to opt out.

Do I really have to get my agreements vetted by a lawyer?

In the case of simple agency agreements for concerts or gigs this isn't strictly necessary, and only if you have problems would you need to consult a lawyer. However, for all songwriting assignments/licences, recording and management agreements, especially 'blankets' or 'exclusives' as opposed to one-offs, you will actually be expected to have taken independent legal advice. Agreements will have a clause, usually towards the end, stating that the agreement could have an important impact on your career and strongly urging you to take expert independent (legal) advice. Often, this will go so far as asking to confirm (warrant) that you actually have taken such advice.

This is to protect the other party from the possibility of you going back to them at a later date and claiming that the agreement was unfair because you did not understand what you were signing or your bargaining position was weaker than theirs. Contracts, or parts of contracts, have been declared null and void in the past as a result of one party having been shown to have not clearly understood what they were signing, and publishers and record companies want to avoid this in the future. And since you ought to take this advice for your own protection, it's fair for them to ask you to do so and to declare that you have.

The expert advice should really come from an entertainment lawyer, not one who is more used to conveyancing, divorce or other areas of the law. Record companies, publishers etc. can suggest three or four to you and leave you to choose, but you'll understand that they

can't suggest just one in case you accuse them in a few years' time of having influenced the advice you got. In practice, once he's acting for you, your lawyer will in any case be bound by his professional standards to act only in your best interests. It is, of course, very important that he be wholly independent, and should not therefore be an employee of your record company, manager or publisher or work for a firm that currently acts for your record company, manager or publisher.

Do I always have to take the lawyer's advice?

No, but you'd obviously be foolish to ignore it entirely. In the end the final decision is your own, and your lawyer is there to help you understand and weigh up the options. Sometimes the advice will be very strongly to reject a contract or a particular clause; at other times you will have to balance accepting one relatively bad clause in order to get a good one elsewhere in the same agreement. Your lawyer may proffer an opinion about what to do in these cases but, again, ultimately it's up to you. You should be aware that it's not unknown for a lawyer to blow your chances with a particular company by asking for too much in advances, royalties or too many concessions in the small print. Make sure he or she knows how much you're prepared to concede, and that they're guided closely by you throughout any negotiations they conduct on your behalf. They'll do the best deal they can for you, but they can't read your mind!

What if I'm under 18?

If you're under 18 (or under 16 in Scotland) then you are technically still a minor, and might find it easier to get out of any deals you make on the grounds of 'immaturity' (though the longer the contract continues without objection after you officially become an adult, the less likely this is). To avoid this, one of your parents or your legal guardian will have to be involved in the negotiations and countersign your agreements, to ensure that you're bound by what you've signed.

How binding are verbal agreements?

Verbal agreements are a very complex area of the law, and one to be avoided wherever possible. In short, if there are independent witnesses to the agreement it is likely to be binding at some level. If you actively fulfil your end of the bargain and so does the other party then it is more likely to be binding, and the longer you allow the terms of the verbal agreement to continue, the more likely again. So if you agree something verbally in front of witnesses, take the money, deliver the recording, accept royalties for five years and then turn round and object, you will be in a weak position. On the other hand, if you agree something in front of witnesses but go no further, then the longer the other party takes to try to enforce the agreement, the less likely it is to be binding.

The major problem with a verbal agreement is all the details it doesn't cover, and while some of these can be assumed, others have a major influence on the actual performance of the agreement. So except in very minor and simple matters, a written agreement is always preferable, and should have a clause stating something along the lines of 'this agreement represents the total agreement between the two parties and can only be altered in writing'. That way, nothing outside the written agreement can be said to be part of it (such as a 'verbal agreement' on a detail not mentioned in the document). If the person offering you such an agreement says, while explaining it, something like, 'Oh don't worry about that', 'this never happens' or 'obviously we'll up the royalty after a little while', you cannot hold him to any of this, and must ask him to have the con-

tract altered to cover these things or else sign it at its face value.

In what ways might VAT affect me?

Value Added Tax is payable on a great many goods and services in the UK, and VAT or an equivalent sales tax exists in many other countries. The only person who cannot claim it back in some way is the 'consumer' at the end of the line. Thus, each member of the chain in the production and sale of a record can claim back some of the tax he has paid by collecting tax himself from the next person in the chain, until it is eventually the record buyer who pays the appropriate tax on the cost of a record. The advisability of putting VAT on the cost of sheet music and books has been under consideration for many years, but records had VAT on them right from their introduction in the UK.

If you are 'in the business', say, as a musician, then you can register for VAT. You can claim VAT from record companies, publishers and the management of venues at which you perform. If you are registered, record companies and publishers are obliged to pay you the additional VAT on top of your royalties if you send them an invoice for it quoting your VAT registration number. At venues, you can charge this if you ask for it initially together with your fee but, if you forget, then you will be in the embarrassing position of having to go back to them and ask, or else work on the basis that the fee you got included VAT in the first place. Although all this VAT you have collected is payable quarterly by you to the government (make sure you get your returns in on time!), you can, of course, before paying it, deduct (if registered) all the VAT you have had to pay on new instruments, stage clothes, recording equipment – in fact, almost everything reasonably necessary to the pursuit of your musical career (but don't push it too far, and do get proper tax advice from your accountant on the latest rulings and regulations).

All this may sound fine but it does have to be properly worked out by your accountant (you'll need to have one if you wish to register for VAT, unless you have enough free time and/or you're good with figures). It is often worth registering even though your earnings don't reach the level where you're obliged to, but it may require an accountant to tell you whether in your particular circumstances this would be a worthwhile step.

Should I get a royalty statement even if nothing is payable?

If something (anything) was earned in the last accounting period but nothing's payable to you because the company haven't yet recovered the advance they paid you, then you should still get a statement. To keep their costs down, and even if your advance is recouped, publishers and record companies tend not to pay out if you're less than £25–£50 'in credit', and will roll the money over period by period until you reach their minimum payment amount. Nonetheless, they should be prepared to pay you if you ask specifically. If you want to receive statements even when no money has been earned in the period, you will need to be sure this is covered in your agreements, otherwise many companies will not send them.

Do I really need an accountant?

Once you have a manager who is receiving and spending money on your behalf, you should definitely have your own accountant, preferably one who understands the entertainment business. Even if you trust your manager implicitly, it's better to have your finances sorted out by someone independent. The advice your accountant can give on tax liability could save you a small fortune. There have been a few horror stories about stars being ripped off by their accountants, but you'd be very unlucky to fall

into the hands of both a crooked manager *and* a crooked accountant. The more questions you ask, within reason, the harder it is for anyone to pull the wool over your eyes. As with lawyers, you can ask an accountant for a rough estimate of his likely charges.

Can I audit my manager/publisher/record company?

Your agreements with all of these should contain an audit clause, which should state that you can appoint someone to audit the company, usually not more than once a year, at their normal address in normal office hours on giving reasonable prior notice. You can't expect them to let absolutely anyone look at their books, so it should be a professional accountant. The clause will usually say that if you don't query any royalty statement within around three years, you lose the right. After six years, the Statute of Limitations allows them to throw away the documentation in any case, though for serious fraud, your lawyer may advise that it will be possible to make claims back beyond this.

Depending on the audit clause, if a deficit of more than a certain percentage (say 10%) is found, they'll be expected to pay your audit fees (your accountant can advise what these are likely to be), the amount of any deficit and a set rate of interest (usually linked to the Bank of England base rate).

It is actually surprisingly rare for audits to be made by individual writers or artists (except for the really high earners). It's not cheap (even quite a small audit can cost several thousand pounds) and you'd normally do it only if you seriously suspected the company of deliberately underpaying you a lot of money (or you're looking for an excuse to call material breach and end the contract early). A really aggressive audit is likely to cast a shadow over the relationship between you and the company you're auditing, especially if it's a smaller company and you don't find much underpayment.

Incidentally, the MCPS do conduct regular audits of record companies on behalf of all writers and publishers, on which they charge 10% commission, and they generally find substantial amounts owing. The MCPS also audit other societies abroad – they call them 'technical visits' – and again, this usually unearths significant unpaid earnings. Where possible, the money these audits recover is paid in respect of the songs used, but mostly it's impossible to identify these and the money is divided pro rata according to your other earnings.

What happens if my manger/ record label/publisher goes broke?

While many regard the music industry as something of a fly-by-night, get-rich-quick business, it's actually much more 'businesslike' than ever before. That said, there are still lots of companies that look good after a couple of hits but have completely disappeared a year or so later. You should therefore make absolutely sure that your contract clearly states that it terminates should the company go bankrupt or into administration, and that any rights (ie. your songs or recordings) assigned or licensed by you to them immediately revert back to you.

If you can't get these clauses in your contract then, in the event that the company goes under, the receiver or administrator may well suspend all activity other than the collection of income due to be collected by it. This means that promotion of your songs or recordings will cease, any money the company collects or has in hand will go to its creditors in strict rotation (with the tax authorities and others way ahead of you in the queue) and, if we're talking about a record company, it's likely that no more CDs will be made and existing stocks will be sold off cheaply. Eventually the assets will be sold (including your songs or recordings). The new owner may do a fine job and your royalties may resume

as before, but you will most likely never recover the royalties that were owed to you by the old company when it went under, or crucially those earned between that moment and when the new company took over (which, in a complex bankruptcy, can be months or years). Sadly, the smaller and newer the company you sign to, the more likely, statistically, this is to happen. That doesn't mean you shouldn't sign to a small or new company. Many are very proactive and prepared to take a risk on a writer or artist whom the majors would shy away from... but the newer or smaller they are, the more insistent you should be about getting your songs/recordings back if they go under. Be warned!

Can any of my earnings be guaranteed?

It used to be the case that managers and some record and publishing companies would write into agreements that the artist was guaranteed a certain level of earnings, or that the artist/songwriter was bound by the agreement until certain earnings had been achieved. The first of these is extremely rare in the modern music business, where the only real guarantees are advance payments that a company is obligated to pay under the terms of the agreement when certain conditions are met. For example, when an artist signs to a label, when an album is released, or when it reaches a certain chart position (and the only absolute guarantees are the advances they pay you on signing!). If you are offered a £1m recording deal, this usually means that the advances will total £1m if, and only if, the label takes up all its options and all the conditions are met. As for the second scenario, these days, if anyone were to offer a deal where you continued to be bound by it until the 'guaranteed earnings' had been reached, you'd be able to claim that it was a restraint of your trade because such a contract potentially has no limit to its term;

hence, you are very unlikely to receive such an offer.

What royalties should I get on sales of DVDs?

As a songwriter, the use of one of your songs in a film or TV production released on video/DVD will be licensed by your publisher (sometimes through the MCPS). There are two types of licence (and two potential streams of income) from a 'videogram' (the name for all types of physical video media). The first is for the 'synchronisation right' and the second is for the mechanical reproduction right. The following varies greatly from territory to territory around the world but, in general, for film both rights are usually bought out as part of the flat fee paid for the synch licence. For television the synch right is usually covered by a mechanical society blanket licence, and the mechanical right is licensed on a royalty basis (that royalty being based on the dealer price and the proportion of the production that features music). Productions specially made for video (such as exercise or instructional videos and the like) will follow the usual charging structure for TV. 'Music only' videos and DVDs (ie. live performances or compilations of music videos) are licensed and attract royalties in a similar way to normal music CDs.

A recording artist will receive a share of buyout fees for uses in film and TV productions released on video or DVD, but rarely a royalty. As for 'music only' products, there are usually no artist royalties payable on uses of individual promo videos, but an artist should certainly receive royalties on sales of long-form videos (whether of live concerts, compilations from promo videos of your singles, or compilations of videos by various artists). The royalties on videos sold by your record company alongside the records and tapes will usually be at the same rate, but remember the cost of making your promo videos will be offset against your royalties – usually half from general royalties and half from sales and uses of the videos on DVD etc.

How are the charts compiled?

The best-selling singles and album charts in the UK are compiled by the Official UK Charts Company (OCC) on behalf of the BPI. They're published in the trade magazine *Music Week* and widely used by the BBC and by other television and radio programmes (though some music papers and broadcasters have their own charts). *Music Week* also publishes airplay, club charts and dance charts, as well as specialist compilation, country, rock and indie charts.

The information on sales comes from 'returns' made by a certain number of retail outlets in the UK ('chart shops') and UK online download retailers.

The charts are broadcast by the BBC on Radio 1 on Sundays, and published a day or two later in *Music Week*, but it is possible to estimate the positions from the 'midweek' information the researchers supply to the industry.

In the US, the definitive Top 100 singles, Top 200 albums and other charts are published in the magazine *Billboard*, but these are based on radio and television airplay as well as sales. The sheer size of the market, and the inclusion of airplay, means that records climb the charts more slowly than in the UK. The airplay is actually so important that it's possible to have a US Top 10 singles hit without even releasing the single! This is becoming more common, as record companies don't want people buying the single if they could possibly sell them a whole album on the strength of the song they've heard and liked on the radio.

How do I get a silver/ gold/platinum disc?

These can be awarded for any single or album that reaches a certain level of sales and are certified by the market research company compiling the charts. In the UK at present sales levels for singles are: silver – 200,000; gold – 400,000; platinum – 600,000; for albums the thresholds are: silver – 60,000; gold – 100,000; platinum – 300,000. Most albums that enter in the Top 10 can expect to go silver after the first few weeks. An album entering at number one can expect to go gold more or less immediately, and almost any album that's been in the charts for three months or so can expect to go platinum. Once the figures have been reached, anyone connected with the record can get one of the relevant discs. They cost about £100 each and your manager, record company and every different publisher of a song on an album will probably all buy at least one for themselves, plus possibly one for the artist or writer. However, you should be aware that nobody actually gets one automatically and free of charge. They are often awarded to such people as the act's lawyers and accountants, and the company that produces them will even make one for presentation to your granny for making the cakes you ate during rehearsals, if you're prepared to pay for it.

What should I know about sampling?

The use of a really distinctive sample, or re-recorded extract, from an earlier song, can make the difference between success and failure. Imagine 'Gangsta's Paradise' by Coolio, 'Hung Up' by Madonna or 'Bittersweet Symphony' by The Verve without the use of samples from an earlier song. On the other hand, samples are frequently used when it would have been almost as easy to write and record something original. The vital thing to remember when you use a sample is that you're using someone else's property, so you need to ask permission from the rights owner. Often, of course, this is the publisher or record company, so if you got permission directly from the songwriter or the artist, it may count for nothing

even if can sometimes help (or may indeed also be needed). They can quite legally demand a large percentage of your entire song/record, even for a tiny sample, though for very small samples you may be able to negotiate a flat fee buyout (more commonly for the recording than for the song copyright). You don't have to agree to their demands of course, as you always have the option to take the sample out of your recording. If the record doesn't work without it, you and your record company may then decide not to release it. But if you go ahead with the release complete with the sample having been refused permission, not having sought it, or before negotiations are complete, then at worst you risk having all copies confiscated and destroyed (along with any money you make), and at best you will be in a much weaker position to negotiate the percentage or buyout fee. Record companies and publishers are usually not too unreasonable, but you can't assume that. They'll be guided to an extent (and governed by their contracts) by their artists or writers, and very broadly, the less the artists/writers of the original song need the money, the more likely they are to say 'no' (often because they get many similar requests).

Remember that it's likely that you guaranteed your publisher and record company in their respective agreements that the song and recording would be 'all your own work', so you're financially liable if they contain bits of someone else's music.

There are arguments as to whether some samples are too insignificant to be an infringement, and the question of whether you've used 'a substantial part' of another song will be brought up in negotiations. In pop music, the entire length of a track is so relatively short that even a few seconds represents a significant proportion of the whole work. Also, the test of whether something is substantial is not only by length but by how important it is to the song in the ears of the average listener, so even a drum loop or a bass line can be substantial enough.

Finally, there's a 'halfway' position, which would be for you to use a bit of someone else's song but re-record it. Again you must ask permission first, but only from the publisher of the original song this time. If, of course, it's your record that's been sampled then the boot is on the other foot, and you and your publisher should try to agree between you how much of the new song you should ask for. You will then generally become a part writer of the new song.

What if the sample is only on one mix of a song?

This does make life complicated, and if it's your song that's been sampled we would suggest that if it's at all likely that the mix containing your sample will be the featured radio edit ('A-side') – in other words, the one everyone plays – you try to ask for a share, albeit a small one, of all the mixes. If you don't then it's quite possible that you'll miss out on performing and broadcasting fees, as the PRS and other societies abroad won't always be able to distinguish which mix was being played. You may even miss out on royalties from sales of compilation albums, though you can at least tell the MCPS and other mechanical societies when you know it's the mix with your sample on it that's included in a particular release.

Incidentally, beware of remixers getting hold of a track of yours that has no samples in it and putting some in. You could suddenly find yourself losing a share of your song, and possibly on all the mixes including the hit radio edit, just because of someone else's actions.

Would my career take off better overseas?

There have been quite a few British artists who have first made it in Continental-Europe, usually Germany or Holland, and you may be able to get a record deal from a major label there and be able to make a good living. There's still a certain mystique about Anglo-American artists on the Continent and this can certainly be used to your advantage. Do remember, though, that lots of records are successful all round Europe but do nothing in the UK. While certain types of music, such as Italian dance music and Scandinavian pop and heavy rock, do have credibility in Britain, often your major label's UK office will either not release or else not get behind a release from one of their Continental-European affiliates. So if your ultimate aim is to make it in the UK, this isn't always the best route. If the opportunity arises, however, it is a possibility you should be aware of.

Then there's the US. Despite America's constant on/off love affair with British culture, and the obvious advantage of a common language, it's not an easy place to launch a career no matter what nationality you are. But it's another possibility, and occasionally, as in the case of the London rock band Bush, UK acts do make it in the US before their home country. It should be noted, though, that even British acts who are already big in the UK often have to go and live in America permanently for a while to make any impact, and the US now has relatively strict rules relating to permission to work.

Do I need a licence to run a mobile disco?

As with live bands, the venues where you play should be licensed by the PRS and PPL and, if you're simply playing records, then you're entitled to assume that you don't need a separate licence. If you were organising a gig yourself somewhere where music isn't normally played, however, then you should make sure a licence is obtained (either by you, the venue or the event organiser). Again, as with bands, most DJs can make steady money (£150 or more for a good mobile disco with lights working on a local level at parties and functions), without having to spend a fortune on new releases every week, provided they play some ABBA or songs from *Grease* etc.! It's possible to get from there to hospital radio and, with a lot of tenacity, from there to local radio and upwards, but it won't, of course, open doors to being a club DJ.

How can I get to become a club DJ?

If you're a mobile DJ who's already buying a lot of current dance music, then it's a matter of being persistent in trying to find the local gigs where you can get to play what you want to play. Most top DJs built up their reputation in one club before 'playing the field'. The better known you get, the more freebies you'll receive from the record labels, especially if you co-operate by filling in their audience response forms and keep in touch with them. Having said that, even top DJs still spend some of their own money on new releases. DJs have, of course, become stars in their own right on the club scene and you could earn substantial fees per performance. Some will do maybe three clubs in one night, although some top DJs deliberately try to preserve their value to clubs by not taking all the work offered. For special nights of the year the prices rocket – you could add a nought to the fees for New Year's Eve. It's not just musicians who can make good money from appearing live.

Once you've got a reputation you could easily spend as much of the summer as you want sunning yourself in Ibiza or Ayia Napa. If you're lucky, you might be able to build up a reputation by being based there first, then start earning big money in the UK too.

Another big source of income, and means of increasing your reputation, is mixing and remixing existing tracks, some of which are re-released on a regular basis with new mixes. There's nothing to stop you as a successful DJ getting together with a producer and putting out

records in your own name; increasing numbers of these have made it into the main UK charts. Equally, it's possible for music stars such as Boy George to move over to being successful DJs, especially when their roots were in the clubs in the first place.

How can I find out more about the music business?

The best answer is to read as much as you can of the music press. The predominant trade magazine in the UK is *Music Week*. It has the full UK singles and album charts, including specialised charts and lists of all new releases, as well as news and views from within the industry, and is a very good place to look for ads for jobs in the business. It also includes full club charts, dance, airplay, alternative and urban charts. The long-running weekly magazine *NME* still contains a lot of information, as do the glossies such as *Q* and *Mojo*. In the US, the major trade magazine is called *Billboard*, and this contains the Top 100 singles and Top 200 album charts, as well as lots of specialist music charts. We've also included a number of helpful websites in our Useful Addresses list.

How could I get a job in the music business?

BA courses in commercial music studies are now available at quite a number of universities and colleges up and down the country, including specialist institutions such as the Brit School or the Academy of Contemporary Music (ACM), which are better known for turning out 'stars'. There is a website called the *Music Education Directory* hosted by the BPI (www.bpi-med.co.uk), which indicates the courses available at these colleges, and information can also be found at the BPI's own website. But remember that no one can guarantee you a job, any more than they can guarantee to make you a star.

The MPA also publishes a regular list of people seeking jobs in the business to all its members, so this is a possible avenue. Both the MPA website and that of *Music Week* have pages dedicated to current vacancies, and from the latter you will be able to glean the names of employment agencies active in this area.

Needless to say, a very large number of people working in the music business are also former professional musicians or singers. It's so popular that lots of people with honours degrees from university are still running errands and making the tea, and can be on much lower than average salaries compared with other businesses. Remember also that most jobs in music are actually administrative and, in many respects, are therefore much the same as in any other business. But even today it's the kind of business in which many top executives earning fabulous salaries started out at the very bottom, so if being in the music business is what you really want, don't be put off.

Have we made you feel that everyone is out to swindle you?

We hope not, because although you'll now know what pitfalls to avoid, it needs to be said that for every crook in the music business there are hundreds of honest people. Even if the first contract you're shown is harshly skewed in favour of the record company or the publisher, it doesn't mean they are out to screw you for every penny they can. Often this is merely a combination of zealous lawyers and the haggling/negotiating principle that you always start with your highest price. Remember, these days equally zealous lawyers will be on your side trying to skew things the other way, so the final contract is likely to be much fairer. For all that, it's nice to know that the contract you've signed is a reasonable one, and also that it really does set out what you think you've agreed to. It's usually easier to create music knowing that you'll be properly paid for it.

CONTRACTS

EXAMPLES OF CONTRACTS, WITH COMMENTS

In this section we have included some shortened versions of a song assignment, an agreement to record one single for an independent producer, a form of management agreement and simple agency and booking confirmation agreements. A full exclusive songwriting agreement can run to 30 pages or more and a long-term artist/record company agreement to around 50 or more, and are much less likely to follow a standard format. You will in any event need to take legal advice before signing all such agreements, and your lawyer can explain the details. Examples of royalty terms have generally been included, but you will know from our earlier comments what you could normally expect to get under such contracts in terms of royalty rates and hard cash.

As we have said, artist management agreements can range from a scrap of paper appointing your next-door neighbour as your manager, to a multi-paged document with an international company that takes a long time to read and even longer to understand. There is no such thing as a 'standard' artist management contract, but again your lawyer can explain the pros and cons. Try to think, 'If I'm immediately successful, am I going to be happy to be bound by this contract?'. If not and you're happy to compromise until you become successful, then try to make sure that the period of time you are committed to the compromises is relatively short.

1. Publishing assignment for specific songs.

For notes and comments on the terms of this agreement see 'Publishing Contracts' section.

AN ASSIGNMENT made this ..... day of .....   between

.... of............ ('the Writer') of the one part and
..................of............ ('the Publisher') of the other part

WITNESSETH:

1. In consideration of the sum of £1 (receipt whereof the Writer hereby acknowledges) and of other good and valuable considerations the Writer with full title guarantee (and by way of assignment of future copyright and rights where appropriate) hereby sells, assigns, transfers and delivers to the Publisher its successors and assigns the whole of the property title copyright and interest vested and contingent and all other rights whatsoever now or hereafter known throughout the Universe ('the Territory') in the musical work entitled: '...............' ('the Work') for a period of .... years from the date hereof ('the Term') including the right to collect royalties and fees outstanding for payment in respect of any uses of rights in the Work prior to the date hereof and the right to collect any royalties and fees accruing during the Term but actually payable within one year thereafter SUBJECT to the rights of the Performing Right Society Ltd. ('PRS') arising by virtue of the Writer's membership thereof but including the reversionary interest of the Writer in such rights expectant upon the termination of the rights of PRS subject to the payment to the Writer by the Publisher thereafter of the share payable by the PRS to the Writer thereof.

2. The Writer hereby warrants and agrees:

(a) that the Work and every part thereof is the original work of the Writer and does not infringe the copyright or any other right whatsoever of any person firm or corporation and is not obscene or defamatory
(b) that he is the owner (subject to the terms of this assignment) of the copyright and all other rights in the Work and has not previously granted transferred or assigned and will not during the Term purport to grant transfer or assign any interest therein assigned hereunder to any other person firm or corporation
(c) that he has the full right power and authority to enter into this agreement and is under no disability in regard thereto
(d) that each and every part of the Work is and will at all times be capable of such copyright protection throughout the Territory as is afforded to works of UK origin
(e) that he has made no representation to or agreement with any third party as to the terms upon which mechanical licences might or will be available in respect of the Work
(f) that he will indemnify the Publisher in respect of any claims demands and expenses arising from any breach of these warranties PROVIDED THAT the Publisher will not compromise or settle any such claims without the prior consent of the Writer such consent not to be unreasonably withheld or delayed. The Publisher is hereby irrevocably appointed the true and lawful representative of the Writer so far as may be necessary to defend and/or institute claims to establish or maintain copyright in the Work.
   In the event of any material breach of any of the above warranties and agreements the Publisher shall be entitled without prejudice to its other rights to suspend payment of royalties hereunder and to pay same into a separate interest-bearing account pending final resolution of such matter in an amount reasonably related to their probable loss.

3. The Publisher shall have the right to make and publish and to authorise others to make and publish new adaptations orchestrations and arrangements of the Work and new lyrics or translations in any language to the music of the Work as the Publisher shall think fit IT BEING AGREED that no major or substantial alterations may be authorised by the Publisher hereunder without the prior written consent of the Writer. The entire copyright and all other rights whatsoever in such modifications and new matter shall be vested in the Publisher for the Term.

4. The Publisher shall use all reasonable endeavours to procure the promotion of the Work it being agreed that if at any time following the expiry of two years from the date hereof the Writer shall serve notice on the Publisher enquiring whether any such promotion has taken place and if within three months from receipt of such notice the Publisher shall fail to provide evidence of such promotion, whether or not as a result of the Publisher's endeavours, then all rights hereby granted to the Publisher shall forthwith revert to the Writer. For the purpose of this agreement 'promotion' shall mean the commercial release for sale to the public of a recording of the Work or inclusion of the Work in a film, television commercial or commercial video production.

5. The Publisher shall pay royalties (excluding performing and broadcasting fees) to the Writer in respect of the Work as follows:

(i) 12.5% per copy of the marked retail selling price of all printed editions of the Work sold in the United Kingdom by the Publisher and paid for to the Publisher (pro rata in the case of collective editions)

(ii) 65% of all net licence fees computed at source and received by the Publisher in respect of the manufacture for sale to the public of recordings of the Work save that such royalty shall be 50% in respect of recordings procured by the Publisher ('Cover Recordings')

(iii) 65% of all sums computed at source and received by the Publisher in respect of synchronisation rights and any and all other uses of the Work (excluding performing and broadcasting) not specified hereunder

(iv) 65% of any and all net royalties received by the Publisher specifically in respect of the Work arising from the imposition of any levy on blank tapes or audio equipment provided that if the Writer shall receive any portion of such levy direct then the Publisher shall only be required to pay the balance necessary to bring the Writer's share of such levy to an aggregate of 65%.

   'Sums received' shall mean all sums received by or credited to the Publisher or its sub-publishers and licensees outside the United Kingdom who may, at the Publisher's absolute discretion, be affiliates associates subsidiaries or parents of the Publisher, less only normal bona fide arms-length collecting society commissions and deductions of any amounts paid to arrangers adaptors and translators subject to local rules and practices or, if none, as agreed by the Writer. The Publisher will use its best endeavours to receive promptly in the United Kingdom from such sub-publishers and licensees any and all sums not retainable by such sub-publishers and licensees hereunder.

6. General performing fees and broadcasting fees shall be divided equally by the PRS between the Writer and the Publisher subject to any allocation for orchestral arrangements or lyrics in accordance with the rules of PRS for the time being in force.

The Publisher further undertakes to pay to the Writer 30% of the 6/12ths total publisher share of all such fees received by the Publisher or its overseas sub-publishers and licensees specifically in respect of the Work. The Writer hereby certifies that for the purpose of PRS rule 1(o) the Publisher is to be treated as exploiting the Work (otherwise than by publishing) for the benefit of the persons interested therein to the extent indicated in the said rule.

7. (a) All copies of the Work (whether sheet editions, mechanical reproductions or otherwise) distributed free for the purpose of propagating and popularising the Work shall be free of all royalties or payments to the Writer

(b) In calculating the Publisher's receipts Value Added or any similar tax forming part thereof shall be deducted therefrom. All payments hereunder are exclusive of VAT which shall be payable in addition to the principal sum upon presentation of a VAT invoice in respect thereof.

8. (a) Royalty statements shall be made up to June 30 and December 31 in each year to include all sums received by the Publisher in that period and sent to the Writer within 90 days thereafter accompanied by a remittance for the amount so found due

(b) All royalty statements and other accounts from the Publisher to the Writer hereunder shall be binding upon the Writer unless specific objection in writing stating the basis thereof is given to the Publisher within three years from the date rendered

(c) If the Publisher shall be unable to procure the remittance to the United Kingdom of monies accountable hereunder to the Writer from any country then it shall at the written request of the Writer and subject to the laws of that country open an interest bearing bank account in the name and under the control of the Writer in such country and pay the Writer's share of such monies into such account and notify the Writer of details thereof.

(d) The Writer shall have the right to appoint a professional accountant to examine and inspect all books and records of the Publisher pertaining to the Work not more than once in any 12-month period during normal office hours on reasonable prior notice. In the event that a deficit of in excess of 10% of total monies in any accounting period is found by such inspection to be outstanding then the Publisher will forthwith pay the cost of such inspection, such cost not to exceed the amount found to be outstanding for payment, together with such amount and interest thereon at 3% above the Bank of England minimum lending rate.

9. The Writer hereby grants the Publisher the right to use the Writer's name, approved likeness and biographical material solely in connection with the publication or exploitation of the Work.

10. The Writer, for himself his heirs and successors in title with the intent that this clause be binding upon them hereby represents warrants undertakes and agrees that he or they will not at any time hereafter assert any moral right in the Work, save for the right of the Writer to be credited as author, or commence or maintain any claim or proceedings in relation to the Work against the Publisher its licensees or successors in title or save as aforesaid perform any of such acts against any other person without the prior written consent of the Publisher. The Writer shall promptly in his name and at the Publisher's request and expense institute or defend any suit action or proceedings which the Publisher shall deem appropriate or necessary for the protection of any moral rights in relation to the Work and if the Writer fails so to do the Writer hereby irrevocably authorises and appoints the Publisher to do any of such acts in the Writer's name. The Writer shall nonetheless fully co-operate with the Publisher in the commencement or defence and maintenance of any such suit action or proceedings and shall hold the Publisher harmless from and against any and all claims costs liabilities and expense arising out of or related to any breach of the Writer's representations, warranties undertakings and agreements contained in this Clause 10.

11. (a) The Writer will on demand at the Publisher's expense execute and sign any documents and do all acts which the Publisher hereafter may reasonably require for the purpose of confirming or further assuring the Publisher's title to the rights assigned or intended to be assigned hereunder.

(b) All notices required to be served hereunder shall be in writing sent to the addressee at his last address notified in writing to the other party by recorded delivery post and shall be deemed served on the date on which it is deposited at the Post Office. Proof of deposit shall be deemed proof of service.

(c) No waiver of any term or condition of this agreement or of any breach of any part thereof shall be deemed a waiver of any other terms or conditions hereof or of any other breach of any part thereof.

(d) Neither party shall have the right to assign transfer or charge this agreement or any of its rights or obligations hereunder without the prior written consent of the other provided that the Publisher may assign this assignment to any third party purchasing all or substantially all of its assets or with whom the Publisher may merge without however relieving itself of its primary liability hereunder it being understood that nothing contained herein shall be deemed to restrict the Publisher's right to licence or assign its rights in the Work to third parties.

(e) The illegality or unenforceability of any part hereof shall not affect the legality or enforceability of the balance hereof.

(f) The provisions hereof constitute the entire agreement between the parties and this agreement may not be modified altered or changed except in writing signed by both parties.

(g) The Writer hereby warrants and undertakes that he has taken independent legal advice as to the terms and conditions hereof.

(h) This agreement shall be construed in accordance with the laws of England whose courts shall have exclusive jurisdiction.

AS WITNESS WHEREOF the parties have hereunto set their hands the day and year first before written

Signed and delivered by the Writer as his Deed:

....

In the presence of:

....

Signed for and on behalf of the Publisher by

....

In the presence of:

....

2. Recording Contract

This is a one-off recording agreement with an independent production company. It lists the royalties you would get (fairly normal) if the company released your records itself, and also what you would get if (as is more likely) it licensed your records to a record company (any AP1 company would be a reasonable definition if the producer objects to 'major').

AN AGREEMENT made this .... day of .... between:

...................of .... (hereinafter called 'the Artist') of the one part and
...................of............... (hereinafter called 'the Company') of the other part

WHEREBY IT IS AGREED AS FOLLOWS:

1. The Artist hereby agrees to render his recording services to the Company for the making of audio and audio-visual recordings and hereby grants and assigns to the Company all copyright and any and all other rights in all the Artist's performances and recordings thereof made hereunder for the Universe ('the Territory') and for the full term of copyright therein and grants to the Company all consents and licences to permit the Company fully to exploit any such recordings made hereunder by any means and in any and all manners. The Artist hereby waives any moral right which he may have against the Company or its licensees. The Artist hereby grants to the Company the right to use his name, approved likeness and biographical material solely in connection with the making and exploitation of recordings hereunder.

2. The Artist shall attend at such times and places as the Company shall reasonably require and render to the best of his ability whether alone or with other artists performances of not less than three musical works. The choice of such musical works, producers (who shall be engaged by the Company) and recording studios shall be specified by the Company but giving due consideration to the wishes of the Artist. The term of this agreement ('the Term') shall commence upon the date hereof and expire upon the date of acceptance by the Company of fully equalised edited two-track stereophonic mixed down tape or disc recordings of the Artist's performances of such musical works which are satisfactory in the reasonable opinion of the Company for the manufacture of records (such recordings being referred to herein as 'the Recordings') together with the original multi-track recordings from which the Recordings were produced. Save as a result of any default by the Artist, the Term shall not extend beyond 6 months from the date hereof. The date of acceptance by the Company shall be deemed to be 45 days following receipt by it of the Recordings together with label copy, any necessary consents and clearances and current Musicians Union numbers of all performers thereon, unless the Company shall give notice within such period of its failure to accept together with the reason(s) therefor.

3. In the event that the Company shall enter into a third party licence agreement in respect of the Recordings then the Company shall pay to the Artist a royalty equivalent to 50% of the Company's 'Net Receipts' which shall mean all fees royalties or other sums received by the Company solely in respect of the Recordings including any so-called synchronisation payments (but excluding any sums payable in respect of the phonographic performance rights or video performance rights in the recordings) less any and all proper and reasonable costs incurred by the Company in the making of the Recordings including without limitation the following:
All costs of tape, equipment, musicians, and singers and any other costs incurred directly in the recording of the Recordings save for costs of the Company's in-house studio and in-house engineer,
Royalties and fees payable to any producer, mixer or remixer of the Recordings,
All reasonable costs incurred by the Company in the conclusion of any licence agreement in respect of the Recordings, it being agreed however that all recording and pre-production costs excluding manufacturing costs but including any sums paid by the Company at its discretion in respect of rehearsals, clothing, hair-styling, choreography, car hire and per diems and any amount by which the agreed recording budget for the Recordings, if any, shall be exceeded through the actions or at the behest of the Artist without the prior written consent of the Company, shall be fully recoupable against all income, save for mechanical royalties payable in respect of the musical works embodied on the Recordings, becoming due to the Artist hereunder, which shall be recouped 'off the top' before the balance of any royalties or advances are divided between the parties hereto as provided for above.

4. In the event that the Company shall manufacture distribute and sell records itself derived from the Recordings then the Company shall pay to the Artist a royalty equivalent to 16% in respect of UK sales and 12% in respect of non-UK sales ('the Royalty') based on 90% of all sales less only bona fide returns calculated on the published price to dealers of records after tax and the packaging deductions listed below and after deduction of any and all reasonable and proper costs incurred by the Company as set out in this Clause and Clause 3 hereof. The term 'records' as used herein shall mean any and all forms of physical embodiment of sound with or without visual images manufactured and/or distributed for sale to the public by any means now or hereafter known.

5. The following packaging deductions shall be applied to the Royalty: 10% for 7" or 12" singles in special sleeves, 15% for single-fold vinyl albums in plain inner bags, 20% for double-fold and gatefold- albums and singles and for CDs in 'jewel cases', 25% for boxed sets, 30% for DVD's
The Royalty in respect of the following categories of records shall be 50% of that stated under Clause 4 hereof: Low price and budget records under 75% of the full price, multi-album packages, audio-visual CDs up to 10,000 units on a format by format, territory by territory and release by release basis, television-advertised records (solely in respect of sales in the country where television advertising takes place), soundtrack albums, compilations and mini-albums
The Royalty shall be 50% of that stated under Clause 4 hereof or 50% of the Company's net receipts whichever shall be the greater in respect of records sold by mail order and through record-clubs on a royalty basis by a bona-fide third party on arms-length terms, records sold to charities, libraries or military bases and so-called premium records.

No Royalty shall be paid in respect of deletions, scrap records and records for which the Company shall receive no payment, picture and/or non-standard shaped discs, free and promotional records actually and solely promoting the Recordings.

The Royalty shall only be paid during the life of copyright of the Recordings in the country of sale and shall be reduced pro rata in respect of records embodying the Recordings and other recordings.

6. Mechanical royalties shall be borne by the Company or its licensees it being agreed however that in respect of sales in the USA and Canada of Recordings embodying musical works in which the Artist has an interest as copyright owner the mechanical royalty payable shall, to the extent of that interest, be limited to 75% of the minimum statutory rate at the date of first release thereof subject to a maximum of 12 times such rate for albums and three times such rate for singles save that the Company will use reasonable endeavours to obtain higher rates and more favourable provisions in respect thereof from any licensee(s) in the USA & Canada in which case such more favourable rates and provisions shall apply. The Artist hereby grants to the Company an all-media worldwide synchronisation licence in respect of music videos free of charge for promotional use in respect of any such musical works and at a one-off non-recoupable fee of £100 in respect of the commercial exploitation of such videos. In all other countries the Artist will procure the grant to the Company of a mechanical licence for such musical works at the prevailing rate.

7. (a) The Company shall account to the Artist all sums due hereunder within 30 days following the Company's receipt thereof from third parties.

(b) The Company shall be entitled to retain reasonable reserves against records shipped but unsold which reserves shall be liquidated within 2 accounting periods of creation thereof (3 in respect of USA & Canada sales) by equal instalments or as liquidated by the Company's licensees.

(c) The Artist shall have the right to appoint a professional accountant to audit the books and records of the Company relating to sales of records hereunder not more than once in any 12-month period upon reasonable prior notice in normal office hours. No statement may be objected to by the Artist more than three years after such statement was rendered.

8. The Company shall originate and pay for all artwork in connection with the sale and exploitation of records derived from the Recordings and the Artist shall be entitled to use any such artwork for merchandising purposes under exclusive licence from the Company on payment of 50% of the cost thereof subject however to any limitations upon the Company's control thereof under any licensing agreements concluded by the Company for the Recordings hereunder. However the Company shall have no so-called 'merchandising rights' hereunder save in respect of the sale and exploitation of records derived from the Recordings.

9. The Artist hereby undertakes not to re-record any musical works embodied in the Recordings for any other party within the period of five years from the date of first release thereof by the Company or its licensees hereunder.

10. In the event that the Company shall produce or procure at its discretion but after consultation with the Artist, the production of a promotional video in respect of any or all of the Recordings then 50% of the cost to the Company thereof shall be treated as an advance to the Artist against income from such promotional video and the remaining 50% against income from any other sources.

11. The Artist undertakes to assist the Company upon reasonable prior notice in the promotion of records derived from the Recordings including without limitation attending at photographic and/or publicity receptions and radio and television appearances, the reasonable and approved cost to the Artist thereof to be reimbursed to the Artist by the Company.

12. The Artist hereby warrants and represents that he is over 18 years of age and has taken full independent legal advice from a solicitor experienced in the music industry as to the terms hereof and that he is free to enter into this agreement and to grant the rights granted herein and the Artist hereby agrees to indemnify the Company against any claims demands or expenses made against the Company as a consequence of the breach of any of the Artist's warranties hereunder which claim, demand or expense has been adjudicated by a court of competent jurisdiction or agreed pursuant to a settlement made with the consent of the Artist.

13. (a) The Company shall be free to license or assign any or all of its rights hereunder.

(b) Unless otherwise stated herein the Artist's consent where required herein shall not be unreasonably withheld or delayed and shall be deemed given within 5 working days of his receipt of written request therefor unless approved or rejected prior to such date.

(c) The Artist undertakes not to render his recording services to any other party during the Term without the prior written consent of the Company, such consent not to be unreasonably withheld.

(d) This agreement shall be construed in accordance with the laws of England whose courts shall have exclusive jurisdiction.

....
The Artist   The Company

132

3. Artist/Manager long-term agreement

Here is the sort of general management agreement you may well wind up with. These terms are reasonably favourable to you. When the deal is first offered it may not contain these limitations on the amount the manager can spend without asking you, the length of time he goes on getting his commission or the extent of the earnings he gets commission on. These are the least 'standard' sort of agreements and both the wording and the terms vary enormously. Many management contracts are much longer than this but they are generally only covering, in more detail, the same points as this one. There might be an additional clause stating that he can renew the term of the agreement for a further period (this should be at most two years more) if you've earned, or else he's advanced you, a stated large sum of money by the time the agreement ends. There is no catch here. If you've made that much money (excluding any income in the 'pipeline') then you're obviously succeeding, and good management is so important that this will almost certainly have been partly down to your manager. If you haven't earned that amount, then you are free to leave or re-negotiate, unless he has such faith in you that he's prepared to pay you that amount anyway just to keep you. It is worth bearing in mind that many artists have happy (and very long and successful) relationships with their management. Some of the accounting provisions (which are common to most music business agreements) in this and the recording agreement are abbreviated, and are more fully set out in the publishing agreement.

AN AGREEMENT made this .... day of ....between
........................of ....hereinafter called 'the Artist' of the one part and
........................of ....hereinafter called 'the Manager' of the other part

WHEREIN IT IS AGREED AS FOLLOWS:

1. The Artist hereby appoints the Manager to act and the Manager hereby agrees to act as the sole and exclusive manager throughout the Universe of the Artist in connection with all his activities in the entertainment industry including but not limited to:
    (a) the performance of musical works in concert, for broadcast via radio television or otherwise, and the recording of performances in films or other audio-visual media and any other media
    (b) the recording of musical works and the exploitation thereof by means of broadcast, sale or in the form of records, audio-visual devices or otherwise
    (c) the composition and exploitation of musical works by any means
    (d) merchandising and sponsorship.

2. This appointment shall be for a period of 3 years ('the Term') from the date hereof IT BEING UNDERSTOOD that in the event that upon the expiration of one year from the date hereof the Artist shall not have entered into an agreement reasonably acceptable to the Artist with a so-called major record company then the Artist shall be entitled to terminate this agreement forthwith.

3. The Manager agrees to use his best commercial endeavours to enhance and develop the career of the Artist in the entertainment industry and generally to render all services customarily rendered by a manager in such industry and in consideration of his services the Manager will be entitled to a fee equal to 20% of all gross monies (subject to Clause 5c hereof and exclusive of VAT or any similar tax) received by the Artist or by a company controlled by the Artist on his behalf during the Term and arising from any of the Artist's activities in the entertainment industry whether as a result of an agreement or arrangement negotiated by the Manager or otherwise and of all gross monies received by the Artist after the expiry of the Term but arising from an agreement entered into or subsequently negotiated during the Term, or in substitution of any such agreement, provided however that the Manager shall not be entitled to a fee in respect of:
    (a) the exploitation of records featuring the performances on master recordings of the Artist recorded after the expiry of the Term or prior to the commencement of the Term if already exploited
    (b) the exploitation of musical works written by the Artist after the expiry of the Term or prior to the commencement of the Term if already exploited

Notwithstanding the foregoing the Manager shall not be entitled to a fee on any monies advanced to the Artist for recording or video costs, tour support, or any third party producers mixers or remixers advances.
    (c) The Manager's fee in respect of income from live concert performances shall be calculated on the net income therefrom i.e. gross income less all bona fide expenses incurred in connection therewith
    (d) The Manager's fee shall be reduced to 10% three years following the expiry of the Term and shall cease to be payable 10 years following the expiry of the Term.

4. (a) The Artist hereby appoints the Manager to collect and receive all monies payable to him during the Term arising from his activities within the entertainment industry prior to or during the Term subject to the terms hereof and the Artist shall irrevocably direct all third parties to make payments accordingly. All such monies shall be paid into a specially designated account in the Artist's name but under the Manager's control and the Manager shall keep the Artist's monies in such account strictly separate from the Manager's income or that of any other artist.
    (b) The Manager shall keep accurate and up to date books of account showing all monies received by him on the Artist's behalf and the Artist shall have the right to inspect such books and records upon reasonable notice during normal office hours.
    (c) The Manager shall be entitled to deduct his fee and any expenses to be reimbursed to him pursuant hereto from monies collected on the Artist's behalf and shall send a statement as at 1st. Jan., lst. April, 1st. July and 1st. October in each year of the Term showing all monies received by him and paid or retained by him during the preceding 3 month period to the Artist within 60 days thereafter and shall pay the balance of all sums due to the Artist simultaneously therewith
    (d) Notwithstanding the above if at any time the Manager shall hold monies in excess of £5,000 he hereby agrees to pay over the excess on demand after deducting his fee and any expenses properly incurred by him hereunder
    (e) After the expiry of the Term the Artist shall render statements and keep books and records of account in respect of receipts by him after the Term in the same manner as set forth in (a) and (b) hereof and the Manager shall have the same right of inspection thereof as is granted under (b) hereof
    (f) All payments to the Manager hereunder are exclusive of VAT which shall be paid by the Artist in addition thereto upon receipt of a VAT invoice from the Manager therefor.

5. The Artist shall bear any commission payable to any so-called 'booking agent' in respect of live performances or to any agent appointed by him in respect of his acting or other activities within the entertainment industry.

6. The Artist hereby grants to the Manager power of attorney to sign agreements for one-off live appearances on his behalf but any other offers of work shall be referred to the Artist for approval and signature of agreements in respect thereof, and the Manager shall not incur any one item of expenditure in excess of £750 without the prior written consent of the Artist, not to be unreasonably withheld or delayed.

7. In the event that the Manager shall become insolvent or is adjudicated bankrupt or shall make any composition with his creditors or in the event that .... (key man) shall cease to be a director of the Manager then the Artist shall have the right to terminate the Term forthwith.

8. The Manager shall be solely responsible for the Manager's normal office expenses. Any other expenses reasonably and necessarily incurred by the Manager specifically in connection with the performance of the Manager's obligations hereunder shall be reimbursed by the Artist within 30 days of the Artist's receipt of the relevant invoices. If the Manager or any employee of the Manager shall travel on the Artist's behalf (in which event the Manager or such employee shall enjoy the same standard of

accomodation, form of travel etc. as the Artist) the Artist shall reimburse the Manager's or such employee's travel, accommodation and subsistence expenses.

9. (a) Any notice to be served by either party hereunder shall be in writing to the last address of the other party notified in writing by recorded delivery and the date of service thereof shall be deemed to be the date upon which such notice was delivered to the Post Office

(b) The Artist shall be solely responsible for his personal tax and national insurance payments and arrangements

(c) The Artist hereby warrants that he has taken independent legal advice on the terms hereof from a solicitor specialising in the entertainment industry and confirms that he has read and understands the terms hereof

(d) This agreement represents the sole agreement between the parties hereto. Any amendment or modification hereto shall be in writing and signed by both parties.

(e) This agreement shall be construed in accordance with the laws of England whose courts shall have exclusive jurisdiction.

Signed by   Signed by

....
The Artist   The Manager

4. Artist Venue Agreement (through an agency)

An Agreement

made this.........day of ....between...............
(hereinafter referred to as ''the Management'') of the one part and........................
(hereinafter referred to as ''the Artiste'') of the other part

WHEREBY IT IS AGREED as follows:-

1. THAT the Management engages the Artiste and the Artiste accepts the engagement to appear as known at the following venue from the date(s) for the period and at the salary set forth below

Date(s) ....

Venue ....

Salary ....

2. IT is agreed that the Artiste shall arrive at .... and perform his/their usual and known act for a period of .... hours divided into .... sessions as arranged with the Management terminating not later than ....

3. THE Artiste shall not without the written consent of the Management perform at any other public place of entertainment within a radius of   miles of the venue during a period of .... weeks prior to and.........weeks following this engagement.

4. THE salary shall be payable by.................. to ....

5. THE Management undertakes to provide adequate dressing room facilities for the Artiste.

AS WITNESS the hands of the parties hereto the day and year first before written.

....
for and on behalf of
  the Management

....
The Artiste

Here is the sort of agreement submitted to an artist or to his manager for him to sign for a specific booking or series of bookings. ('Management' here means the owner of the venue, not the artist's manager.)

This form of agreement is quite normal and acceptable. The ideal form of payment is 'by cash to the Artiste on the night', preferably before you perform, but normally afterwards. If a singer or group wishes to take more than just a couple of roadies or a sound engineer to a venue, it's just as well to check by phone beforehand.

The clause in this particular form of agreement that you must watch out for is Clause 3. The radius is often about 15 miles, and if you are playing at different London suburbs every night for a week it is quite unreasonable for the management of one venue to make you agree to this, especially when you are comparatively little-known and the venues are private functions several miles apart. In such a case, in law this would probably amount to a 'restraint of your trade' and be unenforceable. But it's much better to try to have it deleted before you perform, to save misunderstandings and bad feelings. It really only exists for public concerts where a good turnout would actually be noticeably affected by your being billed to play at another local venue at around the same date.

Another clause that is often included is one in which you undertake that you will not deal directly with the venue for around the next two years and thereby cut out the agency. As we have said, this is quite understandable if it was through the agent that you came to know of the venue in the first place.

5. Simple agreement to perform at a venue

If you are securing engagements yourself and are dealing with a venue that is not regularly booking acts, or where the management is a bit casual as to paperwork, they may ask you to write and confirm a phone booking, in which case the following is really quite adequate in most cases, typed in duplicate, signed by you and sent to the management of the venue. You could add that a cancellation fee of, say, 50% is payable if cancelled less than a month before, but you risk putting yourself in a position where they could expect you to pay them if you suddenly discovered you couldn't make it.

```
                                        Artists address

                                        date



    Dear ...............

    This will serve to confirm that..............(the artist)

    is booked to perform at....................on...........

    ............(date) from...............until..............

    with suitable breaks for a fee of £............... payable

    in cash on the night.


    If you are in agreement with this please sign in the

    place provided below, and return one copy to me.


    Yours sincerely,




    ..............................
    (the Artist)
     read and agreed




    ..............................
    (the Management)
```

QUICK REFERENCE

INSTANT GUIDE TO ROYALTIES

A summary of the royalties and terms that can be expected from publishers, record companies, managers and agents. Royalties, dealer prices, calculations of fees etc. vary substantially between one company and another, one country and another, and from one year to the next, so remember that these calculations of actual money you might receive, like the others in the book, are only a very rough guide to what you might get in any particular situation.

PUBLISHING CONTRACTS

Printed Music (including downloads)

10–15% of the UK retail selling price for all UK sheet music sales of individual songs (pro-rata in folios or music books). If the books are not actually produced by your publisher, however, they'll pay you the same rate as they would on mechanical royalties from what they get from a specialist company – say, 60–85%.

Recorded Music Royalties

60–85% of all record royalties from UK (known as 'Mechanicals'), which the record company pays to the MCPS at 8.5% of the published price to dealers (around 2/3rds of the retail price – 'the rsp') less VAT. On a 70/30 deal with the publisher you might get around 10p per single where you wrote all the mixes, and from around 4p per track generally for a 14-track CD depending on the length of the tracks. So you'd get around £40,000 for 100,000 albums, based on a PDP for a full-priced album of £7. (Bear in mind that the PDP may be up to £1 more, in which case the figures would need to be increased by around 10%). It would be much less for budget compilations (e.g. well below 1p per track for a 40-track £4.99 rsp album). Long-form music DVDs attract a rate at the MCPS of 6.5% of PDP, non-music DVDs (if not bought-out, as music in films commonly is) a rate based on the proportion of music to non music in the film and 8.5% of PDP.

The same percentages apply for overseas mechanicals from an 'at source' deal or a 'receipts' deal, the difference being that for an 'at source' deal you receive your contractual share of what the overseas publisher collects, whereas under a 'receipts deal' you receive your share of what your local publisher received from the overseas publisher (ie. less their commission of, say, 15–30%). So under a receipts deal, a track on a US album should bring in roughly the same rate of royalties as in the UK, but you might be down to as little as 2p per track on a full-price album and, if controlled composition clauses apply (see definition), it might be only around 70% of that.

Your standard mechanical rate will apply (unless you negotiate otherwise) for Internet downloads, which will be licensed by the MCPS at 8% of the gross revenues of the online service.

You'll usually get a slightly lower percentage on 'covers' (records not recorded or produced by you that your publisher goes out and gets).

Other types of mechanicals, such as newspaper giveaways or music-based video games, should attract your standard mechanical rate and are licensed under schemes that you can check out on the MCPS/PRS website.

Performing/broadcasting royalties

60–85% of the total of performing royalties. Join the PRS as soon as you are eligible and you will receive 50% of the total performing royalties directly from them (including of the income collected by foreign societies and passed on to the PRS on your behalf). The publisher (and its overseas sub-publishers) will collect the remaining 50% from the PRS (and the overseas societies) and pay you between 20–70% of that. Again, the receipts or at source contracts will also affect this. So you end up with 60–85%. The obvious advantage of joining the PRS is, therefore, that your publisher will not collect that 50% of performance income and will not be able to count that against your advance (though the terms of your agreement would usually prevent this).

The PRS pays out from less than £1 to over £10 per minute for UK radio broadcasts, depending on the audience size and/or advertising revenue of the radio station, and up to around £150 for your three-minute song on network TV (this rate varies and increases in peak times and decreases off-peak). Do remember that 'sampling' still operates with many local radio stations, unless your song was recorded locally (i.e. specifically used on your local station), in which case tell the PRS if you don't get paid. Otherwise, remember that if your song isn't actually a hit (or maybe only in the clubs) and you don't get plays on national radio, you may miss out on samples on local radio and the income could be lower than expected.

Synchronisation fees

You get 60–85% of these, probably nearer 60% if your publisher went out and got the deal (rather than waited for an agency or film company to ring and ask). Your publisher can get a synch fee of around £30,000 for a year's use in a network UK television commercial for a recent UK hit, around £10,000 for a commercial on network radio, £10,000 for satellite and cable, £10,000 for cinema and perhaps another £12,000 if they want to include television in the Republic of Eire. There will be more money if a company wants to embed the commercial on their website or to use the music on a site tied into the commercial. These figures can vary wildly depending on the international success of the song, whether the licence is exclusive for a period of time, and territories involved. Usually, these figures would be negotiated down substantially,

in fact very substantially, as a sort of group discount, if the user wants all these media. You'd get much more for a really big song, but much less for a 'dormant' song where you and the publisher are happy just to get it used at all. Similar amounts are possible in other major countries, but less than you might think for an international campaign (say, £200,000 for television for a year in the whole of Europe for a well-known song or recent hit, unless it's really big).

You'll get around £10,000–£20,000 for synch use of a song in a film, plus another £3,000 or so for a 'video/DVD buyout', but again this varies hugely according to the importance of the song and film, and could be substantially lower than the bottom of this scale or higher than the top. Competition to get music in films means that this area is substantially less lucrative than you might imagine, but as a one-off bonus and a profile-raiser, it can be valuable nonetheless.

You can expect similar fees for use of a commercial hit in a 'triple A' video game, though unless the game is entirely music based (such as *Singstar*) and covered by the relevant MCPS licensing scheme, then this will include a buyout of mechanicals. It is still most often the case that video game companies use bought-out commissioned music.

An international number one hit can easily bring in upwards of £500,000 from all these sources over, say, 3–5 years (more if it takes off in the US and/or Japan).

Lots of other smaller audio-visual and 'new media' uses are possible, although smaller synch fees will apply.

Miscellaneous

60–85% of miscellaneous (i.e. of everything else the publisher gets).

No deductions

Royalties are paid on 100% of income received by your publisher from sales of records, videos, downloads and printed music etc., with no deductions except for the commissions already deducted by collection societies for their costs.

RECORD CONTRACTS

Royalties on sales

Even for an unknown act, around 16–18% of the published price to dealers (i.e. the wholesale price), maybe around two-thirds of this for foreign sales. For a full-price UK album – your royalty at 16% would be just under £1.25–£1.30 in total, but more like 90p after deductions and reductions, say £90,000 for 100,000 sales. (This is based on a conservative PDP price of £8 but, as we've said, it's possible that the PDP may be as much as £9, and so you'd have to increase these figures by around 10%). If the record company is offering a deal without these deductions, the basic royalty may be only 14–15% but will amount to roughly the same in cash terms.

For a number one dance single your royalty would be around 40p per unit, but again this is before deduction of packaging allowances, free goods etc., which might knock around 30% off. So on a royalty of 16% of PDP you get around 25p per single (say, £25,000 for 100,000 sales). If the record company gives away or sells cheaply a lot of records to chain stores etc., it could be less.

Broadcast performance

PPL will collect this income and divide it equally between you and the record company (in their role as owner of the master) – this can be a five figure sum for a number one hit. You should be able to collect your share directly through PPL or via PAMRA or AURA (phonographic performance royalties for broadcasts and performances of your recordings). These societies will collect similar royalties from sister societies abroad if you authorise them to do so.

Synchronisation fees

For uses of recordings in commercials, films etc. the fees are generally very much the same as for the songs used in them, unless it's a big song and an unknown artist or unless it's very much cheaper for the user to re-record it rather than pay the fee (see under Publishing Contracts). In that case your record company will not ask too much. Of course, if the agency or their client really want you (the famous artist), and not just someone who sounds like you, to be appearing to endorse their product, then you should receive a great deal more. In any event, whether you like the product or not, you should have approval of uses for commercials.

Deductions

Unless you've done a new-style limited deductions deal with an overall lower rate, it's likely that all recording costs, royalties to producer, costs of remixes, even tour support and other money (but not general PR and advertising budget), plus half the cost (anywhere from £10–100,000 or more) of making promo videos, will come out of your artist royalties under your agreement with your record company. Remember, if your first album's big but the second album bombs, you won't get any more artist royalties on the first till they've recovered their losses on the second and so forth. Also, remember that 50% of video production costs come out of your royalties too!

Reductions

Royalties are usually paid on 90% or less of actual sales. Royalties are usually less 20% packaging deductions.

Notes on deals

Try to get a commitment to make at least one album, but there's no particular benefit in being offered a five-album deal, as the second and subsequent albums, and the budgets and advance royalties that go with them, will almost certainly be at the label's option. If the first album flops they won't take up the options, and if it doesn't, you'll most likely be renegotiating in any case.

Remember you should continue to receive royalties on sales and uses of your records long after you've gone to another company.

Don't sign away your publishing or merchandising rights under the same contract as your recording rights even for what look like reasonable fees. (This is not least because the record company would be able to offset income from one against losses on another before you were paid anything at all, even if they could get the same deal from a specialist company for merchandising, as your manager could.)

Remember, the label generally doesn't absolutely guarantee to release your records (an independent producer simply can't), but should guarantee to record a certain number of songs per year or help fund the recordings (at least half the money for each album on signing, or taking up the option, with maybe 25% on delivery of the album and 25% on release). They should also agree to give back the UK rights around six to nine months after you deliver the record if they don't release it, as well as ROW (rest of the world) rights if the local licensees/distributors don't release it within a few months of the UK release date (they should at least agree to license it to a company you nominate if you can find one).

Whether you write your own material or not, there will be 'controlled composition' clauses for US release (see Glossary).

MANAGEMENT AND AGENCY CONTRACTS

The manager's commission will usually be 20%. This will probably be based on gross earnings on publishing and recording deals and on net earnings from live performances (i.e. after costs of putting on the show/tour etc.). The methods of calculation vary enormously.

An agent's commission ought to be around 15% of fees for gigs he secures for you. In your early career, you'll probably collect and pay his commission to him. Later he'll do all the negotiations, collect the fee, deduct his commission and then pay you.

Acts playing music for dancing, theme parties, weddings, cabaret etc. should get £50–£100 per person depending on the venue, distance travelled, duration and time the gig ends. A top-flight band with no record deal could easily make £1,000 with £2,000–4,000 upwards for an act who have had chart hits, even if the line-up isn't original. A dance act with a UK hit could make £1,000–2,000 or more per PA at clubs etc. A really big act on a big US tour can gross £500,000 or even more per performance, but may not make a cent after deducting all expenses.

Acts (if they're not yet well-known) playing prestigious clubs and touring as support for top acts will probably have to pay for the privilege – maybe £150 or so to the club per performance, and £500–£1,000 per night to be on someone else's tour.

Merchandising can be big business. A relatively big act can still get £50,000 or so as an advance from a merchandiser for a tour, against a share of around 30% of the retail price, less taxes and less the 25% that goes to the venue. A merchandiser might hope for a spend of around £8 per head at live concerts, so, for the right sort of acts (which generally means 'rock') you could be looking at around £15,000 for the artist just for one 10,000-seater concert. The more eye-catching your name and logo the better, although if you haven't registered your name/logo, it's likely that you'll get much much less, as there's a lot less protection against counterfeit goods.

Notes

1. As soon as you have a manager and start to earn through him, you need your own independent accountant (preferably not one recommended by your manager, just to be on the safe side).
2. Don't give away too much control of your career for too long to a non-

professional manager, and be absolutely sure he can't claim 20% of your first number one hit under his old agreement!

3. If you're in a band and then leave, you're almost certainly still bound as an individual to all the contracts that you, or your manager, have signed. If you join a band that already has contracts, you will probably be required to become bound by theirs as well.

4. Most management contracts cover all aspects of the music and entertainment business, down to writing articles and books and opening supermarkets. A manager will expect to start receiving your income and keeping a share even on deals that you may already have in place; try to limit or resist this if possible.

5. Don't give him a power of attorney that commits you to any expenditure over a few hundred pounds at one time or that allows him to sign away your publishing, recording or merchandising rights without consultation and approval.

6. Try to negotiate at the start that his share of your income on deals made during his term as manager ceases as soon as possible after he stops being your manager (for example, no more than three to five years at full rate and another five to 10 at half rate). Also, try to ensure that he doesn't get commission on any albums you make or songs you write after he ceases to be your manager (which he might try to do if you remain signed to the record company or publisher who he introduced you to).

Last but by no means least, do get a lawyer to check, and if necessary nitpick, before you sign anything, but remember that unless the deal is utterly dreadful, the lawyer will push only as hard as you want him to. It's worth the money and he may even get the people you're signing with to pay his fee as an advance. Do take away and read any agreements before signing and, if there is anything you don't understand, ask your lawyer. If someone expects you to sign it there and then, it may be unenforceable later, but do you really want the hassle of arguing about it? Ask questions, even if you're afraid they might sound a bit dumb.

Don't just sign the first deal you're offered if you can see, having read this book, that it's not a good one. No matter how tempting it is, don't think that the first company to offer you a deal is doing you a huge favour by signing you up. Very few people will do you a favour that might cost them money – even if you have contacts in the business. Unless your contact is the managing director of the company then you can't really expect them to be in a position to do you a favour anyway. Ultimately, it's down to having enough faith in yourself to believe that you really can make a good living (or a fortune) in the music business, and that if they don't sign you it's their loss. That way, you'll almost certainly get a better deal, if not from them, then from someone else. Keep your head screwed on, and good luck.

Publicity stunt? Oh no... he's just having a quiet swim with his agent.

A LIST OF USEFUL ADDRESSES

The best suggestion for further reading is to keep up with what's being written online and in the newspapers and magazines comprising the British music press. The following list includes some relevant magazine or publisher addresses and websites.

The following list also includes some of the firms of lawyers and accountants who specialise in the music business, some of the various organisations that may be of help to you, and also a list of some of the UK TV broadcasters and production companies.

There are now so many local, digital and Internet radio stations in the UK that a complete list would be pages long. You are probably familiar with your local ones and the addresses of others can be found on the web.

Finally, we've listed some other websites that are part of the new approach to the music business in the digital age.

PUBLICATIONS

BBC Music Magazine
14th Floor, Tower House
Fairfax Street
Bristol BS1 3BN
www.bbcmusicmagazine.com
(0117 927 9009)

Billboard (UK address)
5th Floor 189 Shaftesbury Ave
London WC2H 8JT
www.billboard.biz (020 7420 6003)

Blues & Soul
153 Praed Street
London W2 1RL
www.bluesandsoul.com (020 7402 6869)

City Life
164 Deansgate
Manchester M3 3RN
www.citylife.co.uk (0161 832 7200)

City Living
1st Floor, Weaman Street
Birmingham B4 6AT
www.icbirmingham.icnetwork.co.uk/city living/ (0121 234 5653)

Classic FM Magazine
38–42 Hampton Road,
Teddington
Middx. TW11 0JE
www.classicfm.com (020 8267 5180)

Computer Music
www.computermusic.co.uk
(see Future Publishing)

Country Music People
1–3 Love Lane
London SE18 6QT
www.countrymusicpeople.com
(020 8854 7217)

Dazed & Confused
112 Old Street
London EC1V 9BG
www.dazeddigital.com
(020 7336 0766)

DJ Magazine
Highgate Studios
53–79 Highgate Road
London NW5 1TW
www.djmag.com
(020 7331 1148)

EMAP Metro
4 Winsley St.
London W1R 7AR
www.emap.com (020 7436 1515)

Essential Newcastle
5–11 Causey Street
Newcastle-Upon-Tyne NE3 4DJ
(0191 284 9994)

Folk Music Journal
Cecil Sharp House
2 Regent's Park Rd
London NW1 7AY
www.efdss.org (020 7485 2206)

Future Publishing
30 Monmouth Street
Bath
Somerset BA1 2BW
www.futurenet.co.uk (01225 442 244)

Future Music
www.futuremusic.com
(see Future Publishing)

Guitar & Bass
www.guitarmagazine.co.uk
(see IPC Media)

Hip Hop Connection
PO Box 392
Cambridge CB1 3WH
www.hhcmagazine.com (01223 210 536)

Hit Sheet
31 The Birches
London N21 1NJ
www.hitsheet.co.uk (020 8360 4088)

Kerrang!
www.kerrang.com (see EMAP Metro)

The List
14 High Street
Edinburgh EH1 1TE
www.list.co.uk (0131 550 3050)

Metal Hammer
99 Baker Street
London W1U 6FP
www.metalhammer.co.uk
(020 7317 2688)

Music & Media
50–51 Bedford Row,
London WC1R 4LR
(020 7822 8300)

Music Week
245 Blackfriars Road
London SE1 9LS
www.musicweek.com (020 7921 8346)

New Musical Express (NME)
110 Southwark St
London SE1 0SU
www.nme.com (0207 261 5813)

Performing Musician
(see Sound On Sound)

Q
www.qonline.co.uk (see EMAP Metro)

Songlink International
23 Belsize Crescent
London NW3 5QY
www.songlink.com (020 7794 2540)

Songwriter Magazine
PO Box 46
Limerick
Eire
www.songwriter.co.uk (+353 61 228 837)

Sound on Sound
Media House
Trafalgar Way
Bar Hill
Cambs CB23 8SQ
www.sooundonsound.com
(01954 789 888)

The Stage
47 Bermondsey St,
London SE1 3XT
www.thestage.co.uk (020 7403 1818)

Time Out
251 Tottenham Court Road
London W1T 7AB
www.timeout.com (020 7813 3000)

Top of the Pops Magazine
Room A1136, 80 Wood Lane
London W12 0TT
www.totpmag.com (020 8433 3910)

Uncut
110 Southward St
London SE1 0SU
www.uncut.co.uk

The Voice
8th–9th Flr. Blue Star House
234–244 Stockwell Road,
London SW9 9UG
www.voice-online.co.uk
(020 7737 7377)

SOLICITORS

Bray and Krais
Suite 10, Fulham Business Exchange
The Boulevard
Imperial Wharf
London SW6 2TL
(020 7384 3050)

Clintons
55 Drury Lane
London WC2B 5RZ
www.clintons.co.uk
(020 7379 6080)

Collyer Bristow
4 Bedford Row,
London WC1R 4DF
www.collyerbristow.com
(020 7242 7363)

Davenport Lyons
30 Old Burlington Street
London W1S 3NL
www.davenportlyons.com
(020 7468 2600)

David Wineman
121 Kingsway
London WC2B 6NX
www.davidwineman.co.uk
(020 7400 7800)

Dean Marsh
73a Middle Street
Brighton BN1 1Al
www.deanmarsh.com (01273 823 770)

Engel Monjack
16–18 Berners Street
London W1T 3LN
www.engelmonjack.com
(020 7291 3838)

ELA
2 Queen Caroline Street
London W6 9DX
www.ela.co.uk (020 8323 8013)

Field Fisher Waterhouse
35 Vine Street
London EC3N 2AA
www.ffw.com (020 7861 4000)

Forbes Anderson Free
16–18 Berners Street
London W1T 3LN
(020 7291 3500)

Harbottle & Lewis
14 Hanover Square
London W1S 1HP
www.harbottle.com
(020 7667 5000)

Lea & Co.
Bank Chambers
Market Place
Stockport
Cheshire SK1 1UN
www.lealaw.com (0161 480 6691)

Leonard Lowy & Co.
500 Chiswick High Rd.
London W4 5RG
www.leonardlowy.co.uk
(020 8956 2785)

Magrath & Co.
66/67 Newman Street
London W1T 3EQ
www.magrath.co.uk
(020 7495 3003)

Michael Simkins LLP
45–51 Whitfield Street
London W1T 4HB
www.simkins.co.uk
(020 7907 3000)

Olswang
90 High Holborn
London WC1V 6XX
www.olswang.com
(020 7067 3000)

P. Russell & Co.
Suite 61, 271 King Street
London W6 9LZ
(020 8233 2943)

Robin Morton & Co.
27 Herbert Street
Glasgow G20 6NB
(0141 560 2748)

Russells
1–4 Warwick Street
London W1B 5LJ
www.russellslaw.co.uk
(020 7439 8692)

Schillings
72–74 Dean Street
London W1D 3TL
www.schillings.co.uk
(020 7453 2500)

Sheridans
Whittington House
Alfred Place
London WC1E 7EA
www.sheridans.co.uk
(020 779 0100)

SSB
91 Peterborough Road
London SW6 3BU
www.ssb.co.uk (020 7348 7630)

Taylor Wessing
50 Victoria Embankment
London EC4Y 0DX
www.taylorwessing.com
(020 7300 7000)

Teacher Stern Selby
37–41 Bedford Row
London WC1R 4JH
www.tsslaw.com (020 7242 3191)

Tods Murray LLP
Edinburgh Quay
133 Fountainbridge
Edinburgh EH3 9AG
www.todsmurray.com
(0131 656 2000)

ACCOUNTANTS

Baker Tilly
2 Bloomsbury Street
London WC1B 3ST
www.bakertilly.co.uk (020 7413 5100)

Bevis & Co
6 West Street
Epsom
Surrey KT18 7RG
www.bevisandco.co.uk
(01372 840 280)

Bowker Orford
15–19 Cavendish Place
London W1G 0DD
(020 7636 6391)

Brebner Allen & Trapp
180 Wardour Street
London W1F 8LB
www.brebner.co.uk (020 7734 2244)

Carnmores Royalties Consultants
Chelsea Business Centre
73–77 Britannia Road
London SW6 2JR
(020 7384 3216)

Deloitte & Touche
180 Strand
London WC2R 1BL
www.deloitte.co.uk
(020 7936 3000)

**Entertainment Accounting
International**
26a Winders Road,
London SW11 3HB
(020 7978 4488)

Ernst & Young
1 More London Place
London SE1 2AF
www.ey.com (020 7951 2000)

Freedman Frankl & Taylor
31 King Street West
Manchester M3 2PJ
www.fft.co.uk (0161 834 2574)

Gelfand Rennert Feldman & Brown
1b Portland Place
London W1B 1GR
(020 7636 1776)

Grant Thornton
Grant Thornton House
Melton Street
London NW1 2EP
www.grant-thornton.co.uk
(020 7383 5100)

Harris & Trotter
65 New Cavendish St.
London W1G 7LS
www.harrisandtrotter.co.uk
(020 7467 6300)

KPMG
31 Fishpool Street
St Albans AL3 4RF
www.kpmg.com (01727 733 000)

Newman & Co
1 Pratt Mews
London NW1 0AD
www.newman-and.co.uk
(020 7554 4840)

MMG @ MGR
55 Loudoun Road
St John's Wood
London NW8 0DL
www.mmguk.com (020 7625 4545)

O J Kilkenny
6 Lansdowne Mews
London W11 3BH
(020 7792 9494)

Prager & Fenton
8th Floor, Imperial House
15–19 Kingsway
London WC2B 6UN
www.pragerfenton.co.uk
(020 7632 1400)

PricewaterhouseCoopers
1 Embankment Place
London WC2N 6RH
www.pwc.com (020 7583 5000)

RSM Robson Rhodes
186 City Road
London EC1V 2NU
www.rsmi.co.uk (020 7251 1644)

Saffery Champness
Lion House
Red Lion St.
London WC1R 4GB
www.saffery.com (0207 7841 4000)

Sedley Richard Laurence Voulters
1 Conduit St.
London W1S 2XA
www.srlv.co.uk (020 7287 9595)

Sloane & Co
36–38 Westbourne Grove
Newton Road
London W2 5SH
www.sloane.co.uk (020 7221 3292)

BROADCASTERS & PRODUCTION COMPANIES

Anglia
Anglia House
Norwich
Norfolk NR1 3JG
www.itvlocal.com/anglia
(01603 615 151)

BBC East
St Catherine's Close
All Saints Green
Norwich NR1 3ND
www.bbc.co.uk/england/lookeast
(01603 619 331)

BBC North
Woodhouse Lane
Leeds
W. Yorks LS2 9PX
www.bbc.co.uk/england/
looknorthyorkslincs (0113 244 1188)

BBC North East
Barrack Road
Newcastle-upon-Tyne
Tyne & Wear NE99 2NE
(0191 232 1313)

BBC North West
Oxford Road
Manchester M60 1SJ
www.bbc.co.uk/england/
northwesttonight (0161 200 2020)

BBC Northern Ireland
Ormeau Avenue
Belfast BT2 8HQ
www.bbc.co.uk/northernireland
(028 9033 8000)

BBC Scotland
40 Pacific Quay
Glasgow G51 1DA
www.bbc.co.uk/scotland
(0870 010 0222)

BBC South
Havelock Road
Southampton SO1 OXQ
(023 8022 6201)

BBC South West
Seymour Road
Plymouth
Devon PL3 5DB
www.bbc.co.uk/england/spotlight
(01752 229 201)

BBC TV Centre
Wood Lane
London W12 7RJ
www.bbc.co.uk (020 8743 8000)

BBC Wales
Broadcasting House
Meiron Road
Bangor LL57 3BY
www.bbc.co.uk/wales (01248 370 880)

BBC West Midlands
Pebble Mill Road
Birmingham B5 7QQ
(0121 432 8888)

Big Eye Film & TV
Lock Keepers Cottage
Century Street West
Manchester M3 4QL
(0161 832 6111)

Border
Television Centre
Carlisle
Cumbria CA1 3NT
www.border-tv.com (01228 525 101)

Carlton (Central)
Television House
Nottingham NG7 2NA
www.carlton.com/central
(0115 986 3322)

Carlton UK
101 St. Martins Lane
London WC2N 4AZ
www.carlton.com (020 7240 4000)

Carlton (Westcountry)
Western Wood Way
Langage Science Park
Plymouth
Devon PL7 5BG

Channel 4
124 Horseferry Road
London SW1P 2TX
www.channel4.com (020 7396 4444)

Endemol UK
Shepherds Building Central
Charecroft Way
London W14 0EE
www.endemoluk.com
(0870 333 1700)

Five
22 Long Acre
London WC2E 9LY
www.five.tv (020 7691 6610)

GMTV
London Television Centre
Upper Ground
London SE1 9TT
www.gmtv.co.uk (020 7827 7000)

Granada Manchester
Quay Street
Manchester M60 9EA
www.granadatv.co.uk
(0161 832 7211)

ITV London
London Television Centre
Upper Ground
London SE1 9LT
www.itvregions.com/london
(020 7620 1620)

ITV Wales
Television Centre
Culverhouse Cross
Cardiff CF5 6XJ
www.itvregions.com/wales
(029 2059 0590)

Landscape Channel
Royal Oak Lane
Crowhurst
E. Sussex TN33 9BX
www.landscapetv.com (01424 830628)

Meridian
Television Centre
Northam
Southampton SO14 0PZ
www.meridiantv.co.uk (023 8022 2555)

Mike Mansfield TV
5th Floor, 41–42 Berners Street
London W1T 3NB
www.cyberconcerts.com (020 7580 2581)

Ministry Of Sound TV
103 Gaunt Street
London SE1 6DP
www.ministryofsound.com/tv
(0870 060 0010)

MTV
17–19 Hawley Crescent
London NW1 8TT
www.mtv.co.uk (020 7284 7777)

Music Box
30 Sackville Street
London W1X 1DB
www.music-bx.co.uk (020 7478 7300)

Music Choice
91 Brick Lane
London E1 6QL
www.musicchoice.co.uk (020 3107 0300)

Pearson
1 Stephen Street
London W1P 1PJ
www.pearsontvarchive.com
(020 7691 6000)

RTE
Donnybrook
Dublin 4
Eire
www.rte.ie
 (+353 1208 3111)

S4C
Parc Ty Glas
Llanishen
Cardiff CF4 5DU
www.s4c.co.uk
(029 2074 7444)

SKY Music Channels
Unit 4, Grant Way
Isleworth
Middlesex TW7 5QD
(020 7805 8526)

Southampton Television
157–187 Above Bar Street
Southampton SO14 7NN
www.southamptontv.co.uk
(023 8023 2400)

Tyne Tees
Television Centre
City Road
Newcastle-Upon-Tyne NE1 2AL
www.itvregions.com/tyne_tees
(0191 261 0181)

UTV
Havelock House
Ormeau Road
Belfast BT7 1EB
www.utvlive.com
(028 9032 8122)

Yorkshire Television
Television Centre
Leeds LS3 1JS
www.yorkshiretv.co.uk
(0113 243 8283)

INDUSTRY BODIES

ACM (Academy of Contemporary Music)
Rodboro Buildings, Bridge Street
Guildford GU1 4SB
www.acm.ac.uk
(01483 500 800)

AIM (Association of Independent Music)
Lamb House
Church St
London W4 2PD
www.musicindie.com
(020 8994 5599)

APRS (Association Of Professional Recording Services)
PO Box 22
Totnes TQ9 7YZ
www.aprs.co.uk (01803 868600)

ASCAP (American Society Of Composers Authors & Publishers)
8 Cork Street
London W1X 1PB
www.ascap.com (020 7439 0909)

AURA (Association of United Recording Artists)
1 York Street
London W1U 6PA
www.aurauk.com (020 7487 5640)

BACS (British Academy of Composers & Songwriters)
26 Berners St.
London W1T 3LR
www.britishacademy.com
(020 7636 2929)

BARD (British Association Of Record Dealers)
(see ERA)

BMI (Broadcast Music Inc.)
84 Harley House
Marylebone Road
London NW1 5HN
www.bmi.com (0207 486 2036)

BMR (British Music Rights)
26 Berners Street
London W1T 3LR
www.bmr.org (020 7306 4446)

BPI (British Phonographic Industry)
Riverside Building, County Hall
Westminster Bridge Road
London SE1 7JA
www.bpi.co.uk (020 7803 1300)

The Brit School for Performing Arts & Technology
60 The Crescent
Croydon CR0 2HN
www.brit.croydon.sch.uk
(020 8665 5242)

BVA (British Video Association)
167 Great Portland Street
London W1W 5PE
www.bva.org.uk (020 7436 0041)

CatCo
1 Upper James Street
London W1F 9DE
www.catcouk.com (020 7534 1331)

Christian Copyright Licensing
PO Box 1339
Eastbourne
E. Sussex BN21 1AD
www.ccli.co.uk (01373 417 711)

ERA (Entertainment Retailers Association)
1st Floor, Collonade House
2 Westover Road
Bournemouth BH1 2BY
www.eraltd.org (01202 292 063)

IFPI (International Federation Of Phonograph Industries)
10 Piccadilly
London W1J 0DD
www.ifpi.org (020 7878 7900)

IMRO (Irish Music Rights Organisation)
Copyright House, Pembroke Row
Lower Baggot Street

Dublin 2
Ireland
www.imro.ie (+353 1 661 4844)

MCPS (Mechanical Copyright Protection Society)
29–33 Berners Street
London W1T 3AB
London SW16 1ER
www.mcps.co.uk (020 7580 5544)

MMF (Music Managers' Forum)
(see BMR)
www.musicmanagersforum.co.uk
(0870 8507 800)

MPA (Music Publishers Association)
6th Floor, 26 Berners Street
London W1T 3LR
www.mpaonline.org.uk (020 7580 0126)

MPG (Music Producers Guild)
71 Avenue Gardens
London W3 8HB
www.mpg.org.uk (020 3110 0060)

Musicians Union
60–62 Clapham Road
London SW9 0JJ
www.musiciansunion.org.uk
(020 7582 5566)

PAMRA (Performing Artists Media Rights Association)
161 Borough High Street
London SE1 1HR
www.pamra.org.uk (020 7940 0400)

PPI (Phonographic Performance Ireland)
1 Corrig Avenue
Dun Laoghaire
Co. Dublin,
Eire
www.ppiltd.com (+353 1 280 5977)

PPL (Phonographic Performance Ltd.)
1 Upper James St
London W1F 9DE
www.ppluk.com (020 7534 1000)

PRS (Performing Right Society)
www.prs.co.uk (see MCPS)

RadioCentre
77 Shaftesbury Avenue
London W1D 5DU
www.radiocentre.org (020 7306 2603)

VPL (Video Performance Ltd.)
1 Upper James Street
London W1F 9DE
www.vpluk.com (020 7534 1400)

Worshipful Company of Musicians
6th Floor, 2 London Wall Buildings
London EC2M 5PP
www.wcom.org.uk (020 7496 8980)

OTHER WEBSITES

www.3barfire.com
www.bandname.com (Band name registration)
www.bandfamilytree.com
www.benedict.com (Copyright)
www.bpi-med.co.uk (Music In Education directory)
www.britishunderground.net (Support for artists and micro-labels)
www.clickmusic.com
www.edirol.com (Roland)
www.entsweb.co.uk
www.gearsearch.com (Equipment)
www.inthecity.co.uk (Trade fair)
www.manchestermusic.co.uk
www.midem.com (Trade fair)
www.mp3.com
www.mudhut.co.uk (Unsigned artists)
www.musesmuse.com (Songwriting tips & tools)
www.musicroom.com (Sheet music & equipment)
www.rightswatch.com (Taking unlicensed music off websites)
www.sheetmusicdirect.com (Digital sheet music)
www.showmehowtoplay.com
www.songlink.com
www.useyourears.co.uk
www.yahama.com (Yamaha)

GLOSSARY OF TERMS

Here's an alphabetical list of some of the words and phrases you may come across in the music business. If a term is not defined here you may well find it in the general index. Forgive us if there are some you already know and completely take for granted – it's possible that someone else may not.

A&R

Artists and Repertoire. The A&R manager of a label is the man or woman to see with your demos. They decide which artists get signed to the company's roster and what tracks they should release (or acquire and promote, in the case of publishers).

Advances

Payments made to writers and artists or expenses paid out by a company on your behalf or to create or promote your music or recordings. They should not have to be paid back unless, possibly, to buy yourself out of a contract (non-returnable) but they will be recovered by the company from royalties due to you (i.e. you don't get paid anything more until the royalties you would have got equal the advance payment).

Album deal

A deal with a record company whereby they undertake to make (or give you the money to make) and release at least one album. More likely to be offered to rock acts than dance acts.

AP1, AP2A, AP2

These are the licensing schemes offered to actual mainstream record labels by the MCPS to collect the songwriters' and publishers' royalties for the songs they use on their records. AP1 covers not only the major labels but most labels that have had several hits – they pay on what they sell once they've sold it. AP2A is for smaller labels that pay on how many they press but don't have to pay in advance. AP2 is for everything from quite established small but successful labels right down to very small specialist labels pressing 500 CDs of each album (which is why the MCPS charges publishers about three times as much to collect from AP2 as from AP1 companies). There are lots more schemes – for record clubs, cover mounts on newspapers and magazines, 'premium' albums advertising something etc. and, although they're not 'mainstream' record sales, they can bring in a great deal of money.

Arrangers

The term used of writers who make arrangements or adaptations of traditional music. It also refers to people within the business whose job it is to take down music from records for printing, who prepare scores for recording sessions, broadcasts, bands and so forth. There are far fewer than there used to be years ago, but it's a very specialised skill and, as you can imagine, such people are skilled musicians in their own right.

Arms-length

Meaning particularly a deal with an international publisher or record company – they guarantee that if your song or record is licensed to one of their own affiliated companies overseas, the terms are no worse for you than if it had been a totally separate UK company doing the deal with those overseas companies. The same applies where a UK management company signs a writer/artist to a recording/publishing deal with their affiliate.

Assignability

Refers to a clause in your contract that governs what happens if the company you're signed to is bought by another. Most of the time this is permitted, but some artists have clauses allowing them to terminate or renegotiate, and it can be important if you begin as a major signing to a small company one year only to find yourself a very small fish in a bigger company's pond the next.

A-side Protection
A guarantee in your agreement that if you only wrote, produced or mixed the feature track (radio edit) on a single your royalties won't be 'diluted' by the inclusion of other 'throwaway' tracks or mixes, some of which might be longer than yours and therefore attract a higher share of the mechanical royalties on sales of the record.

Ayants Droit
The owners of the rights to songs, recordings, merchandise etc. Most often used in publishing to refer to the original (usually foreign) owners.

Black Box
The term for income that some collecting societies have 'left over' or unallocated (see 'non-member') after making payments to their members and sister societies abroad. It is then divided among their own members. Estimates of the amounts involved and the ways they are calculated vary wildly, but are often highly exaggerated.

It's fashionable for writers to ask for a share of 'black box' equal to the proportion of their earnings to the publisher's total earnings. As this would enable you to calculate what the publisher's total earnings are, this is usually resisted. Some mechanical right societies will send publishers separate 'black box' statements for individual writers or original publishers if requested. These are called 'editions', and you could ask for a share of 'black box' based on these, though if the society makes a charge, as some do, then it may simply not be worth it. Your publisher shouldn't have a problem with giving you your specified share of income from these.

Blankets
The term used for exclusive agreements under which all the songs you write or recordings you make for a period of time will go to the one company. Remember that once that period is over, the company will usually go on owning those songs or recordings for much longer. Publishing companies may be prepared to do a deal just for one song, but record companies will almost always want a blanket agreement. Also used to describe the agreements between collection societies.

Bonus
Generally refers to an amount paid to a songwriter or artist that will not be recouped from his royalties (i.e. not an advance). These are very much less common than advances and you should not expect to be offered bonuses. The term 'chart bonus' (a payment made when your single or album reaches a certain position), however, will usually just mean an additional advance.

Bootlegged Records
Bootleg recordings are usually ones made illegally at live concerts, especially where otherwise unrecorded material was played. Pressing plants in the UK work together with the BPI and MCPS to try to spot anyone trying to duplicate unauthorised recordings of an artist. Bootleggers themselves often escape the punishment of the law and it's the sellers who attract attention. However, if caught in the act of recording, bootleggers risk not only prosecution but loss or damage of their equipment and even physical assault. One groundbreaking band in the early Eighties avoided the problem by recording every single concert they gave and making available tapes of the most recent 24-hours' worth of live material. It goes without saying that they were not signed to a major label, as no such label would have had the administrative capacity to deal with such a project. Although this wasn't their aim, however, it was an excellent marketing ploy and it got around some of the bootlegging problem.

Breakers

Records 'bubbling under' in the charts with sales increasing but not yet enough to push the record into the charts. Not applicable to the UK, where most records, after five or six weeks of advance promotion, enter the charts at their highest position on the strength of advance orders then drop down, sometimes dramatically. In the US, there is an entirely separate chart published by *Billboard* of records by artists who have never made the charts but are looking like entering in the near future.

Bullet

Mark shown against records making good progress up the US *Billboard* trade magazine's weekly charts.

CAE numbers

(see IPI numbers)

Collecting Societies

In the UK there are two main writer/publisher societies, which have now come together for their back office operations as the MCPS-PRS Alliance, often just referred to as "the Alliance". The PRS basically licenses all forms of public performances of songs (broadcasts, live concerts, music streamed on the Internet etc.) and the MCPS licenses the reproduction of songs on all forms of sound-carrier (CDs, DVDs, music downloaded from the Internet etc.). A totally separate company, PPL, collects royalties for record companies, artists and musicians when recordings, rather than just the songs, are performed and broadcast, and its sister organisation, VPL, does the same for videos and DVDs. Thus broadcasts of records on television and radio etc.

involve the PRS and PPL. There are affiliated societies to all of these in most other countries (notably ASCAP, BMI and SESAC, operating as rival performing rights societies in the US).

Compilation shows

Musical theatre shows in which the music used was not written for the show but 'interpolated' into it at a later date. Many successful ones are based on the lives and/or music of well-known artists of the past such as *Buddy* (Buddy Holly), *Mamma Mia* (ABBA) or *We Will Rock You* (Queen).

Writers and publishers, get a share of the box office receipts from each performance of the show, as with musicals, but whereas the publisher always collects directly for musicals where the music was written for the show, compilation shows are sometimes licensed by the PRS, sometimes by the publishers with PRS consent. In practice, the usual rate is about 4–5% of the gross box office receipts pro-rated across the musical works in the show. With a long-running and successful show such as the ones mentioned above, this can be a highly lucrative income stream. As with synch licences, songwriters often have prior approval for the context in which their music is used, especially if the words are changed or translated.

Container Allowance

Permits record companies to deduct a further percentage (usually around 20% for CDs) before paying artist royalties. It is meant to recompense record companies for the cost of manufacture of jewel cases for CDs, cardboard sleeves for vinyl etc., though these usually cost next to nothing to produce nowadays. Especially high deductions are usually made for any new format on which your album is released. In some cases, as with CD when it was first introduced, the mechanical royalties payable to publishers and songwriters are also reduced for a limited period, to allow for high development and manufacturing costs at the start (a similar reduced rate has, more recently, been offered to commercial music download sites for similar reasons). These reduced rates are eliminated over time, but usually not quickly enough for writers' and publishers' liking.

Contract Year

A term used in contracts meaning a year commencing with the effective date of the contract rather than January 1 (unless of course that happens to be the date of the contract anyway). It makes sense for contracts to be dated (or effective) from the beginning of a half year or quarter, as this makes a much clearer break point at the end of the contract.

Controlled Compositions

The system whereby US record companies try to ensure that their copyright and artist royalties together do not exceed a certain amount on records where the artist is also the writer. The artist's contract will state that, if his publisher holds out for more than a certain royalty per track, generally 75% of the statutory US royalty rate when the record was first delivered or released there, then the excess will be deducted from the artist royalty. Your publisher may have the right to comment on such clauses but, in practice, he won't be able to get it changed without prejudicing your negotiations as an artist with the record company, even, in some cases, if you signed the publishing agreement first and therefore that should really take precedence. In the UK, the record companies are not able to negotiate such deductions with the copyright owners of the songs and, as a writer, you or your publisher will always get the full mechanical royalty rate.

Counterfeits

These are CDs, videos or DVDs illegally re-recorded from the original releases or copies of the master tapes and pressed up to look exactly like the genuine article, but without any royalties having been paid. Some are sold at a discount to unsuspecting or opportunist dealers, and it is virtually impossible even for the record or video companies concerned to tell them apart from the real thing. Others are sold on street corners and are usually just re-recorded from discs or tapes and the quality, even with digital recordings, can be appalling.

Cover-mounts

Some contend that "cover-mounts" help CD sales, others that they devalue music; that's a discussion you will need to have with your record company. As an artist you may get no royalties from albums given away with newspapers etc. – it all depends on your contract. At one time these were generally back-catalogue tracks of little value, but increasingly in recent years they have been compilations of valuable hit material or of live recordings of hits by major artists, and some artists/record labels have taken it one step further and used cover-mounts as a means of launching a new album for nothing (see 'Freebies'). There's no set amount that the company and artist receive from the newspaper for this. The songs on freebies are licensed at special mechanical royalty rates by the MCPS, so you will get royalties for your song from your publisher and, although the rate may be low, the number pressed may be so large (millions for cover-mounts with national newspapers) that one track could be worth around £20,000 to the writer/publisher. Writer/publisher permission is not needed to include your song on a cover mount in the UK, but it is required on the Continent, and is also required in the UK if the cover-mount CD/DVD is advertising a product (see under 'Premiums').

Cover

A recorded version of a song other than the original recording. Under most publishing agreements you get a slightly lower royalty on covers. These may be described as all recordings where you yourself were not involved as artist, producer, mixer or remixer, or they may have to be recordings specifically procured by the publisher, which, in a lot of cases these days, could include your own recording if it was your publisher who secured its release, unless you ensure that it's specifically excluded.

Cross-collateralisation

Also known as cross-recouping, this is where advances paid to you by the same company for different things (such as publishing and recording) are recoupable against royalties due to you from both types of activity. This means that any advance paid to you relating to one type of activity is

recoupable against royalties due to you from another type – if, for instance, you have your publishing with the same company as your recordings. They pay you a £10,000 advance on each. In the first year you earn £10,000 royalties on your songs, but only £2,000 on your recordings (maybe someone else recorded one of your songs and it sold better than your recording). In the next royalty period you earn £2,000 royalties on your publishing and £2,000 on your recordings. If your advances are not cross-collateralised you would receive £2,000 for publishing royalties and remain £6,000 unrecouped on recordings. Whereas if your advances are cross-collateralised you would receive nothing until you earned a further £4,000 from either activity.

Obviously, this is key when it comes to the new style cross-media or '360' deals, where big artists who are not perhaps selling so many records any more are doing deals that include revenue from live performances and merchandising. For them this makes a lot of sense as they have money in the bank to live on, but for smaller artists, if you take the example above you can see that this can make a significant difference to your annual income.

Crossover

Apart from being a hi-fi term, this is mainly used

to describe records from the specialist charts, dance, rock, club, country, classical, independent etc. that go on to become mainstream hits.

Cue sheets

Lists, prepared by film, television and other audio-visual production companies, of all the musical works in the production. Against each piece of music should be the writer, publisher, length of the use and whether it is vocal or instrumental, featured or background. Featured (or visual) means it should be audible to the characters on screen, including when the music is actually (or seemingly) performed by them, and sometimes attracts a higher fee for the use. Cue sheets are sent to the PRS and other performing right societies so that when the film or programme is broadcast, they know how to divide up the royalties. So it's vital if you have your songs placed in a film or if you compose the score that the production company gets the cue sheet right. Your publisher will have limited power to alter it once it's with the societies. Often, every separate piece of specially written music is listed, eg. Singer enters the room: 32" IB; Singer calls his agent: 10" VV; Singer leaves the room: 1"15" IB and so on... (IB meaning 'instrumental background' – i.e. no vocals and not audible to the people on the screen, and VV meaning 'vocal visual' i.e. audible to the people on the screen).

Custom Pressing

Generally refers to pressings made by one record company's pressing plant for the benefit of its company in another country or for another record company.

Cut-off Periods

Some record companies, publishers and other bodies operate cut-off periods whereby your statement of money earned from, say, July 1 to December 31, may actually be cut-off at the end of November and therefore not include some big Christmas sales that you may have been expecting. You will of course get those royalties in the next Jan-June statement, which itself may be cut-off at the end of May.

Dealers

The usual term for record shops and online outlets. There are over 5,000 in the UK of varying sizes, plus many 'outlets' such as petrol stations and supermarkets, where impulse buying keeps sales up on budget products. Some acquire their stocks from 'one-stops' who keep stocks of product from most record companies. Some of these actually decide which records should go to certain outlets and 'service' them exclusively, usually with middle of the road records. By

using one-stops, some retail outlets can receive records from different companies at only slightly more than the normal dealer price, thus saving time and avoiding delivery charges added by some record companies to small orders. In the US, similar companies are known as rack jobbers.

Delivery

The term used for the final completion of an album to the satisfaction of a record company or for handing over new songs or demos to a publisher. Highly relevant to songwriter/artists, as the rate on which they're paid US mechanical royalties (even decades later) is frequently dependant on the date of delivery of their album to the record company.

Direct Injection

Plugging an electric instrument (eg. bass guitar) straight into the mixing desk in a recording studio, instead of recording it into a microphone in front of a speaker in the studio. These days, as you probably know, apart from vocals and acoustic drums virtually everything is direct injected.

Doubling

Playing more than one instrument at a session, performance etc.

DRM (Digital Rights Management)

A term used for the embedded encryption in many

commercially available music downloads, usually limiting the number of times or devices the file can be copied to. Initially seen as a way for record companies to beat the challenge of piracy (and especially peer-to-peer networks) in the digital age, it has now been abandoned by many record companies, as the limitations were felt to be suppressing sales. Many music users were reported to be reluctant to pay for music that they could only use on a particular computer or portable player.

Drop-in

Re-recording part of a track of a recording in a studio, commencing part of the way through without having to start from the beginning.

Dubbing

Re-recording from one recording medium to another, eg 24-track tape to CD. Broadcasters pay small dubbing (or mechanical) fees for the use of the song and the recording when they re-record music onto the soundtracks of their programmes.

Electronic Press Kit

Usually on DVD, this is one of the terms to describe press material (a compilation of tracks, interviews etc.) sent by your record company to the press and media to promote you.

Exports

Like royalties, these are sometimes treated as local sales and sometimes as sales in the country of destination. Small quantities are usually treated as local sales for calculating mechanical royalties for the songs involved. The artist contract may well say that exports are treated as foreign sales, which may well be at 50% of the royalty you get for UK sales, or it may even spell out the royalty rate applying to any exports of your recordings.

Fiduciary Duty

This is the 'good faith' that a manager in particular has to show to you in doing the best deals he can for you in respect of publishing, recording, merchandising etc., even if the deals are with companies he has an interest in. If that's the case, there's no reason not to sign with him provided you and your lawyer are happy that these deals really are on 'arms-length' terms, meaning that they're every bit as good as you could get if you were doing each one individually. Remember that you also have a fiduciary duty, for example to the record company to finish your album on time (as long as the time scale was reasonable) or deliver the number of songs your Exclusive Songwriter Agreement specified in a given year.

Fixer

Someone who acts as an agent for session musicians and brings the required musicians together, usually for broadcasts or recordings or for UK tours for foreign artists.

FLR (First Licence Refusal)

A flag available when registering works with certain mechanical collection societies (such as the MCPS), which allows the publisher or writer to have a say on the first recording of the work made available to the public. Once one recording has been made available, any artist can cover your song (so long as they or their record company pay the mechanical royalties and as long as they don't alter it in any way), so if you or your publisher want to make sure a particular recording is first to market in the right territory you can use this FLR to make it happen.

Freebies

These are generally records distributed free to members of the public who subscribe to record clubs, mail order organisations and the like. The usual principle is 'buy a certain number, get one free, or at a very low price'. If the free album happens to be the only one in the offer by you then it's unfair if you don't get paid artist royalties, whereas if the other albums are all by you, it matters less. Increasingly, artists are looking at freebies as a means of launching new product. Prince gave away

his new *Planet Earth* CD as a cover-mount in the newspaper *Mail On Sunday*, and the band Radiohead (almost) gave away their *In Rainbows* album by allowing fans to download it for whatever they thought it was worth (the average, it seems, was 6p!). See also 'Cover-mounts'.

Ghosting
The practice (increasingly unusual) of having experienced musicians playing behind a band on stage without being seen, or playing instead of a group at a recording session just in case the regular group members make a mistake, which could be costly in studio time wasted. As the general standard of musicianship improves, and as more boy/girl bands make no pretence of playing instruments, it is becoming much less common.

Grading
The practice of some performing right societies of paying less than normal royalties for a performance or broadcast of an arrangement of a public-domain song, depending on the amount of new material contained. This is no longer the case in the UK and many other countries.

Grand Rights
This has no legal definition but is taken to mean the 'Dramatico-Musical Performance Right', in other words, music or

songs that form an integral part of what's happening on stage. In the UK it is the right to license a performance of an opera, ballet or musical or of a number of songs from the same overall work, generally live on stage (meaning songs that were originally written specifically for that overall work). On the Continent the definition is taken to cover compilation shows (see definition), which in the UK, are not generally considered Grand Right uses per se but are generally licenced on a similar percentage of box office basis.

Graphic Rights
Generally refers to the right to reproduce the actual music and lyrics of a song, not as hard copy but on magnetic media, for example in video karaoke, or on CD-ROM, video game, DVD etc. Where

these can be downloaded and printed out, then of course they are very likely taking sales away from printed music and song-books. It's hard to regulate on the Internet, but for karaoke etc. in the UK the MCPS' mechanical licensing scheme has an additional 2% of the price added on to the normal mechanical royalty for the songs included.

Hyping
Really just exaggerating the merits of a record or artist, but also used to refer to chart-rigging. This involves record companies either buying their own records from shops they believe are making 'returns' to the chart compilers, or sending quantities of free copies of records to those shops in the hope that they will try harder to sell them, or else in the hope of a 'you

Sid – do we have 2000 copies of 'Why don't you lerv me no more?'

scratch my back...' relationship with the shop concerned. Now that charts include not only physical sales but also downloads and an element of airplay, there are more ways than ever before for the charts to be corrupted in this manner (for example 'pay for play' at radio stations); then again, the same technology makes it all the easier to catch the cheats. Every few years stories appear in the press exposing such practices, but in truth it's not at all common; after all, in the end it's so much more profitable to actually sell music than to pretend that you have, and a record company doing this risks heavy penalties, including having its records removed from the chart, and it can do the artist's profile possibly irreparable harm.

IPI Numbers

Formerly a nine digit number called the CAE Number, these are the 11-digit code numbers allocated to every writer or publisher member of a collecting society. Every songwriter member of the PRS, including the authors of this book, has his or her own number. The use of this number by the collecting societies, especially in conjunction with the ISRC and ISWC codes (see below) should ensure that the writer is correctly identified as the person who should receive royalties on his or her works.

ISWC/ISRC

These stand for International Standard Work Code and International Standard Recording Code, and are gradually being introduced so that all collecting societies around the world can allocate money for uses of songs or recordings to the correct parties and lessen the chances of the money going astray because a work or record was wrongly identified. Plans are in progress for these numbers to be embedded in all legitimate digital content, so that every use and sale can be automatically and accurately recorded and ultimately paid on.

Jingles

Mostly written by specialist writers for specialist publishers, or directly for advertising agencies or the facility houses that make commercials. Some are taken from Production Music libraries (see 'Library

Recordings') and synch licensed at around £1,000 or so per 30 seconds for a year's use on UK network television for a commercial (for the song and recording). These each might have cost upwards of £20,000 if the client/agency had used a normal commercial track. Broadcast performance fees are, however, still licensed by the performing right societies at the same rate as commercial music, so the total revenue from a frequently aired commercial can still be very lucrative.

Incidentally, if an altered or parody lyric is used especially for tracks in commercials, you should try to ensure that the writer of that doesn't get a share of the broadcasting fees or the copyright of the resulting derivative work, and your publisher should specify this in the contract.

Key Man Clause

This is a clause in your agreement that says that if

the particular person who signed you and enthused about you leaves the company, then you can give notice that you wish to terminate the agreement. It's much more likely to be agreed to by smaller companies and by management than publishing or recording companies.

Lease Tape Deal

An agreement under which an independent producer of a master recording licenses it to a record company. The artist would usually be signed to the independent producer, who would pay him his royalty out of what the record company pays him under the lease. The producer may give the artist a split of around 50/50 (up to about 70/30) of profits instead of a royalty. These days of course, it's likely that the recording won't be on tape at all but on some form of digital medium.

Library Recordings

A recording in the catalogue of a Production Music Library, formerly known as background or mood music libraries. These days, a number of former 'pop' writers or even 'classical' composers write and produce albums for library companies (sometimes using a pseudonym), though most production music is still composed by specialists in this field. Their music is used by producers of

films, television, commercials etc. who don't want to commission their own music or use existing 'commercial' songs, which can be much more expensive. The rates they pay are laid down by the MCPS and cover the synch use of both the music and the recording. The writers are usually not signed exclusively to one publisher but album by album, though most have a regular publisher.

The terms of acquisition of such music (they are hardly ever songs, with words) are virtually the same as those for the ordinary songwriter, but new writers would probably only get a 50/50 split of the all-important synchronisation fees and just their 50% writer share worldwide of performing fees, plus an advance to help pay for the cost of making the album. The library publishers, although they produce CDs, do not release the music for sale to the public as a rule. Pressings of library recordings are sent free of charge to potential users, such as TV production companies and advertising agencies, who then only pay when some of the music is actually used. There are a small number of specialised production music library publishers in the UK. Increasingly, it is possible to access and license this music via specialist websites belonging to library publishers, or using specialist software

provided by companies who gather together the music of as many libraries as they can (their key service being the 'one stop' nature of their software and additional mood or era categorisation).

The intention is that this music can be used quickly and cheaply where time or budget doesn't allow for a specifically composed or commercial piece to be used, and most likely otherwise no music would be used.

Long-form video

Music videos other than promo videos for singles, usually either live or else compiled from individual promo videos and sold to the public.

Long-stop

One term used to describe the date upon which a 'contract year' terminates no matter what. For example, if an album is to be released within a year of the start of an agreement but is released after that year ends, the company doesn't have to take up its option (and usually pay a substantial advance) for the next year/next album until the first album is released, or a few months after. Without the long-stop – say, two or three years from when the agreement began – that first 'year' could continue forever.

Masters, Master Tapes

Finished recordings of sufficient quality for CDs

to be pressed up from them. Sound quality has improved so much through digital technology that even home-made demos can usually be remixed in a studio into finished masters.

Matching Offer

This is a provision, usually in recording or songwriting agreements, under which you agree to give your existing record company or publisher, at the end of your deal with them, the right to match any offer from a new record company/publisher for your services. It's always easier for your current company to come up with a new deal for you (better royalty splits etc.), firstly because they know how much you've been earning (though you can always tell your new publisher/record company this) and secondly because they can pay an advance based on their ability to recover part of it (if you let them) from money you've already earned under the first deal that hasn't reached you yet (pipeline income).

If a new record company/publisher comes up with a much better offer (in the light of the above), then as long as that company is trustworthy (some that are not will make a great offer but simply not honour it when the time comes) it's worth looking seriously at changing over to them. However, there really is a

'trust' in the music business between certain artists/writers and their record companies, publishers and managers that goes beyond advances and promises of fortunes to come. If you do have to give your existing company the right to match an offer from a new one, you should reasonably expect to give it around 10 working days to match the offer in writing.

Musical Directors/ Music Supervisors

A Musical Director co-ordinates the music in plays, musicals, television programmes, films, recording sessions, etc. and is generally the leader of the band or orchestra performing. A Music Supervisor performs a similar role in film and TV but the emphasis is on finding and placing music in the production, rather than being directly involved in its creation.

Mechanicals

The royalties payable to the owners of the copyright in a song on a recording, earned by the sales or uses through downloading direct to home of the recordings.

Merchandising

Term used to describe the making and selling of any non-musical goods associated with the name, logo or image of an artist.

MIDEM

An annual gathering in winter in the South of France

for music industry executives from around the world to make contacts and finalise deals for songs and recordings etc., as well as debate matters of international importance to the music industry. The biggest such gathering in the UK is In The City, which is usually in Manchester though it has moved around. There are other similar gatherings in the US such as SBSW (South By South West) in Austin, Texas. These events also tend to showcase both signed and unsigned acts, so it's well worth asking your record company if there's any possibility of you appearing there.

MIDI Files

Actually stands for Musical Instrument Digital Interface and is the normal method of synching up drum sounds and keyboards from the computer in a studio. In some countries, MIDI files are sold either on physical media or over the Internet in the form of specially prepared backing tracks for acts to play along to live. In the US, it was considered that these should be treated just like normal audio discs for royalty calculation. In the UK, however, the MCPS has a specific scheme for this and similar products like karaoke CDs & DVDs.

Min/Max formula

This is a method of calculating the amount that a

publisher, record company etc. should pay as an advance to take up an option for additional songs, albums etc. Generally it is a certain percentage of the amount earned during the first period or by the first album (including earnings in the pipeline) at the time the option is due, subject to a minimum of maybe 75% of the advance paid for the first period/album and a maximum of maybe 150% of that advance.

Non-Member
Usually used to describe the status of a songwriter vis-à-vis a performing right society. A non-member writer will not be able to directly collect his share of performing fees in many countries of the world, and in certain territories it may not be possible for his publisher to collect that share on his behalf either. Non-member shares may well end up as so-called 'black box' money if they remain uncollected for too long.

Non-needletime
A certain small amount of broadcasters' time on air is given over to the playing of music that does not require a licence from PPL (see 'Collecting Societies' earlier). This includes production music from library publishers, demo recordings and other recordings in which the rights are owned by companies that are not members of PPL

and therefore don't qualify for payment. For them, it's a way of getting some airplay on which PRS royalties are nevertheless paid for the broadcasting of the songs, even though nothing, or just a nominal amount, is paid for the use of the recordings.

On hold
Where songs are submitted by writers and publishers for an artist to record, the artist or their management is likely to ask for a hold on the song if they like it. This means they don't want you to pitch it to anyone else till they've had a chance to record it. Of course, songs can be on hold for years till they finally get onto an album and it can be tricky knowing when to say 'time's up'. Unless you desperately want the artist holding it to record your song, your publisher would normally start pitching it again once you know that the first artist has finished their album and not used it.

Orchestrations
Printed copies of songs arranged for the whole or part of an orchestra. These are very expensive to produce, and whereas they were once even considered essential to launch a new mainstream pop song, they are now very rarely made by publishers themselves, although bands and orchestras sometimes make their own, with the

publishers' permission. Some small private firms are also licensed by publishers to make and sell or hire out small quantities, generally for brass and dance bands.

Overrides
Percentage points given to someone on songs or recordings in return for some assistance. A common example would be a publisher producing a master tape of an artist/songwriter and approaching a record label with it. The label, if it wants to sign the artist, may then insist that the publisher actually sells them his masters in return for what it cost to record them, plus an override royalty of, say, 2–4%. The label will be asked to pay this directly to the publisher and may deduct it from your artist royalty on these particular tracks under your agreement with them. If it's subsequently remixed, then the override may be reduced.

Parallel Imports
Records coming into one country from another at a lower price to the dealers than the locally released copies of the same record. Under EU rules, imported records and tapes can be sold in UK record shops, and if, because of the prevailing exchange rates for example, the imported records are cheaper, then it's these that will be selling, and your artist royalty

rate may be a lot lower on these imports than it would have been on the UK release. It's actually quite normal and reasonable, however, that in some cases a record company in one country will prefer to test the market in another country with a few exports before doing a licensing deal with a company in that second country, under which the local company will press and release the recording there on their own label. As a writer, your local publisher (or the local mechanical rights society) may or may not collect copyright royalties on imported discs for they have often been paid in the country of export.

Parody

Generally humorous versions of songs, but can also refer to any alteration of the lyric of a song for use in an advertising campaign or other use. For reasons mentioned in the Songwriting Section, parodies are referred to in the US as derogatory

treatments of songs. Some have been very big hits in the past.

Pay for Play

The practice where some venues charge bands to play, rather than the other way round. It may be expressed as a charge to use the house PA system, whether you want to or not (and in small venues you probably don't). Alternatively, you have to pay in advance for a certain number of tickets, which it's then up to you to sell. Also used as a UK term for Payola (see below).

Payola

An American term for the practice of record companies, publishers, an artist or manager bribing disc jockeys or radio producers to broadcast certain records. Broadcasting authorities and companies set rules to determine where reasonable business relations, lunches and small gifts end and payola begins.

Per diems

Living expenses paid to artists by managers or record companies, generally while recording or touring, at so much per day.

Performing Fees

The more general term for all royalties received through the PRS and its affiliated performing right societies worldwide, including broadcasting royalties and royalties for digital diffusion of songs.

Pipeline income

Generally refers to money that a publisher, record company etc. knows has been earned (perhaps it has been received by a foreign sub-publisher or licensee, or by the MCPS from a record company) but that hasn't actually been received by them yet and therefore isn't actually due to be paid to you in the next accounting. It's sometimes possible to negotiate regular payments each royalty period taking pipeline income into account, but, since it complicates accounting, companies are reluctant and it may almost be more trouble than it's worth to the artist.

Pirates

Not to be confused with bootleggers. Pirates abound in countries where copyright is not rigidly enforced. The pirate usually gets a record or DVD and makes low-quality copies from it without authority. In some countries, books, including songbooks, are also pirated and counterfeited. Piracy is bad in Eastern Europe, Russia and the Indian sub-continent, but is particularly rife in the Far East and Middle East and, of course, online. Technically, anyone using peer-to-peer networks or bit torrents to download copyright material is a pirate, and the recording industry, especially in the US, has been very aggressive of late in pursuing even these small-time pirates.

Playlist

Associated with radio stations. The producers who put together the programmes meet regularly with other station executives to hear new record releases and decide whether to give them airplay in their programmes, and also to decide which records should be removed from the previous list. Often, this decision is based not only on whether or not they like the record, but also on the target audience of the radio station or the show.

The principal daytime shows, which are largely composed of songs from the playlist or the current charts, are sometimes known as strip shows because of the way they are put together. There are still plenty of plays to be had by non playlisted tracks, though usually not at peak times. Obviously, if your record gets on a playlist it can lead to good sales and airplay income, but the diversity of radio stations – both traditional and online – means that the playlist, while still extremely important, is less powerful than it once was.

Power of Attorney

This is the right, given by artists to record companies and managers and by writers to publishers, to sign contracts on their behalf. This should always be limited for certain rights and circumstances, and it shouldn't include any agreement for a writer/artist's long-term services (anything more than about a guaranteed maximum of six months), and in any case should be carefully perused by your lawyer before you agree to the grant of this right. Under some management agreements it can go much further, and allows the manager to spend unlimited sums of money (recoupable against the artist's earnings) on behalf of the artist, and to negotiate and sign, without reference to the artist, long-term record and publishing deals. Undoubtedly it is helpful, especially if you become successful, to have someone else sign the minor deals on your behalf (otherwise you'd have no time to create the music that powers the business). Yet power of attorney is a potentially dangerous tool in the wrong hands; as well as fraud, plain honest bad decisions can really harm you professionally and financially. For this reason, always ensure that power of attorney is limited in artist agreements to certain types of agreement and circumstances, and in management agreements that the manager is not able to commit the artist to any expenditure above a certain limit.

Premiums

Releases that are designed to promote a product, usually by being given away free in return for the public sending in a number of vouchers collected from the product packaging or in a newspaper or magazine. Artists' and writers' contracts should give them the opportunity to decline premiums if they object to them (particularly if they're promoting certain products or causes of which the artist disapproves), though there is usually plenty of money to be made from them. Unlike covermounts, where there is a laid-down royalty for use of the songs, the royalty per song for premiums is negotiated by the individual publisher.

Pressing and Distribution (P & D) Deals

These are agreements under which independent record companies can have their records pressed up and distributed to UK dealers under one agreement with a specialised pressing plant/distribution company, who will normally take around 30% of the PPD (published price to dealers) of the records they handle.

Pressing Plant

A record, DVD or CD factory. The major companies have generally sold off their own pressing and distribution affiliates, and these functions are performed by independent pressing plants, used by indie and major labels alike.

Promo copies

Record companies will send out a certain number of copies of a new release for promotional purposes free of charge. They will not pay artist royalties on these even if they wind up supplying large quantities free or very cheaply to chain stores to encourage sales. Limits on permissible numbers of promo copies are usually made explicit in both recording and publishing contracts. The mechanical rights societies have a strict policy; for example, the MCPS only allow 1,500 copies to be pressed and distributed free of mechanical royalties to writers/publishers before the record company have to start paying the full mechanical rate.

Promoter

Person or company arranging tours and engagements for artists.

Public Domain

No longer afforded copyright protection, a recording or song 'in the public domain' may be used freely without royalties being due. Works and recordings do not necessarily go into the public domain at the same time in all territories of the world, and just because a recording of a work is out of copyright, it doesn't mean the song itself is too. There are complex rules governing when a copyright enters the public domain and all too often they are misunderstood.

Racking

The sale of CDs on racks in supermarkets, petrol stations etc.

Recoupment

A record company or publisher will usually pay an 'advance' to an artist/writer, which they will then expect to 'recoup' from his share of royalties and fees or other income they collect in respect of his recordings/songs. So if you have a 50/50 deal and £100 is collected, then £50 will count towards recouping your advance. Recording advances will usually include all recording costs and consequently will usually be recouped much later than publishing advances.

Release Sheets

Also known as 'dealer mailings', these are simply sheets (or more commonly emails these days) sent to every record shop in the country by most major record distributors every week, telling the retailers what records are being released and any good reason why the retailer should be sure to order a supply (i.e. previous record was number one, forthcoming tour by artist in certain areas etc.).

Retention Period

The period of time after a contract expires during which the publisher or record company is entitled to collect income on and license your works or recordings.

Returns

Two meanings. One, unsold records returned by the shop to the distributor. Two, information as to uses of songs, e.g. a BBC return to the PRS will show songs used in a particular programme.

Ripping

The act of converting the high-quality music or audio-visual file on a CD or DVD to an often lower quality but more compact format such as MP3, WMA or ATRAC. These files can then be stored on a hard drive and streamed to other computers or devices such as games consoles, or transferred to and used on portable music players such as an iPod or mobile phones. Files created in this way, though initially usually of lower quality than CD, can be copied endlessly without loss of quality, unless they have embedded DRM copy protection.

Rolling advance/ Roll-over advance

This is a method of paying advances whereby as soon as the initial advance is recouped by the publisher or record label, a further advance becomes payable, and another when that is recouped, and so on. This continues until either the deal is a year or two from its end or until the deal ends. If it's the former, then at the end of the term the songs or recordings revert to the artist; if the latter, then either the term of the deal or the period for which existing works or recording are retained (retention period) is extended either for a set period or until recoupment.

Sleeper
A record that becomes a hit months or years after its initial release with no further publicity from the record company.

Split copyright
A song in which more than one publisher controls a share, usually because the co-writers are under contract to different publishers. This was almost unknown till the Seventies. Now it's more or less standard and creates problems when, for example, the song is wanted for use in a film or commercial or even for printing in a songbook. All writers and publishers must clear their individual shares before it can be used. As you can imagine, this can get even more complicated where, for example, a song was written by five members of one act and includes a sample of a song written by five another writers. Incidentally, if, in this example, the film company only wanted the part of the song that didn't include the sample, it would not be unusual for the sample writers and

publishers to be involved anyway (another reason for not using samples unless they're really likely to make or break your record).

Sub-Publishing
Most publishers acquire world rights in a song from a writer and then appoint other publishers outside their home territory, in return for a share of the local royalties, to administer the rights in their part of the world. Of the traditional publishers only the so-called 'majors', plus one or two of the bigger 'independents', actually have their own people operating in all the major territories of the world. Otherwise, in general Fred Smith Music (UK) may have a subsidiary called Fred Smith Music in, say, Brazil, but actually it's really being run by, for example, Universal or Peer in Brazil. A new model of publisher, acting merely as a collection agent rather than the traditional collecting and promotion agent, may be argued to have reach from its home territory to the rest of the world through direct memberships of foreign societies.

As regards Ireland, it's quite normal for a UK publisher to collect money directly through the collecting societies rather than to appoint a sub-publisher there, but an independent Irish publisher with an international hit

may sometimes appoint a sub-publisher for the UK.

Tax Exiles
The higher rate of UK tax can be seen as especially harsh on those who earn a large sum of money in a relatively short time (and then perhaps little more for the rest of their lives), and this causes a regular flow of writers, musicians and singers from the UK to take up residence in countries with more favourable tax laws. Writers, whose earnings from hits tend to be spread over a longer period than recording artists, tend to be less affected by this problem. Your accountant will advise you whether it's worth leaving the country. If you are a 'tax exile', you can still spend a good proportion of the year in the UK but you mustn't, under any circumstances, exceed the limit, or your tax residence may shift back to the UK. This is the reason why The Rolling Stones were unable to tour the UK a few years back, when a change in the rules meant that they'd have lost money by being in the UK for too much of the year. Ireland actually has specific tax breaks for creators of intellectual property such as songwriters.

Term
Used in contracts to mean both the length of time an agreement is valid for and clauses covering the actual royalty rates payable, the types of rights

169

granted, the advances payable etc.

Test pressings

As you would assume, these are a few copies of a pressing supplied in advance to the record company to ensure that the sound is as expected before a pressing plant goes ahead with duplicating large numbers. You should get to hear the test pressing if at all possible, as it may sound significantly different from the original master you heard in the studio.

360 deals

A newer type of deal under which an artist makes available to one company the revenue generated by all of their activities including recording, publishing, live performance and merchandising. The company will handle the management of all the relevant rights, collect all the relevant fees and pay an advance based on expected earnings. The idea is that the artist can get themselves a higher advance and the company can spread the risk. (Say a major artist has declining record sales but a huge live following, then even if their next album fails to sell, the company will recoup on the nonetheless successful accompanying live tour.)

Video or synch buyout

The practice of film companies and other audio-visual producers wishing to clear the rights in a song or recording they want to use without ever again having to go back to the copyright owner to ask for rights for another new form of CD rom or DVD for example, and without having to pay royalties on sales of videos etc. Sometimes, limited buyouts are granted based on copies sold or produced or territory or term.

Publishers and record companies are naturally reluctant to grant buyouts in broad terms, but increasingly in film synch contracts, terms such as 'all media which may hereafter be invented' are appearing, as film companies generally insist, and the value of placing a work in a high-profile film is seen as higher in promotional terms than the royalties being bought out. Smaller productions and TV production companies are more flexible, preferring not to pay a high buyout fee and to share the risk by accepting liability for mechanical royalties or further synch fees.

White labels

Pressings, generally 12-inch vinyl pressings of dance tracks, for distribution to DJs and specialist record shops. To maintain the artist and label cred, these contain minimal information about who has put them out. Some do get sold, but the object of the exercise is to create the interest and test the market before the official release, rather than necessarily to make money. Needless to say, if your white labels are broadcast there's a good chance you won't get paid unless there's enough information for whoever is making the programme returns to the PRS to enable them to recognise what the track is. But then the object is to get the club-goers to like them and try to buy them, and if they do, then you'll probably get a commercial release and won't mind losing a bit of money on the white labels themselves.